FROM NUREMBERG TO H

From Nuremberg to Hollywood

The Holocaust and the Courtroom in American Fictive Film

JAMES JORDAN

VALLENTINE MITCHELL
LONDON • PORTLAND, OR

First published in cloth in 2016 by Vallentine Mitchell
paper edition in 2021

Catalyst House,
720 Centennial Court,
Centennial Park, Elstree WD6 3SY, UK

814 N. Franklin Street
Chicago
IL 60610, USA

www.vmbooks.com

British Library Cataloguing in Publication Data:
An entry can be found on request

ISBN 978 0 85303 874 0 (cloth)
ISBN 978 1 912676 89 7 (paper)
ISBN 978 0 85303 866 5 (ebook)

Library of Congress Cataloging in Publication Data
An entry can be found on request

For Sidney (1994-2010)

Contents

Introduction

> In the aftermath of such 'indecent' dying, the courtroom as mise en scène for a comprehension of [the Holocaust's] enormity seems pitifully inadequate.
>
> Lawrence Langer[1]

> What are we living for if we need movies to tell us? Movies are there for themselves. To be enjoyed, so that you can laugh, so that you can cry, so that you can think. Everything else is just bullshit.
>
> Marcel Ophuls[2]

For seventy years, across proceedings as different as the International Military Tribunal at Nuremberg in 1945–46 (hereafter the IMT) and the libel case brought by David Irving at the London High Court over fifty years later, the courtroom has provided the setting for more than just a legal judgment in respect of the Holocaust. As Lawrence Douglas has shown in *The Memory of Judgment: Making Law and History in the Trials of the Holocaust* (2001), this formal, institutionalized and controlled environment has also been the forum for an increasingly nuanced, often intentionally pedagogic, examination of the Holocaust's history and its legacy. Moving chronologically forward from the IMT and the trial of Adolf Eichmann in Jerusalem in 1961 – the two trials which continue to echo loudest in the memory – to the cases against Klaus Barbie, John Demjanjuk and Ernst Zundel, Douglas has explored how the events of the courtroom have impacted beyond their legal context. The IMT, for example, provided a record of atrocity which would inform historians for decades to come, while Eichmann's trial not only influenced subsequent dialogue, but was conceived and 'staged to teach history and shape collective memory'. In turn, the latter trials have also been both historically and legally didactic, with the prosecution in the Zundel case, for example, seeking 'to enlist the coercive power of the law to protect historical truth and sacral memory from hateful distortion'.[3]

Taken in order, the cases cited in Douglas's book chart, therefore, both the law's relationship to the Holocaust and the development of 'Holocaust consciousness' across the century, examining how the meaning of the trials has altered as the Holocaust has grown in prominence the further it has moved into the past. Douglas's work also evidences how the trials themselves have changed. Trials of perpetrators – initially trials of recognizable figures such as Hermann Goering and Albert Speer, faces and names well known to a viewing audience – have become trials of the elderly and, in the case of John Demjajnuk, for example, concerned with identification as much as the crimes themselves. Indeed, Holocaust trials are no longer necessarily about establishing the guilt of a suspected perpetrator. The high-profile cases involving Irving and Zundel have seen Holocaust denial at the centre of proceedings as the courtroom has become the scene for an examination of the past in order to protect its memory for the future as the Holocaust itself has been put on trial.

There now exists a corpus of judicial proceedings that chronicles not only society's desire for justice in the face of such crimes, but also its changing understanding of those crimes, how they are remembered and how that memory is to be safeguarded. Moreover, the trials reveal the different ways in which the presentation of evidence has changed in an effort both to satisfy the demands of credibility for the courtroom and to overcome the challenges faced in trying to prove a crime which has been considered beyond the limits of representation. 'Together', as Douglas writes in the conclusion to his introduction, 'these trials reveal the imaginative range of legal efforts directed towards mastering the problems of representation and judgment posed by the Holocaust – and the shortcomings of those efforts.'[4]

Given the visibility, drama and significance of these courtrooms it is perhaps unsurprising that analogous to this sequence of trials, Hollywood and American film more generally have consistently utilized the law and the dialectic of the courtroom in order to represent and engage with the Holocaust and its memory. The most famous of these films probably remains Stanley Kramer's all-star *Judgment at Nuremberg* (1961), but there have been many others, and just as the real-life trials have changed in response to the evolving relationship to the Holocaust, so too has the cinematic courtroom. These films, as will be discussed in the following pages, are confronted by the challenges of representation which beset all Holocaust films, but there are other specific challenges faced by courtroom films. On one level this book provides a cultural history of those films, examining the relationship between fact and fiction through an analysis of the factual trials and their fictive counterparts, exploring how genre creates meaning and unpacking the advantages and limitations of the courtroom in respect of representing the horror of the Holocaust. In particular, it explores how the films in question present and represent evidence, focusing on key scenes to discuss not only what is depicted, but also how and why.[5] For that reason, it is a book grounded not in historiographical debates but film analysis, with close reading of images rather than archival study, although historical contextualization is key to understanding the relationship between film and history.[6] Together these individual studies demonstrate how the depiction of the Holocaust in the cinematic courtroom has altered since the 1940s in films that are themselves evidence of America's changing understanding of the Holocaust. In so doing, this brings together the law, the Holocaust and the cinema, asking questions of the transmission of the role of witnessing from the fictive audience (the imagined) to the audience of the fiction (the real) and our relationship to an event which is now in the final stages of its transition from being an event in living memory to one beyond it.

The Courtroom in American Film

It has often been noted that the language and structure of the court and the setting of the courtroom are ideally suited to drama: 'Traditionally and situationally, judicial proceedings are dramatic. Aristotle noted the importance of forensic oratory as a special device of legal rhetoric; playwrights have always appreciated the dramatic value of a trial scene; lawyers have always been cognisant of rhetorical presentations.'[7] It is unsurprising, therefore, that the courtroom drama has long been a cinematic staple, with Carol Clover suggesting that it was as early as 1907 that American cinema began transforming 'the courtroom into a movie theatre and the jury into a film audience'.[8] Those earliest courtroom films, like most films of the time, were technically unsophisticated by today's standards and offered 'little more than mildly diverting entertainment', but by the 1920s and 1930s, aided by the introduction of sound and other technological advances, and by the expansion of domestic and international markets, films had grown in complexity and popularity.[9] Courtroom dramas such as *Madame X*

(USA, Lionel Barrymore, 1929) – one of the earliest films to utilize the recurrent drama of an accused parent being defended by his/her offspring, which would feature in the Holocaust courtroom dramas of the late 1980s and early 1990s – and *The Life of Emile Zola* (USA, William Dieterle, 1937) became big box office hits across America.

In these early films the sanctity of the law was normally above reproach, with the on-screen proceedings affirming an accepted moral code under the rule of law. Indeed, it was an attitude codified in Hollywood's Production Codes established in 1934 by the Motion Picture Producers and Distributors of America, more commonly known as the Hays Office: 'Law, natural or human, shall not be ridiculed, nor shall sympathy be created for its violation ... Crimes against the Law ... shall never be presented in such a way as to throw sympathy with the crime as against law and justice or to inspire others with a desire for imitation.'[10]

This faith in the law began to be questioned in the introverted and morally ambivalent post-war world of film noir, and then more explicitly by the confrontational social-comment courtroom dramas of the 1950s and 1960s, such as *12 Angry Men* (USA, Sidney Lumet, 1957) and *Anatomy of a Murder* (USA, Otto Preminger, 1959), coinciding with firstly the threat to Hollywood posed by the (House) Un-American Activities Committee and then the relaxation of the Production Codes.[11] While the mid-1960s to mid-1970s witnessed a waning of the popularity of the cinematic courtroom in Hollywood (possibly because 'public appetite had been sated by the television serial', such as *Perry Mason*),[12] the genre proved resilient and returned in the 1980s and 1990s in a string of popular films including *The Verdict* (USA, Sidney Lumet, 1982), *The Accused* (USA, Jonathan Kaplan, 1988), *Jagged Edge* (USA, Richard Marquand, 1985), *Presumed Innocent* (USA, Alan J. Pakula, 1990) and *Reversal of Fortune* (USA, Barbet Schroeder, 1990). Once more the cinematic courtroom depicted social dilemma and minority group issues, often examining the conflict of public and private responsibility. In the final ten years of the century, the courtroom remained a constant presence on both the small and big screen, with the irreverent approach of shows such as *Ally McBeal* seeming to exist unproblematically alongside message-movies such as *Philadelphia* (USA, Jonathan Demme, 1993) or *Erin Brockovich* (USA, Stephen Soderbergh, 2000). This popularity across genre and medium has been maintained into the twenty-first century, with *Boston Legal* and *Law and Order* being just two examples of the courtroom's continued presence, playfulness and popularity.

The courtroom is, therefore, a setting that has lent itself to the cinema for virtually all of the twentieth century. But it is more than just a setting; it is an established genre, one that has its own dynamic and conventions which consciously and unconsciously influence audience preconceptions and understanding. But how does the genre respond when faced with the prospect of prosecuting and representing the Holocaust, an event often said to be beyond representation and at odds with the organizing principles of narrative and testimony, two of the key components of the courtroom? To return to Lawrence Langer's quote that opens this book, what does the cinematic courtroom have to offer an event of the complexity of the Holocaust?

Film and the Holocaust

In trying to answer that question, this book makes a contribution to the well-established debates as to the ability of popular cinema, a medium most readily identified as being for the purpose of 'mass entertainment', to reproduce and represent the Holocaust without abusing or traducing the memory of the event or its victims.[13] Such has been the perceived challenge of the Holocaust to the fictive film-maker in particular that Omer Bartov once asked: 'Can fiction films be made of the Holocaust? ... Is memory, rather than either historical fact or fiction, the most immediate, sincere, and authentic element in Holocaust reconstruction? And if so, how can memory be represented in film, and at what price?'[14] This debate is true, in a sense, of all historical films, but it is foregrounded by the specific challenges faced in recreating the Holocaust, an event of such horror that it is said to defy representation, to be an event 'at the limits'.[15] In one of the first book-length studies devoted to the study of 'cinema's images of the unimaginable', Ilan Avisar summarized that the Holocaust poses for the film-maker the three questions of 'representation, presentation and comprehension. The first involves the aesthetic problematics of achieving an adequate representation of the original reality. The second is more political in nature, referring to the need to present correctly the role and the identity of the participants ... [while] the third involves ... trying to understand why it happened.'[16] The Holocaust, therefore, is a challenge for the film-maker at the point of both conception and reception, with some of the more recurrent questions pertaining to realism and authenticity. For Roberto Benigni, director and star of the controversial Oscar-winning 'Holocaust comedy' *Life is Beautiful* (Italy, Roberto Benigni, 1997), fiction, artistic licence and non-realistic representation play an important role in cinema's understanding and reconstruction of the Holocaust: 'According to what I read, saw and felt in the victims' accounts, I realized nothing in a film could ever come close to the reality of what happened. You can't show unimaginable horror – you can only ever show less than what it was. So I didn't want audiences to look for realism in my movie.'[17] And yet even while there have been an increasing number of films which have moved beyond realism and into the realm of 'Holocaust impiety', most of these films, because of their historical origins, continue to locate themselves within the factual and historical, even if only to prove to the audience that film is no longer bound by the demands of historical accuracy.[18] But freedom from accuracy is not freedom from history, and the majority of 'Holocaust films' tend to remain grounded in history and 'realism' for, as Lawrence Langer argued twenty years ago in respect of literature,

> When the Holocaust is the theme, history imposes limitations on the supposed flexibility of artistic license ... Holocaust facts enclose the fiction, drawing the reader into an ever-narrower area of association, where history and art stand guard over their respective territories ... The Holocaust in fact resists displacement by the Holocaust in fiction, as if the artist were guilty of some unprincipled violation of a sacred shrine.[19]

What is clear from the stances of Benigni and Langer (stances which are not necessarily antithetical), and films such as *Inglorious Basterds* (USA, Quentin Tarantino, 2009) and *Everything is Illuminated* (USA, Liev Schreiber, 2006),[20] is that even when Holocaust films look to the surreal and magical, they continue to reference the historical, not only for the film-maker but also the viewer.[21] It is an observation which foregrounds the fact that the manner in which cinema 'represent[s] or avoid[s] representing the Holocaust is of major importance for the protection of the memory of the event itself'. Film, that is, is integral in helping to establish and shape 'an element of memory for a public who might otherwise remain uninformed about the event' and has a palpable influence on popular perceptions and memory.[22]

A powerful example of this is the case of Binjamin Wilkomirski and his phantom memoir *Fragments*. According to Elena Lappin, the origins of Wilkomirski's book – and his memories – were to be found in film:

> I suspect (the proof is impossible) that his knowledge of Majdanek is at least partly based on the German documentary, *Der Prozess*, which contains detailed descriptions of the camp, powerful witness accounts by both guards and inmates, and, unusually, a harrowing section on the children who were there. Wilkomirski often refers to his memories as being film-like. They are, I believe, more than that; they are, I believe, derived from films.[23]

If Lappin is correct, then Wilkomirski's knowledge has been gleaned not just from a film, but specifically from a courtroom film, where the presentation of the material as evidence and testimony provided him with a register and context with which to be able to persuade many experts that his memoir was authentic. His memoir, that is, may not have been real, but it was realistic or, rather, a realistic representation of a representation. In an age of simulacra, vicarious witnessing, prosthetic memory and postmemory, he was able to replicate the horror using the shadows of the cinema as his guide, thereby provoking difficult questions of how we know and understand the Holocaust, especially once it has passed from living memory.

The following chapters are grounded in the tension between film, truth, history and memory that is suggested by Wilkomirski, exploring how the fictive representations of the courtroom have drawn on and (mis)represented the real-life trials as well as the Holocaust across seventy years. This has not been a static relationship. All films, even documentaries such as *Der Prozess*, are cultural composites and reconstructions that resonate with the contemporary aspirations, fears and preoccupations of the environment of their creation. Films, that is, reflect and shape the memory of the contemporary world as well as that of the historical.[24] In the case of the Holocaust, therefore, they 'comment not only on the murdered Jews of Europe but also on the ideological climate in which the films themselves are produced, distributed, and reviewed'.[25] Nowhere is this more evident or contentious than in America. Here the plethora of films, alongside all of the books and other forms of commemoration which feature the attempted extermination of European Jewry, stand 'as a tribute not only to the Holocaust but to the American willingness to remember' an event that neither happened in America nor involved, directly, the majority of Americans.[26]

This adoption of the Holocaust into American life – known by some as its Americanization – is not unproblematic. 'On one level', writes Hilene Flanzbaum, editor of a collection of essays on the subject,

Americanization 'simply groups the many ways that the Holocaust has been represented in American culture; on another, it is political and theoretical quicksand, providing all the pitfalls of postulating about history, nation, and ideology'.[27] It is on this second level that there is considerable disagreement. Those who use Americanization purely as a pejorative term argue that while this appropriation affords the Holocaust increased accessibility, it also displays a continued tendency towards the universalization, redemption and trivialization of genocide that often marginalizes the specificity of the Jewish suffering and avoids confronting the full horror of the reality. This version, argues Lawrence Langer in his seminal essay on the subject, insists that the Jews of Europe have not all died in vain, trying instead 'to parlay hope, sacrifice, justice, and the future into a victory that will mitigate despair'. In so doing, he memorably concludes, Americanization 'permit[s] the imagination to cope with the idea of the Holocaust without forcing a confrontation with its grim details'.[28] This is, as Flanzbaum explains, a criticism not only of American film, but of America on a larger scale: 'For some it automatically signals America at its worst: crassness, vulgarisation, selling out.'[29] For the film-maker, the most emblematic examples of Americanization are *The Diary of Anne Frank* (USA, George Stevens, 1959), with its insistence on telling a story of romance rather than horror; the 1978 miniseries *Holocaust* (NBC, Marvin Chomsky, 1978), which brought the genocide into people's homes through the story of one family; and, most recently, *Schindler's List* (1993), Steven Spielberg's award-winning version of the story of 'the good German' that focused on rescue and redemption. The worldwide success and influence of Spielberg's film has galvanized more awareness of the Holocaust than virtually any other text, reaching an audience which might otherwise have remained uninterested.[30] It is now used as a pedagogic tool in schools and has left a legacy in the form of the Shoah Foundation, but for all those who consider it a masterpiece there are others who find it too trivial in its treatment of the Holocaust and too misleadingly redemptive in its narrative to merit such adulation. It is, in short, deemed to epitomize the Americanization of the Holocaust.[31]

From Nuremberg to Hollywood: The Courtroom in American Fictive Film

The following pages add to these debates by considering how Americanization, the courtroom and the Holocaust have converged in fictive film as the courtroom of the twentieth century has moved from Nuremberg to Hollywood. In particular, it examines how the courtroom bears witness to these horrific crimes, and how it presents and represents evidence of the Holocaust so as to satisfy the demands of an audience which is positioned as judge and/or jury, 'not as passive spectators, but as active ones, viewers with a job to do'.[32]

Kathy Eden, in her analysis of poetic and legal fiction, has argued that these debates over the power of evidence and narrative in the courtroom have their roots in classical Greece: 'Demosthenes ... assures the jury that no narrator of the events can make the horror of the outrage committed as vivid as it was either for those who suffered it or even for those who witnessed it with their own eyes', but for Aristotle, the poet or dramatist 'must make the Audience feel that they, like the jury, can see for themselves the events exactly as they occurred'.[33] This book returns regularly to that debate, looking at how the cinematic courtroom presents its evidence in the pursuit of historical realism and credibility. In most cases the films under discussion are fictional constructs that aspire to realism by replicating the appearance and content of the judicial proceedings, with the factual origins often being explicitly referenced on-screen. These fictive courtrooms, fuelled by their desire for accuracy, authenticity and approbation, adhere to the language, developments and arguments prevalent in the real-life courtroom, but does that come at a cost in terms of representing the crime?

The case studies that follow demonstrate how in seeking an answer to these challenges the evidence used in the cinematic trial has shifted from the once shocking, then iconic, but eventually overused black-and-white footage of liberation to the representation of the Holocaust through the use of oral testimony delivered by Jewish survivors from the witness box. In a sense this builds on the debates seen over the different approaches of *Schindler's List* and *Shoah* (France, Claude Lanzmann, 1985), a documentary which famously refuses to use documentary footage. Both films bypass the images of liberation, but they do so in contrasting ways: Spielberg challenges 'the traditional view of the Holocaust as confined to the realm of the unimaginable', even going so far as to 'break the taboo of explicitly imagining the Holocaust and the gas chamber'. Lanzmann, on the other hand, partly because of his distrust of archive footage (especially those images for which he is unable to identify a source and location of unquestioned accuracy), 'resurrect[s] the Holocaust through the words of the witnesses and through images of absence, images of tranquillity and beauty at what were sites of destruction'.[34] While Spielberg therefore reconstructs the past afresh for the audience, Lanzmann is reliant solely upon witness memory in the present to recall the past, challenging us 'to hear and see the witnesses and like a judge to make up our own minds about the stories they relate'.[35]

Arranged chronologically, the following is divided into two sections that are delimited by the two real-life courtroom proceedings – the IMT at Nuremberg in 1945–46 and the Eichmann trial in Jerusalem in 1961 – that have had the greatest influence on American film's representation of the Holocaust. The first section deals with those films made before 1961, from the first films to frame the Holocaust through the formal process of law, including one that pre-empts the IMT, to the moment of Holocaust awakening in American culture that coincided with the Eichmann trial. The second section moves from 1961 to the present day, exploring how the representation and expectations of the film-maker have changed in the years that have followed.[36]

While this is primarily a study of the images themselves, it is also grounded in history and the relationship between film, the Holocaust and the courtroom in real-life. The book begins, therefore, with an evaluation of the use of film as evidence at the IMT, a 'factual' moment that established the subsequent use of liberation newsreel as the pre-eminent evidence in the fictive. In total, the American prosecution showed five films at the IMT and together they reveal in microcosm a synopsis of the problems of interpretation and authenticity that would suffuse the American cinematic courtroom's own subsequent representations of the Holocaust and its legacy. In a sense this treats the IMT not only as a legal precedent and visual paradigm, but as the first film-set. The methodology employed here is replicated throughout, focusing on key moments and not necessarily analysing the meaning of the films as a whole.

The subsequent chapters, therefore, offer close textual analysis of certain scenes alongside historical contextualization, including reference to the filmic trials' factual precursors. Chapter 1 provides an introduction to the representation of the persecution of European Jewry in American film before and during the Second World War. It focuses on *None Shall Escape* (USA, André de Toth, 1944) the first American film in which the Holocaust and the post-war courtroom converge. In many ways this film stands alone from the other works under consideration as it predates both the liberation of the camps and the IMT, the two most significant moments in respect of the early filmic courtroom's representation of the Holocaust. As a result of this it has, I will argue, a freedom of expression in representing the crimes of the Nazis that is absent elsewhere.

Chapter 2 considers American cinema's first post-war attempts to bring the Nazis to trial in *The Stranger* (USA, Orson Welles, 1945), *Sealed Verdict* (USA, Lewis Allen, 1948), *Verboten!* (USA, Sam Fuller, 1959) and *Judgment at Nuremberg* (USA, Stanley Kramer, 1961). In particular it examines the ways in which all four films seek authority and authenticity through their use of newsreel footage as evidence, exploring how the meaning of these films changes in tandem with the altered understanding of the footage and its uses.

The second section of the book covers 1961 to the present, examining how the expectations of the film-maker have continued to change and the consequences of this for how the Holocaust is represented. It offers a brief description of the use of film as evidence at the Eichmann Trial before examining those films inspired by the trial and its manner of articulation of the past. Chapter 3 begins with *Operation Eichmann* (USA, R.G. Springsteen, 1961), a film in which the story of Eichmann's life and capture is retold through an imagined version of Eichmann's trial. This marks the beginning of the return of the Jewish witness, something which is continued in *QB VII* (USA, Tom Gries, 1974), in which the Holocaust survivor takes to the stand to bear witness to the past. *QB VII* marks a shift away from the Hollywood version of the past to a more televisual and domestic version as the Holocaust enters more into the public consciousness. This is also addressed in the second case study, a discussion of the American Film Theatre's production of Robert Shaw's *The Man in the Glass Booth* (USA, Arthur Hiller, 1975), a film which draws its inspiration from the Eichmann trial but is increasingly removed from its factual precursor as the imagination gains a firmer hold over the Holocaust courtroom. This film does not use diegetic documentary film as evidence – meaning that it does not use the on-screen projection of film within film in replication of the earlier trials – but, like *QB VII*, uses a combination of the aural and visual, sounds and images which are increasingly part of a shared palette of atrocity, as triggers for questions of memory, identity and identification, issues which are all tied to the trauma of the central witness.

These questions continue to be paramount in Chapter 4 in *Music Box* (USA, Costa-Gavras, 1989), a film which seeks to expose an elderly American citizen as a once brutal perpetrator. Based on a story that resembles that of John Demjanjuk, the Ukrainian-American who was deported to Israel to stand trial in 1988, it is a film which presents a synthesis of film and testimony as visual and spoken evidence converge to provide proof of the guilt or innocence of its accused for the audience.[37] It also features a trial on American soil under American law, and that domestication of the Holocaust can also be seen in *Perry Mason: The Case of the Desperate Deception* (even though it is set in France) and the two films discussed in Chapter 5. *Skokie* (USA, Herbert Wise, 1981) and *Never Forget* (USA, Joseph Sargent, 1991), made for television either side of *Music Box* and *Desperate Deception*, are separated by ten years, but they are both based on actual cases and share the common thread of empowerment through American citizenship.

The final chapter presents the end of the century and an evaluation of the Turner network's dramatization of the IMT in *Nuremberg* (USA/Canada, Yves Simoneau, 2000), a two-part miniseries produced in Canada for American television that sees the Holocaust, film and the courtroom come full circle to return not only to the trial of the Nazi leaders, but to the use of newsreel footage as evidence. Whereas in the IMT of 1945 the Holocaust was conceptually absent and tendentious, by the year 2000 it has attained a more prominent place within the trial. In this version of the IMT, the prosecution case focuses more on the murder of the Jews of Europe as memory of the process of justice is distorted by a desire to reflect the Holocaust's contemporary presence, rather than its historical absence. Although the voice of the Jewish witness is once again denied his/her opportunity to speak, there is a significant Jewish presence. An epilogue brings this study into the twenty-first century by considering two transatlantic productions from 2008: *The Reader* (USA/Germany, Stephen Daldry, 2008) and the Anglo-American television production *God on Trial* (UK/USA, Andy DeEmmony, 2008).

Ultimately, the debates in this book are not 'simply' about the Holocaust, but about our dialogue with evidence and how we create and recreate the past in the present. The book concludes by addressing directly the question that has been posed implicitly throughout. No representation of the Holocaust 'can claim to be wholly free of bias, distortion, and the limitations of the conventions within which it operates', but is that compounded or ameliorated by the courtroom genre? What does a representation of a representation, one which operates within the conventions and restrictions of the courtroom mise en scène reveal about the Holocaust and how it continues to resonate?[38] Moreover, in using the courtroom to depict the Holocaust, the film-maker aspires to authenticity, but what happens when the demands of historical fact are pulling in different directions? If the courtroom misrepresented or misunderstood the Holocaust, then should the film-maker replicate or correct? Does the authenticity of the judicial setting and proceedings distract the audience from the apparent impossibility of an authentic representation of the crime? That is, if the Holocaust is an event at the limits, then do the formulaic conventions of the courtroom – both in fact and in the fictional shadows – help explain the past or protect us from it?

NOTES

1. Lawrence L. Langer, *Admitting the Holocaust: Collected Essays* (Oxford: Oxford University Press, 1996), p.177.
2. Marcel Ophuls, *The Late Show*, BBC2, tx. 18 December 1990.
3. Lawrence Douglas, *The Memory of Judgment: Making Law and History in the Trials of the Holocaust* (New Haven, CT, and London: Yale University Press, 2001), p.3.
4. Douglas, *Memory of Judgment.*
5. Carol J. Clover, 'God Bless Juries!', in Nick Browne (ed.), *Refiguring American Film Genres: History and Theory* (Berkeley, LA: University of California Press, 1998), p.257.
6. For an introduction to the tensions between film and history see Robert A. Rosenstone, 'History in Images/History in Words: Reflections on the Possibility of Really Putting History into Film', *American Historical Review*, 93, 5 (December 1988), pp.1173–185; Robert A. Rosenstone (ed.), *Revisioning History: Film and the Construction of a New Past* (Princeton, NJ: Princeton University Press, 1995); and Robert A. Rosenstone, *Visions of the Past: The Challenge of Film to our Idea of History* (Cambridge, MA: Harvard University Press, 1995).
7. Pat Carlen, *Magistrates' Justice* (London: Martin Robertson, 1976), p.19.
8. Cited in Clover, 'God Bless Juries!', p.255.
9. Douglas, *Memory of Judgment.*
10. Steven Powers, David J. Rothman and Stanley Rothman, *Hollywood's America: Social and Political Themes in Motion Pictures* (Boulder, CO: Westview Press, 1996), p.106.
11. Ibid.
12. Phil Hardy (ed.), *The BFI Companion to Crime* (Berkeley, CA: University of California Press, 1997), p.91. For more on the cultural and theoretical use of the courtroom see Jerome Frank, *Courts on Trial: Myth and Reality in American Justice* (Princeton, NJ: Princeton University Press, 1949); Lance W. Bennett and Martha S. Feldman, , *Reconstructing Reality in the Courtroom: Justice and Judgment in American Culture* (New Brunswick, NJ: Rutgers University Press, 1981); John Denvir (ed.), *Legal Reelism* (Urbana and Chicago, IL: University of Illinois Press, 1996); Lawrence M. Friedman, 'Law, Lawyers and Popular Culture', *Yale Law Journal*, 98, 8 (June 1989), pp.1579–606; Robert Harriman (ed.), *Popular Trials: Rhetoric, Mass Media, and the Law* (Tuscaloosa, AL: University of Alabama Press, 1990); Steve Greenfield and Guy

Osborn, 'Lawyers in Film: Where Myth Meets Reality', *New Law Journal*, 143, 6629 (17 December 1993), pp.1791–92; 'The Living Law: Popular Film as Legal Text', *Law Teacher: Journal of the Association of Law Teachers*, 29, 1 (1995), pp.33–42; 'Where Cultures Collide: The Characterization of Law and Lawyers in Film', *International Journal of the Sociology of Law*, 23 (1995), pp.107–30; 'Film, Law and the Delivery of Justice: The Case of Judge Dredd and the Disappearing Courtroom', *Journal of Criminal Justice and Popular Culture*, 6 (2), 1999, pp.35–45; Stephen Greenfield, Guy Osborn and Peter Robson (eds.), *Film and the Law: The Cinema of Justice*, second edition (Hart, 2010); and Stefan Machura and Peter Robson (eds), *Law and Film* (Oxford: Blackwell, 2001).

13. See Lawrence L. Langer, *The Holocaust and the Literary Imagination* (New Haven, CT, and London: Yale University Press, 1975), p.1; and Langer, *Admitting the Holocaust*, p.83. See also Sidra DeKoven Ezrahi, *By Words Alone: The Holocaust in Literature* (Chicago, IL: University of Chicago Press, 1980); Saul Friedlander (ed.), *Probing the Limits of Representation: Nazism and the Final Solution* (Cambridge, MA: Harvard University Press, 1992); Geoffrey Hartman (ed.), *Holocaust Remembrance: The Shapes of Memory* (Oxford: Blackwell, 1994) and *The Longest Shadow: In the Aftermath of the Holocaust* (1996; Basingstoke: Palgrave Macmillan, 2002); Neil Levi and Michael Rothberg (eds), *The Holocaust: Theoretical Readings* (Edinburgh: Edinburgh University Press, 2003); Robert Eaglestone, *The Holocaust and the Postmodern* (Oxford: Oxford University Press, 2004); Christopher Bigsby, *Remembering and Imagining the Holocaust: The Chain of Memory* (Cambridge: Cambridge University Press, 2006); and Brett Ashley Kaplan, *Unwanted Beauty: Aesthetic Pleasure in Holocaust Representation* (2007).. These are just a few of the many books which now address the issue of Holocaust representation in the arts. The first introductory texts on representing the Holocaust with specific reference to film were Ilan Avisar, *Screening the Holocaust: Cinema's Images of the Unimaginable* (Bloomington, IN: Indiana University Press, 1988); Judith Doneson, *The Holocaust in American Film* (Philadelphia, PA: Jewish Publication Society, 1987); and Annette Insdorf, *Indelible Shadows: Film and the Holocaust*, 3rd ed. (Cambridge: Cambridge University Press, 2002). More recent texts to continue the discussion of film and the Holocaust include Joshua Hirsch, *Afterimage: Film, Trauma and the Holocaust* (Philadelphia, PA: Temple University Press, 2004); Libby Saxton, *Haunted Images: Film, Ethics, Testimony and the Holocaust* (London: Wallflower, 2008); Jean-Michel Frodon, *Cinema and the Shoah: An Art Confronts the Tragedy of the Twentieth Century* (New York: SUNY Press, 2010); Lawrence Baron, *Projecting The Holocaust Into The Present: The Changing Focus of Contemporary Holocaust Cinema* (Lanham, MD: Rowman & Littlefield, 2005); and Jenni Adams and Sue Vice (eds), *Representing the Perpetrator in Holocaust Film and Literature* (London: Vallentine Mitchell, 2012).
14. Omer Bartov, 'Spielberg's Oskar: Hollywood Tries Evil', in Yosefa Loshitzky (ed.), *Spielberg's Holocaust: Critical Perspectives on Schindler's List* (Bloomington, IN: Indiana University Press, 1997), p.51.
15. Friedlander (ed.), *Probing the Limits*.
16. Avisar, *Screening the Holocaust*, p.x.

17. Interview with Roberto Benigni, http://filmeducation.org/live/5_10/holo11.html. See also Sue Vice, *Holocaust Fiction* (London and New York: Routledge, 2000), pp.4, 169 n.10.
18. Matthew Boswell, *Holocaust Impiety in Literature, Popular Music and Film* (Basingstoke: Palgrave Macmillan, 2011), passim. I'm thinking here not only of Tarantino's film, but also the recent trend of science fiction/fantasy/horror films such as *Iron Sky* (Finland/Germany/Australia, Timo Vuorensola, 2012) and *The 25th Reich* (Australia, Stephen Amis, 2012) which continue to play with ideas such as the 'Space Nazi' and time travel.'
19. Langer, *Admitting the Holocaust*, pp.75–6. See also André Pierre Colombat, *The Holocaust in French Film* (Metuchen, NJ, and London: Scarecrow Press, 1993), p.3.
20. For more on the book of *Everything is Illuminated*, see Jenni Adams, *Magic Realism in Holocaust Literature: Troping the Traumatic Real* (Basingstoke: Palgrave Macmillan, 2011), esp. pp.21–49.
21. One thinks here, for example, of the controversy surrounding the accuracy – or not – of Mel Gibson's *Braveheart* (USA, 1995) or Oliver Stone's *JFK* (USA, 1991). See Robert Brent Toplin, 'The Filmmaker as Historian', *American Historical Review*, 93, 5 (December 1988), pp.1210–27; and Robert Brent Toplin, *History by Hollywood: The Use and Abuse of the American Past* (Urbana, IL: University of Illinois Press, 1996).
22. Colombat, *Holocaust in French Film*, p.3; Judith Doneson, '*Holocaust* Revisited: a Catalyst for Memory or Trivialization?', *Annals of the American Academy of Political and Social Science*, 548 (1996), p.71; Judith Doneson, 'From Hitler to Heimat: The Return of History as Film', *Holocaust and Genocide Studies*, 6, 2 (1991), p.207.
23. Elena Lappin, 'The Man with Two Heads', *Granta*, 66 (1999), p.61.
24. In a sense this is a truism: all films resonate culturally and politically with the aspirations, fears and preoccupations of the environment of their creation as much as, if not more than, the event they are attempting to depict.
25. Sara R. Horowitz, 'The Cinematic Triangulation of Jewish American Identity', in Hilene Flanzbaum (ed.), *The Americanization of the Holocaust* (Baltimore, MD, and London: Johns Hopkins University Press, 1999), pp.142–66, esp. pp.145–46; Gary Crowdus (ed.), *The Political Companion to American Film* (Chicago, IL, and London: Fitzroy Dearborn, 1994), p.xi; and Peter Novick, *The Holocaust and Collective Memory: The American Experience* (London: Bloomsbury, 2001).
26. Novick, *Holocaust and Collective Memory*, pp.2–11, 20–22. See also Doneson, '*Holocaust* Revisited', p.76; and Doneson, *Holocaust in American Film*, p.5.
27. Flanzbaum, *Americanization of the Holocaust*, p.2. See also Judith Miller, *One by One: Facing the Holocaust* (New York and London: Simon & Schuster, 1990); and Ilan Avisar, 'Holocaust Movies and the Politics of Collective Memory', in Alvin H. Rosenfeld (ed.), *Thinking about the Holocaust after Half a Century* (Bloomington, IN: Indiana University Press, 1997), pp.38–58.
28. Langer, *Admitting the Holocaust*, pp.158–9.
29 Flanzbaum, *Americanization of the Holocaust*, p.7.
30 Doneson, '*Holocaust* Revisited', p.71.

31. Loshitzky (ed.), *Spielberg's Holocaust*, p.5. Many works on Holocaust representation deal with the phenomenon of *Schindler's List*, of which the collection of essays edited by Loshitzky remains one of the most articulate and provocative. See also Frank Manchel, 'A Reel Witness: Steven Spielberg's Representation of the Holocaust in *Schindler's List*', *Journal of Modern History*, 67, 1 (March 1995), pp.83–100; and 'Mischegoss: *Schindler's List*, Holocaust Representation and Film History', *Historical Journal of Film, Radio and Television*, 18, 3 (1998), pp.431–36.
32. Clover, 'God Bless Juries!', p.257.
33. Kathy Eden, *Poetic and Legal Fiction in the Aristotelian Tradition* (Princeton, NJ: Princeton University Press, 1986), p.73.
34. Yosefa Loshitzky, 'Holocaust Others: Spielberg's *Schindler's List* versus Lanzmann's *Shoah*', in Loshitzky (ed.), *Spielberg's Holocaust*, pp.104–18, esp. pp.110–11.See also Shoshana Felman, 'In an Era of Testimony: Claude Lanzmann's *Shoah*', *Yale French Studies*, 79 (Spring 1991), pp.39–81; and the same author's 'The Return of the Voice: Claude Lanzmann's *Shoah*', in Shoshana Felman and Dori Laub (eds), *Testimony: Crises of Witnessing in Literature, Psychoanalysis, and History* (New York: Routledge, 1992), pp.204–83.
35. Simon Louvish, 'Witness', *Sight and Sound*, 4, 3 (March 1994), p.15.
36. In so doing, this structure suggests that the other trials, particularly the German trials of the 1960s, historically important for European memory, did not have palpable impact on American film and memory, although this would feature in *The Reader*, one of the films discussed in the epilogue.
37. A brief introduction to Demjanjuk's case is provided in Douglas, *Memory of Judgment*, pp.185–87, 196–97, 209–11. For a lengthier discussion, see Yoram Sheftel, *The Demjanjuk Affair: The Rise and Fall of a Show-Trial* (London: Gollancz, 1994).
38. Bartov, 'Spielberg's Oskar', p.53.

Part One

The Nuremberg Precedent

The trial of the 'major war criminals' before the International Military Tribunal at Nuremberg from 20 November 1945 to 1 October 1946 was, to quote from an RKO Pathé News report of the trial's opening day, 'an epic event in the progress of mankind'.[1] Here for the first time an international body sat in judgment on senior politicians and military officers of an opposing nation which had been defeated in war.[2] Throughout the trial, the murder of the Jews of Europe, a complex combination of separate but linked events that has become known most familiarly as the Holocaust, would feature regularly and often, but it was seldom the specific focus of the prosecution's case. In fact, as Donald Bloxham has argued persuasively in his work on the IMT and its legacy, the subsumption of the crimes against the Jews within the criminality of the Nazi regime as a whole was indicative of the Allies' more general 'failure … to recognize the unique nature of the fate of European Jewry'; it was a lacuna which would continue to be seen long after the trial was concluded.[3] And yet in some ways the trial marked a considerable 'turning point' with regard to what we now know as the Holocaust. 'After Nuremberg', concluded Michael Marrus, 'the murder of European Jewry could be authoritatively pointed to as an established fact of great historical importance.'[4] In particular, the substantial body of oral and documentary evidence produced for and by the trial, 'expedited the compilation of histories of Nazism, and helped to conceptualize "the Holocaust" for a relatively small number of intellectuals in the direct aftermath of the war'.[5] The trial, and the body of evidence produced both for and by it, remains one of the foremost points of reference for Holocaust scholars.

In the immediate post-war period, and extending in different ways over the remainder of the twentieth century, the IMT also exerted a considerable influence on the film-maker's depiction of Nazi crimes, including the extermination of the Jews of Europe. In this respect, however, it was not the documentary record that would have the most salient and enduring of influences – although the transcripts themselves have been an important part of the fictive echo – but rather the IMT's use of film as witness, and in particular the use of the now emblematic footage of liberation.

Liberation footage – the 'centrepiece of Americans' initial encounter with [the Holocaust]' – had first been seen by the American public in April and May 1945 when 'all five of the nation's major newsreels devoted most of their reports to the exposure of "Nazi atrocities"'.[6] The conflicting instructions given by the seemingly authoritative commentaries that accompanied those first newsreels revealed the degree to which witnessing through film was already being constructed as morally imperative, repugnant and compelling. As Thomas Doherty summarized in 1993:

> Fox Movietone News provided a cautionary preface: 'These scenes of horror are an awesome indictment of Nazi bestiality. To the civilized mind such inhuman cruelty is incredible. We show these films as documentary evidence and warn you not to look at the screen if you are susceptible to gruesome sights.' Exposing the furnaces and half-cremated corpses at Buchenwald, Universal Newsreel took a different tack. 'Don't turn away,' orders commentator Ed Herlihy. 'Look.'[7]

Moreover, the content of the films themselves was problematic. Omer Bartov is simply one of several critics to have noted that they 'inevitably represent the victims as horribly emaciated, only quasi-human creatures, and if they express sympathy for the human debris of Nazi racial policies, they do not arouse empathy'.[8]

Lawrence Douglas, Peter Novick and Jeffrey Shandler have all shown that these films failed to explain the crimes on display or to engender any understanding of who was being murdered and why, marginalizing the Jewish victims 'in such a manner as to obscure any suggestion that Nazi terror was directed against Jews as a group'.[9] On one level, therefore, the purpose of these films was not one of exposition, but rather to extend the act of liberation to include the audience watching in the cinema, allowing the American public to witness vicariously the shock of discovery for themselves. The newsreels intentionally anathematized the Nazis as, to quote Jeffrey Shandler, 'the act of witnessing for American audiences [was codified] as unpleasant, shocking, repulsive, yet arousing, compelling, necessary, and ultimately redemptive'.[10] And yet many of the same images, re-edited but similarly codified, were reused within the year at the IMT as the prosecution sought to prove 'incredible events by credible evidence'.[11] 'These films were so powerful and compelling that they would exercise control over the imagination of film-makers for many years to come, becoming the most enduring of Nuremberg's legacies, not only in what was shown but also how.'

The American Prosecution's Use of Film at Nuremberg

The French, Russians and Americans all used film in evidence at the IMT, with the Soviet footage including the iconic images of the liberation of Auschwitz.[12] This was a deliberate choice, indicative of the size of the task faced by the prosecution, and the faith in the medium as evidence. As Serge Fuster, Assistant Prosecutor for the French Republic at Nuremberg, explained to the court before presenting film as evidence for the first time, 'we have used pictures in preference to words, since pictures can make clear in an instant something which it takes time to put into words. In this way we hope we have contributed towards making plain the truth'.[13] The relationship between the truth and the camera was never as straightforward – indeed, the truth is rarely plain – something that was evident in each of the five films shown by the Americans that together presaged the problems of credibility and authenticity that would beset the fictional courtrooms that followed.

The first of the five American films to be screened and the one best remembered and most often referenced today was *Nazi Concentration Camps*. Shown to the court on 29 November 1945, this compilation of images filmed by the Americans and British during liberation was 'the [American] prosecution's most dramatic evidence of the Nazis malignancy'.[14] As described to the packed courtroom by Commander James Donovan, the hour-long film had been compiled from footage taken

> by allied military photographers as the allied armies in the West liberated the areas in which these camps were located. The accompanying narration is taken directly from the reports of the military photographers who filmed the camps. While these motion pictures *speak for themselves* in evidencing life and death in Nazi concentration camps, proper authentication of films is

> contained in the affidavits of the United States Army and Navy officers to which I have referred.[15]

Onto the screen shortly thereafter, provoking near-unanimous horror, came the now familiar and iconic images of the liberation of Dachau, Buchenwald and Belsen. It was a seminal moment: 'By providing a visual register of atrocity', Lawrence Douglas has concluded, '*Nazi Concentration Camps* crossed a threshold of representation from which there was no turning back.'[16] Over the course of the next hour, some of the most graphic and disturbing images were played in a carefully constructed narrative that made hardly any reference by name to the treatment of the Jews of Europe and, while the proceedings condemned the actions seen on the screen, the images themselves received little by way of further explanation – a situation that remained largely unchanged until the work of Douglas and Shandler fifty years later.

Even at this point the power of the image was evident in its impact rather than content, with the focus of discussion being on the response of the accused. Some spoke of how the horror of these images was heightened by the fact that they had not seen them before, but that was not the case for everyone. Those defendants who had been held in custody at Bad Mondorf had already been shown film of the liberation of Buchenwald. This was not to evidence the horror of the camp but rather 'to jog [their] memories back to the reality of the grave situation'. At this screening, Colonel Burton Andrus, the 'Nuremberg jailer', told the fifty-two prisoners present: 'We are showing them to you, not to inform you of what you already know, but to impress on you the fact that we know of it, too.'[17] It was an earlier indicator of how film would be used in the initial post-war years.

On the morning of 13 December 1945, two weeks after *Nazi Concentration Camps* had been shown, Thomas Dodd, Executive Trial Counsel for the United States, reluctantly returned to the 'sickening evidence of the brutality of the concentration camp'. So aware was he of the power of the recently shown images that he recommended that the tribunal take a short recess prior to returning to the film. After the recess, in language which, with the benefit of hindsight, was indicative not only of the power of the images, but of self-censorship, Dodd continued:

> I should like to direct your attention briefly to the treatment which was meted out in these camps. The motion picture … which was shown to the members of this High Tribunal has

> disclosed the terrible and savage treatment which was inflicted upon these Allied nationals, prisoners of war, and other victims of Nazi terror. *Because the moving picture has so well shown the situation, as of the time of its taking at least, I shall confine myself to a very brief discussion of the subject.*[18]

That is, less than a month after the initial showing of these images, the horror of the newsreel footage was already arresting dialogue. As Commander Donovan had explained in his introduction, while these pictures spoke 'for themselves in evidencing life and death in Nazi concentration camps', the unquestioned acceptance of these images did nothing to explain what life and death in the camps was like, who these people were or why they were there. It was a failure that would be replicated to varying degrees by the cinematic courtroom in the decades to come.

The American prosecution's second film, *The Nazi Plan*, was shown on 11 December 1945. This differed considerably in purpose, subject matter and origin to *Nazi Concentration Camps*, although in common with its more famous predecessor this too contained only fleeting mention of the Nazis' treatment of the Jews. This second film consisted of 'captured moving pictures' drawn from the thousands of feet of footage collected by the Allies as they overran former Nazi strongholds'. The prosecution had added subtitles to facilitate comprehension, but otherwise 'all film presented and all German narration heard [was] in the original form as filmed by the Nazis'.[19] Images shot for the glorification of Hitler and as a visual libation to the Reich, including an extended montage from *Triumph of the Will*, Leni Reifensthal's masterpiece which idolized the Nazis in their 1934 pomp, were now presented as evidence of the Nazis' crimes.[20] It was evidence to which the prosecution would regularly return, for *The Nazi Plan* was to be proof of both individual complicity in, and collective adherence to, the crimes against peace and the 'Common Plan' or conspiracy of which all the defendants were accused.[21]

Shown in one sitting over the course of nearly four hours, *The Nazi Plan* consisted of four parts, dividing the history of the Nazi Party into manageable and clearly defined sections. Parts 1 and 2 were respectively entitled 'The Rise of the NSDAP [Nationalsozialistische Deutsche Arbeiterpartei], 1921 to 1933' and 'Acquiring Totalitarian Control of Germany, 1933 to 1935'. These films would, Donovan told the court, 'enable us to re-live those years in which the Nazis fought for and obtained the power to rule all life, in Germany'.[22] Part 3 would then show the 'Preparation for Wars of Aggression, 1935 to 1939' before the film concluded with Part 4: 'Wars of Aggression, 1939 to 1944'. The opening image showed Alfred Rosenberg, one of the leading proponents of Nazi racial ideology, dressed in full Nazi Party uniform. This on-screen image of a confident Rosenberg, taken from a Nazi film in which he narrated the story of the Nazi Party's early years, was very different to the dishevelled figure seated in the Nuremberg dock. Moreover, this footage, originally used as Nazi propaganda, was intercut with silent footage of Nazi parades and acts of physical violence, juxtaposing Nazi propaganda with images of cruelty and persecution. Part 2 then demonstrated how the Nazis took and maintained control of Germany, including footage of the anti-Semitic boycott of 1 April 1933. It concluded with the extended compilation of images from *Triumph of the Will*.

The film's second half presented a further shift in Nazi aspirations from 1935 onwards as consolidation became expansion. The final images of Part 3 presented Hitler before the Reichstag in April 1939, mocking Roosevelt's plea that Germany halt its expansion and adopt a policy of non-aggression. On the screen in the courtroom that day, members of the Reichstag could be seen and heard to laugh derisively as Hitler listed one by one those countries under threat, the loudest laugh being reserved for the mention of Palestine. As the film entered its fourth and final phase, 'occupation' became 'invasion', but the war would soon turn in favour of the Allies, and the wars of aggression would become a fight for survival. The film's penultimate segment showed the People's Court in Berlin and the trial that condemned those accused of taking part in the 20 July 1944 plot to assassinate Hitler. Footage of Presiding Judge Roland Freisler's invective and prejudice were shown to underpin the proceedings of the IMT as dignified and reasoned, with Robert Cooper, special correspondent with *The Times*, noting that such images were powerful propaganda for the tribunal:

> if the defence really thought they were getting a raw deal they were provided with an eloquent contrast by a few filmed scenes from the Nazi People's Court ... Thousands of feet of film, taking in all ten hours to show, had been found recording incidents arising from the plot, and the short extract displayed in court produced in some ways one of the most dramatic moments at the whole trial.[23]

As a whole, *The Nazi Plan* provided compelling evidence of the development of a sequence of individual but connected events in which each of the accused was at some point implicated. In fact, so compelling was the finished film that one American observer called it 'terrific!' and enthused that it could possibly win an Academy award.[24] To the prosecution's dismay, the defendants, too, 'enjoyed [the film] hugely'. Göring, for example, would later tell Gustav Gilbert, the Allied psychologist at Nuremberg, that he felt sure that after seeing the film even Justice Jackson would want to join the Party.[25]

Two days after the brief respite provided for the defendants by *The Nazi Plan*, Thomas Dodd, as part of 'the presentation of War Crimes and Crimes against Humanity, starting with exploitation of forced labor, concentration camps, persecution of the Jews, and Germanization and spoliation in occupied countries', produced in court tattooed skin and shrunken heads from Buchenwald which had been referenced and seen in *Nazi Concentration Camps*.[26] Later that same day, Major William F. Walsh (Assistant Trial Counsel) would ask the court's permission to show 'a very short motion picture, perhaps one of the most unusual exhibits that will be presented during the Trial'. This short, blurred and silent film was the most explicit of the films shown by the United States, and as its title *Original German 8-Millimeter Film of Atrocities against Jews* suggests, it was unambiguous as to the identity of the victims, if less certain about its provenance. Once more Commander Donovan introduced the film:

> This is a strip of motion pictures taken, *we believe*, by a member of the SS and captured by the United States military forces in an SS barracks near Augsburg, Germany, as described in the affidavits now before the Tribunal. We have not been able to establish beyond doubt in which area these films were made, but we believe that to be immaterial. *The film offers undeniable evidence, made by Germans themselves, of almost incredible brutality to Jewish people* in the custody of the Nazis, including German military units. *It is believed by the Prosecution* that the scene is the extermination of a ghetto by Gestapo agents, assisted by military units ... This film was made on an 8-millimeter home camera. *We have not wished even to reprint it*, and so shall present the original, untouched film captured by our troops. The pictures obviously were taken by an amateur photographer. Because of this, because of the fact that part of it is burned, because of the fact that it runs for only 1½ minutes, and because of the confusion

> on every hand shown on this film, we do not believe that the Tribunal can properly view the evidence if it is shown only once. We therefore ask the Tribunal's permission to project the film twice as we did before the Defense Counsel.[27]

While the film was being rewound, Donovan read out parts of the attached affidavit, providing a breakdown of its contents 'in order to direct the Tribunal's attention to certain of the scenes'. The film was then reshown and placed in the permanent record – although, in keeping with the reluctance to reprint the film itself, the published *Documents in Evidence* does not include any stills from the film. The film is a powerful evocation of the horror of the treatment of the Jews, but once more the opportunity for exposition was overlooked as the images curtailed engagement. As Donovan's words made clear, this was not simply happenstance but a conscious decision on behalf of the prosecution.

The final two films to be shown by the Americans were both presented as evidence in the individual cases against Hitler's former bankers Hjalmar Schacht and Walther Funk. It had been apparent throughout the trial that Schacht did not consider himself to be guilty, and clearly he resented even the suggestion that he should be held accountable, particularly as he had been held in a concentration camp since the attempt on Hitler's life in July 1944. Yet Schacht, president of the Reichsbank until his resignation in 1939, had been present throughout the Nazis' rise to power – a fact that had been made evident by *The Nazi Plan*. On 3 May 1946 the American prosecution presented its fourth film as evidence of the vigour with which Schacht had supported Hitler.[28] It was proof, Robert Jackson claimed, that Schacht's status within the Nazi hierarchy was more ambiguous than the accused himself suggested.[29] In this film, also shown twice because of its brevity, Schacht could be seen congratulating Hitler upon the Führer's triumphant return to Berlin in July 1940 subsequent to the defeat of France. It was an image that was at odds with Schacht's claims that by 1939 he was already a man out of kilter with the Führer's views.[30]

While the previous films provoked concerns about origin, construction, intention and depiction, the Schacht footage, as Dr Dix (Schacht's counsel) argued in court, initiated a more fundamental question with regard to interpretation: 'these pictures give no pleasure to the observer, and certainly not to Schacht either. But they do not prove anything. In a natural evaluation belonging to a normal average experience of life, I consider these pictures without any value as evidence, either pro or contra.'[31] While neither Schacht nor his counsel denied the authenticity of the footage, they questioned whether the film could be unequivocally understood. Again, it was a precursor to the questions of interpretation that would be duplicated by the fictive courtroom.

A similarly fundamental problem of how to evaluate the evidence was posed by the last film presented by the Americans, a film which once again contained images that would resurface regularly in subsequent movies even though their status was unclear. Speaking from the witness stand on the 6 May 1945, Walther Funk, Schacht's successor as president of the Reichsbank, denied repeatedly that he had ever done business with the SS. In particular, he was careful to emphasize that the bank had never been involved in the dissemination of belongings from concentration camp inmates.[32] When asked about such procedures, he replied that he 'did not know' whether gold-filled teeth such as these had ever been received by the bank and denied any knowledge of the Reichsbank having accepted any such 'jewels, monocles, spectacles, watches, cigarette cases, pearls, diamonds, gold dentures' as a deposit.[33] In response, the following day, Thomas Dodd showed the American prosecution's final and in some ways most problematic film:

> Right now, since you do not seem to recall that you ever had any or saw any such materials as I have described in your vaults, I ask that we have an opportunity to show you a film which was taken of some materials in your vaults when the Allied Forces arrived there. I would ask, Mr President, that the defendant be permitted to come down, where he can watch the film, *so that his memory will be properly refreshed.*[34]

Pictures were then shown which, Dodd told the court, had been 'taken in Frankfurt when the Allied Forces captured that city and went into the Reichsbank'. These offered proof of the 'jewellery, eyeglass frames, dental gold, and other gold articles in great abundance, taken by the SS from Jews, concentration camp victims, and other persons', which were found there. Although there was as yet no affidavit to accompany the images, Dodd assured the president of the tribunal that one would follow, confirming 'the circumstances under which the film was made, who was present, and why'.[35]

Once again the defence counsel objected to the film's inclusion as evidence, arguing on this occasion that this scene was staged. Funk himself denied all knowledge of such items: 'I have never seen anything of this sort ... I never saw a single item such as these shown in the film, and I cannot imagine where these things came from, to whom they belonged, and to what use they were put.'[36] There was some truth in this: the images were indeed of uncertain tenability and their use as evidence was a calculated risk. As a memorandum sent the previous December had suggested, 'gold articles and teeth might be seen [but] there was no solid proof that they had been taken from concentration camp victims'.[37] Funk offered a similar assessment:

> I was completely confused by this film and most deeply shocked. Photography and especially films are always very dangerous documents because they show many things in a light different from what they really are. I personally have the impression, and I believe the Prosecution will probably corroborate this, that all these deposits of valuables and this entire collection of valuable items came from the potassium mines where, at my instigation, all gold, foreign currency and other valuables of the Reichsbank had been stored away when, because of a terrific bombing attack on Berlin, we were no longer able to work in the Reichsbank.[38]

In an attempt to forestall such objections, the prosecution had arranged for a number of witnesses to attest in person to the footage's authenticity. These witnesses were far from convincing. For example, Albert Thoms, an official who worked in the vaults of the Reichsbank in Berlin, confirmed simply that these were 'typical' of the approximately seventy to seventy-seven 'Melmer' deliveries (as these shipments were termed), although the original shipments were not so plentiful.[39] Also called was Emil Puhl, vice-president of the Reichsbank from 1939 until Germany's surrender, whose affidavit had already been produced by the prosecution. Puhl was asked to confirm that the 'steel vaults of the Reichsbank looked as they were shown in this film'.[40] This he did: 'The film was taken in front of the safes of our bank at Frankfurt-on-Main, the usual safes with glass doors, behind which one could see the locked cases and containers, which had apparently been deposited there. It was the usual picture presented by such strong rooms.'[41] But, Puhl continued, he 'had the impression that the things of which we are now talking had been put there expressly for the purpose of taking the film' and that the safe had been empty when the Americans arrived.[42] Indeed, Rebecca West noted that at Puhl's own trial an official of the bank also asserted that at the time the Americans arrived the safes were completely empty:

> A few days after the occupation some US lorries had pulled up at the door of the branch and the manager requested to hand over Reichsbank bags which were then filled with gold teeth, jewellery, etc., taken from the lorries and put in the empty safes. After these safes had been filled cameramen appeared and made a film of their contents.[43]

The use of these images was clearly dubious even if the footage was intended only to illustrate 'typical' deposits. As Tusa and Tusa have concluded in their account of the IMT, the prosecution could be thankful that their 'bluff was not called' in respect of this evidence.[44]

These five films underlined the American prosecution's apparent faith in film's ability to present undeniable evidence even though this was not always the case. That is, at Nuremberg the camera, considered reliable and credible in its anamnesis, provided testimony that was presented as seemingly objective and irrefutable. But the use of such films was not straightforward, highlighting the problems of comprehension, repulsion, provenance, interpretation and authenticity, as well as film's ability to manipulate and be manipulated through narrative and editing. And yet, in the utilization of newsreel and liberation footage as evidence, Nuremberg established parameters for the representation of Nazis' crimes and atrocities that the film-maker would replicate for decades to come, including newsreel compilations as evidence in order to gain authenticity and approbation from a referent that signified both the crime and the formal process of justice. Suffused with authenticity by virtue of both form and forum, the evocative and recognizable images of liberation in particular became for the film-maker the pre-eminent courtroom proof of the Holocaust, as 'fact' permeated 'fiction' in the search for verisimilitude and accuracy. It was a presence that assisted in the filmic courtroom's occlusion of the Jewish survivor and other witness testimony while simultaneously establishing a compelling image of 'the victim'. Many of these same issues, including the use (and fallibility) of film as evidence and the absence of the Jewish survivor, were to be found in André de Toth's *None Shall Escape*, the first Hollywood film to place the Nazis on trial. And yet this film, produced prior to both the IMT and the liberation of the camps, also displayed a freedom of imagination in respect of the crimes that would be hard to find in the first decade after 1945.

NOTES

1. RKO Pathé News, 'The Hitler Gang Goes on Trial', November 1945. See also Ann Tusa and John Tusa, *The Nuremberg Trial* (London: BBC Books, 1995), p.14.
2. The charges are taken from the indictment as read out in court on the trial's opening day. See *The Trial of the Major War Criminals before the International Military Tribunal* [hereafter *IMT*], Nuremberg, 1947, vol. 2, p.29. For a brief introduction to the background to the trial and how it has been represented, see Tusa and Tusa, *Nuremberg Trial*; Telford Taylor, *The Anatomy of the Nuremberg Trials: A Personal Memoir* (London: Bloomsbury, 1993); and Werner Maser, *Nuremberg: A Nation on Trial*, trans. Richard Barry (London: Allen Lane, 1979). For the specific consideration of the trial's impact on public awareness and understanding of the Holocaust, see Michael R. Marrus, 'The Holocaust at Nuremberg', *Yad Vashem Studies*, 26 (1998), pp.5–41; Donald Bloxham, *Genocide on Trial: War Crimes Trials and the Formation of Holocaust History and Memory* (Oxford: Oxford University Press, 2001); and Lawrence Douglas, *The Memory of Judgment: Making Law and History in the Trials of the Holocaust* (New Haven, CT, and London: Yale University Press, 2001). There are many other works on the IMT which provide details of the cases and challenges faced, including Leon N. Goldensohn, *The Nuremberg Interviews: Conversations with the Defendants and Witnesses* (New York: Alfred A. Knopf, 2004); Guénaël Mettraux (ed.), *Perspectives on the Nuremberg Trial* (Oxford: Oxford University Press, 2008); and Kim C. Priemel and Alexa Stiller (eds), *Reassessing the Nuremberg Military Tribunals: Transitional Justice, Trial Narratives, and Historiography* (New York: Berghahn Books, 2012).
3. Bloxham, *Genocide on Trial*, p.2.
4. Marrus, 'Holocaust at Nuremberg', p.5; Bloxham, *Genocide on Trial*, p.81.
5. Bloxham, *Genocide on Trial*, p. 2. See also Tusa and Tusa, *Nuremberg Trial*, pp.70, 101; and Marrus, 'Holocaust at Nuremberg', p.19.
6. Jeffrey Shandler, *While America Watches: Televising the Holocaust* (New York and Oxford: Oxford University Press, 1999), p.5. The significance of newsreel as witness is addressed in K.R.M.Short and Stephan Dolezal (eds), *Hitler's Fall: The Newsreel Witness* (London: Croom Helm, 1988).
7. Thomas Doherty, *Projections of War: Hollywood, American Culture and World War II* (New York: Columbia University Press, 1993), pp.247–49.
8. Omer Bartov, 'Spielberg's Oskar: Hollywood Tries Evil', in Yosefa Loshitzky (ed.), *Spielberg's Holocaust: Critical Perspectives on Schindler's List* (Bloomington, IN: Indiana University Press, 1997), p.53.
9. Douglas, *Memory of Judgment*, p.57. Peter Novick argues that this response to the liberation footage in itself is perhaps unsurprising, given that only one-fifth of the inmates were Jewish in those camps liberated by the Americans. See Peter Novick, *The Holocaust and Collective Memory: The American Experience* (London: Bloomsbury, 2001), pp.63–65.
10. Shandler, *While America Watches*, p.15. See also Novick, *Holocaust and Collective Memory*; and particularly Barbie Zelizer, *Remembering to Forget: Holocaust Memory Through the Camera's Eye* (Chicago, IL, and London: University of Chicago Press, 1998), for an analysis of the way in which these

images have continued to influence the representation and understanding of the Holocaust.

11. Robert Jackson, cited in Lawrence Douglas, 'Film as Witness: Screening *Nazi Concentration Camps* Before the Nuremberg Tribunal', *Yale Law Journal*, 105 (1995), p.452.
12. Douglas, 'Film as Witness', pp.449, 451–53. See also G.M. Gilbert, *Nuremberg Diary* (London: Eyre & Spottiswoode, 1948), pp.95–96; Boris Polevoi, *The Final Reckoning: Nuremberg Diaries*, trans. Janet Butler and Denis Bradbury (Moscow: Progress, 1978), pp.180–85; and Tusa and Tusa, *Nuremberg Trial*, p.198. See also Chris Penfold's discussion of the filming of the liberation of Auschwitz in his excellent thesis, 'Elizaveta Svilova: Female Authorship in Soviet Cinema', (unpublished PhD thesis, University of Southampton).
13. Fuster, 5 February 1946, *IMT*, vol. 7, pp.12.
14. Douglas, 'Film as Witness', pp.449. This essay offers an extensive evaluation of the film, its images and impact. See also a revised version in Douglas, *Memory of Judgment*, pp.11–37, passim; and Shandler, *While America Watches*, pp.20–22.
15. My emphasis. 29 November 1945, *IMT*, vol. 2, p.431–32. *Nazi Concentration Camps* is entered into the record as document 2430-PS, Exhibit USA-79.
16. Douglas, 'Film as Witness', pp.457–68, passim.
17. Burton C. Andrus, *The Infamous of Nuremberg* (London: Leslie Frewin, 1969), pp.54–55. For more on the defendants' state of mind see Douglas M. Kelley, *22 Cells in Nuremberg: A Psychiatrist Examines the Nazi Criminals* (New York: Greenberg, 1947); and Gilbert, *Nuremberg Diary*, passim.
18. My emphasis. 13 December 1945, *IMT*, vol. 3, pp.493–94.
19. 21 November 1945, *IMT*, vol. 2, pp.101–02.
20. Footage from *Triumph of the Will* had been used in newsreels and films long before the IMT. It was featured, for example, in Frank Capra's *Why We Fight* series (USA, 1942–45); *Hitler's Children* (USA, Edward Dmytryk, 1942); and *Mission to Moscow* (USA, Michael Curtiz, 1943). It had even been used already at Nuremberg when, at a private screening before the trial began, Burton Andrus had shown it to Rudolf Hess, Hitler's increasingly erratic former deputy, in the hope that it would trigger a palpable cognitive response from Hess. See Taylor, *Anatomy of the Nuremberg Trials*, p.150; Maser, *Nuremberg*, p.80; and Polevoi, *Final Reckoning*, p.92.
21. 26 July 1946, *IMT*, vol. 19, p.425. For other subsequent mentions of the film, see Maxwell-Fyfe, in the case against von Ribbentrop, 9 January 1946, *IMT*, vol. 5, p.4; 15 January 1946, vol. 5, pp.281–82, 285, to show the individual responsibility of von Schirach for 'Crimes against the Peace, War Crimes, and Crimes against Humanity as they concern directly the Common Plan or Conspiracy'; 7 February 1946, *IMT*, vol. 7, p.124, for Hess's direct participation in the early years of the NSDAP; 9 July 1946, *IMT*, vol. 18, p.68, in the case against Rosenberg; 19 July 1946, *IMT*, vol. 19, p.42, regarding Defence Counsel Franz Exner's condemnation of Judge Freisler; 19 July 1946, *IMT*, vol. 19, p.62, in the case against Seyss-Inquart; 11 March 1946, *IMT*, vol. 11, p.116, in cross-examination of Milch; 29 March 1946, *IMT*, vol. 10, p.235, Von Ribbentrop on the witness stand referred back to the speech he made which had been shown in the courtroom and 'presented as proof of the duplicity of German diplomacy';

and 15 March 1946, *IMT*, vol. 11, pp.351–52 during the cross-examination of Herman Göring.
22. *IMT*, vol. 3, p.400.
23. R.W. Cooper, *The Nuremberg Trial* (Harmondsworth: Penguin Books, 1947), p.30.
24. Cited in Robert E. Conot, *Justice at Nuremberg* (London: Weidenfeld & Nicolson, 1983), p.197.
25. Gilbert, *Nuremberg Diary*, p.41; and Taylor, *Anatomy of the Nuremberg Trials*, p.200.
26. 11 December 1945, *IMT*, vol. 3, pp.399–401. This provided a physical connection between the courtroom, the crimes and the films, confirming the latter's integrity.
27. 13 December 1945, *IMT*, vol. 3, pp.532–36.
28. 3 May 1946, *IMT*, vol. 13, pp.22–23.
29. 26 July 1946, *IMT*, vol. 19, p.427.
30. 1 May 1946, *IMT*, vol. 12, pp.462–63. See also the comments made about the film by Lord Shawcross, the head of the British prosecution, in his closing remarks on 27 July 1946, *IMT*, vol. 19, p.519; Airey Neave, *Nuremberg: A Personal Record of the Trial of the Major War Criminals in 1945–46* (London: Grafton Books, 1989), p.214; and Cooper, *Nuremberg Trial*, pp.260–66.
31. 15 July 1946, *IMT*, vol. 18, pp.305.
32. In fact, Funk had already confessed his guilt in this respect to Burton Andrus, governor of the Nuremberg jail. See Andrus, *Infamous of Nuremberg*, pp.55–56.
33. 6 May 1946, *IMT*, vol. 13, p.161.
34. 7 May 1946, *IMT*, vol. 13, pp.169–70. My emphasis.
35. Description taken from the affidavit of Emil Puhl, dated 3 May 1946. Cited in evidence, 7 May 1946, *IMT*, vol. 13, pp.169–70. Once again the filmic images were shocking to those present in the courtroom. Defendant Hans Fritzsche would later write of how he and his fellow defendants 'sat flabbergasted' as the screen showed the 'horrible pictures'. See Gilbert, *Nuremberg Diary*, p.203.
36. 7 May 1946, *IMT*, vol. 13, pp.167–69; and Gilbert, *Nuremberg Diary*, p.203. The necessary affidavits were later provided by Captain Sam Harris, 'who arranged to have the pictures taken', and 'the photographer who actually took the picture': 28 May 1946, *IMT*, vol. 13, p.601.
37. Memorandum to Robert Storey, executive trial counsel for the United States, cited in Tusa and Tusa, *Nuremberg Trial*, pp.348–49.
38. 7 May 1946, *IMT*, vol. 13, pp.203–04. See also Justice Lawrence's comments to Jodl, 5 June 1946, *IMT*, vol. 15, p.414.
39. 15 May 1946, *IMT*, vol. 13, pp.600–04.
40. Doctor Sauter, 11 May 1946, *IMT*, vol. 13, p.433.
41. Puhl, 15 May 1946, *IMT*, vol. 13, pp.560–05.
42. 15 May 1946, *IMT*, vol. 13, pp.560–05.
43. Ibid., pp.569–70; and Rebecca West, *A Train of Powder* (London: Macmillan, 1955), p.251.
44. Tusa and Tusa, *Nuremberg Trial*, pp.348–49.
45. Shandler, *While America Watches*, p.18; Douglas, 'Film as Witness', pp.468–69.

1

André de Toth's None Shall Escape (1944): Bearing Witness to the Holocaust in the Courtroom before Liberation, before Nuremberg

Life is goddam black, and I photograph life.

André de Toth[1]

In *Screening the Holocaust*, one of the first books to present an understanding of the way in which the Holocaust has been represented on screen, Ilan Avisar described how in the initial years of Hitler's chancellorship, Hollywood, fearful of generating an 'anitsemitic backlash' at home and alienating the lucrative German market abroad, 'was extremely cautious in its handling of Nazi Germany'.[2] At a time when the film industry was still restricted by the draconian and repressive guidelines of its extensive Production Code, the studios 'punctiliously abided by Article X ... which stated: "The history, institutions, prominent people and citizenry of other nations shall be represented fairly. No picture shall be produced that tends to incite racial bigotry or hatred among peoples of differing races, religions or national origins." '[3] The general consensus among film historians remains that it was not until the release of Warner Brothers' *Confessions of a Nazi Spy* (USA, Anatolé Litvak, 1939) that Hollywood produced an overtly anti-Nazi film which challenged this guarded approach. In this respect, and with one eye on what is to come, it is significant that *Confessions* was based on a real-life court case and, indeed, one that had its on-screen denouement in a courtroom. The film's origins were deemed crucial in allowing it to challenge both the actions of Hitler's Germany and Hollywood's production system: as a 'film that was based on fact – revealed and confirmed in a US courtroom no less – it could not be accused of breaking the "National Feelings" clause of the Production Code'.[4] Although it is not a courtroom drama as such – too much of the film takes place beyond the confines of the court for that to be the case – *Confessions* can be seen as the starting point of the relationship between the cinema, the courtroom and the attempted extermination of the Jews of Europe. This is not only because of the subject matter and setting, but because it predicts *The Nazi Plan* through its inclusion of a montage of archival footage in evidence of Nazi aggression.

The action of *Confessions*, a film which exposes a Nazi spy ring working in the United States in the late 1930s, opens in 1937, at a rally in New Jersey for 'Nazis and Nazi Sympathizers'. At the lectern, Doctor Kassel (Paul Lukas) speaks of his desire for an America of 'German blood and culture', affirming that he wants this as a German, a citizen of the United States and a reserve officer in the US Navy. He urges the assembled crowd to 'destroy our enemies ... we Germans must save America from the chaos which breeds in democracy and racial equality'. As the film progresses towards war, Kassel travels to Germany. His journey is portrayed through a montage of newsreel footage, which is imposed over a globe depicting the expansion of Nazi Germany to the south of Africa, into the Atlantic and across into Eastern Europe. A voice-over provides a narrative to what is being shown:

> Arriving in Germany, Doctor Kassel finds a totally different Fatherland from the one he left ten years before. Following faithfully the programme of the bible of Adolf Hitler, *My Battle*, the Nazi Party had created a new fascist society based on a devout worship of the Aryan superman. A new fascist culture imbued with the glorification of conquest and war. A fascist system of life where every man, woman and child must think alike, speak alike, and do alike; a rigidly censored press with all news coloured by the Ministry of Propaganda; a fascist literature shorn of its greatest writers and poets; a new religion ridiculing the brotherhood and equality of man before God; a fascist economy with its watchword 'cannon' and not 'butter'; a fascist philosophy with a supreme command: 'blind obedience to the Fatherland'. For six long centuries men throughout the world had fought their

> way out of the dark ages of mediaeval barbarism but in six short years Hitler's Nazis cast their ominous shadow over the entire earth.

The spy ring is eventually broken through the combination of a vigilant Scottish postman who grows suspicious at the frequency and type of correspondence, and an industrious Federal Bureau of Investigation agent named Renard (Edward G. Robinson). In the film's denouement, four spies (with fourteen unseen others) are seen being placed on trial before a Grand Jury. This presents the chief prosecutor, Attorney Kellogg (Henry O'Neill), with the opportunity to describe the charges brought against the accused – 'little cogs in a vast intricate machine' – as the screen segues into another montage of Nazi propaganda. Returning to the courtroom, the film's final message is delivered by Kellogg as he stares directly into the camera, addressing both the jury and the audience watching in the cinema: 'But there are some who will say that there is nothing to fear, that we are immune, that we are separated by a vast ocean from the bacteria of aggressive dictatorships and totalitarian states but we know – ' and then a final montage again uses a combination of archive newsreel and original footage to map Germany's continued expansion and provide the background for Kellogg's warning: 'America is not simply one of the remaining democracies, America is democracy, a democracy that has the God-given inspiration of free men determined to defend forever the liberty which we have inherited in our Bill of Rights of the Constitution of the United States.' The courtroom is engulfed in cheers. As the café owner in the epilogue reminds both the American public and Nazi Germany, 'one thing they found out here though: This aint Europe!' 'Thank God for such people', reflects Renard as the film ends.

Even within this film – clearly anti-Nazi and aimed at the American domestic market – there is no explicit mention of the Jews as victims of the Nazi persecutions, with Judith Doneson suggesting that the film 'does not concern itself at all with the Jewish problem' and may have harmed the chances of those Jews seeking immigration into the United States.[5] Instead, there is a reliance on euphemism and universalism, with the Nazis portrayed as 'striving to shatter that attitude of tolerance and respect for minority rights [found in the United States] which entitled people to consider themselves as civilised human beings'. The closest the film comes to being explicit is when Renard searches Doctor Kassel's offices and discovers filing cabinets full of biographies of 'some of the most important men in America ... all classified according to blood and race', which list ancestry back to the third and fourth generation. These are, according to Kassel, 'to preserve Americanism' and to protect democracy from 'the insidious international conspiracy of desperate subhuman criminals, greedy for world power. It is obvious that these criminals need to be removed from public life.' The reference is clear but the language is not, meaning that although voiced by Kassel, the film relies on the audience's ability to recognize an anti-Semitic motif.

It is widely felt that of the films produced by Hollywood between 1933 and 1940 only Charlie Chaplin's *The Great Dictator* (USA, 1940) unequivocally addressed the treatment of the Jews in contemporary Germany, a move which earned Chaplin considerable disapproval within the industry.[6] Even after America entered the war in December 1941, Chaplin's film remained one of the few films to engage directly with the fate of the Jews. In the 1940s, Hollywood, assigned a wartime duty and overseen by the War Activities Committee of the Motion Picture Industry and the Office of War Information (OWI), replaced its staple of the social drama with the propaganda film in which the Nazis were either outwitted by the public or defeated by the military. The Nazis themselves, who remained distinct from the 'ordinary' and 'good' Germans in an echo of the pre-war period which sought to differentiate, were now caricatured as the overconfident and smug spy; the robotic, passionless follower of orders; or the self-aggrandizing leader who was little more than a glorified gangster, as parodied perhaps most famously in Brecht's *The Resistible Rise of Arturo Ui*.[7] The Nazi persecution of the Jews remained in the margins as Hollywood, in the spirit of wartime positivism and still wary of America's own prejudices, focused on winning the war and avoided explicit and prolonged confrontation with the plight of European Jewry.[8]

As the pioneering work of Kenneth Short and Judith Doneson has noted, it was against this taciturn backdrop and amid increasingly frequent reports from Europe of fresh and worsening atrocities that in early 1943 the American Jewish Congress (AJC) made 'a direct approach to leaders of the Motion Picture industry' for a picture that dealt specifically with the Nazi 'extermination program' that was threatening to destroy a 'whole people'. Having been rebuffed by the industry, the AJC made a similar request directly to the OWI. Once again the request was declined. As an often-quoted letter to the AJC dated 5 February 1943 from Lowell Mellett, chief of the Bureau of Motion Pictures at the OWI, confirmed, the prevailing feeling in

Hollywood was that 'it might be unwise from the standpoint of the Jews themselves to have a picture dealing solely with Hitler's treatment of their people, but interest has been indicated in the possibility of a picture covering various groups that have been subject to the Nazi treatment. This of course would take in Jews.'[9] Although the OWI continued to express its concern that any film that dealt with anti-Jewish behaviour (particularly anti-Semitism in the United States) would not be in the best interests of the war effort, almost exactly one year to the day after Mellett's letter, Columbia released *None Shall Escape* (USA, André de Toth, 1944), the first American film in which the Holocaust and the issue of post-war justice converge in the setting of the courtroom. A small-budget film which, while adhering to the Hollywood model outlined by the OWI, takes a 'surprisingly radical stance on anti-semitism [sic] and the Holocaust', the film is an exposé of the horrors of Germany that focuses on the plight of the Jews while also offering a psychoanalytical assessment of the Nazis and a very early engagement with the ability of the camera to *show* the truth.[10] Made in late 1943 from a shooting script completed in June of the same year, it had no dominant factual precedent for visual representation of crime or retribution to which it felt compelled to adhere or from which it could draw 'authenticity'. Moreover not bound by any precursor in terms of representing either the crimes or the process of justice, it displays a freedom of interpretation that would disappear after the war. *None Shall Escape* uniquely generates its authenticity through the use of human witnesses – both on and off screen – from whose memories the persecution and then slaughter of a group of Polish Jews is graphically recreated in flashback as the film-maker's visual imagining of the Holocaust – and not documentary footage – appears as courtroom evidence. It is a reliance on memory, supported through the creativity and accepted truth of the camera, which would disappear in the wake of the IMT amid concerns over the credibility of firstly memory and then film.

None Shall Escape (1944)

> The time of this story is the future.
> The war is over.
> As was promised, the criminals of
> this war have been taken back to

the scenes of their crimes for trial.
In fact, as our leaders promised –

NONE SHALL ESCAPE.

Made before the end of the war, before Nuremberg and before the point of liberation, *None Shall Escape* is the story of a fictional Nazi war criminal on trial before an international tribunal in post-war Warsaw.[11] The chronology is crucial. Filmed at a time when 'Most war movies were about fighting "the Japs" ... and there was no assurance the Allies would beat the Axis', *None Shall Escape* was, to quote from the film's promotional publicity, 'the most prophetic picture of our time!'[12]

A piece of wartime propaganda set in the post-war future, *None Shall Escape* was the second Hollywood movie to be directed by the self-styled 'Hungarian-born, one-eyed American cowboy' André de Toth.[13] A graduate of law from Budapest University and already an experienced film-maker before coming to America, de Toth knew 'well every scene he ... put into the film', having witnessed and filmed the horrors of Nazism first-hand in his native Hungary and across occupied Europe, including the traumatic invasion of Poland.[14] These experiences – as victim, witness and film-maker – would now inform *None Shall Escape*, an anti-Nazi, pro-American film with a distinctly European feel in its visual composition and its open-ended and often downbeat storyline.

The film was based on an original story written by Alfred Neumann and Joseph Than, two Europeans with 'fresh wounds' who, according to de Toth, 'wore the identical masks of refugees, ingratiating smiles and discreet tear drops in the corner of their eyes. A silent unwritten plea.'[15] The screenplay, 'Lebensraum', had been adapted in the summer of 1943 by Jewish author Lester Cole, the noted left-wing writer and later one of the 'Hollywood Ten'.[16] For Harry Cohn, the redoubtable president of Columbia Pictures, the involvement of the 'red troublemaker' Cole was a considerable risk in terms of time and money. Cohn, with his usual tendency for understatement and reticence, warned that Cole would go 'politically overboard. It would be a waste of money; they'd have to rewrite.'[17]

Although the final shooting script for *None Shall Escape* was, as Cohn had anticipated, politically committed, it was considered sufficiently uncontroversial to be approved by both the OWI and the Polish Information Office in Washington, DC, with one reviewer for the OWI noting that, although potentially ' "preaching hate" at a time when we [the US] will be studying how to rehabilitate the whole German nation', the film was 'timely'.[18] In featuring the question of post-bellum retribution, *None Shall Escape* was indeed timely. It had been on 21 August 1942 that President Roosevelt had informed the American people that 'the time will come when they [the Axis powers] shall have to stand in courts of law in the very countries which they are now oppressing and answer for their acts'. Later that same year, Roosevelt intimated for the first time that post-war retribution was to be made an objective concomitant to winning the war:

> I now declare it to be the intention of this Government that the successful close of the war shall include provision for the surrender to the United Nations of war criminals ... It is our intention that just and sure punishment shall be meted out to the ringleaders responsible for the organised murder of thousands of innocent persons and the commission of atrocities which have violated every tenet of Christian faith.[19]

It was not until November 1943, however, concurrent to the production of *None Shall Escape*, that the Moscow Declaration, 'the theoretical cornerstone of postwar crimes policy', detailed how those responsible for war crimes were to be returned to the scene of their crimes, to be 'judged on the spot by the peoples whom they have outraged'.[20] These words would now adorn the film's promotional posters as de Toth brought the Nazis to Hollywood to stand trial in front of an international tribunal for the first time. At a time when, the Moscow Declaration notwithstanding, the Allies had failed to reach an agreement on their post-war policy for the Nazis, de Toth was assured in his intent.[21] As he would recall on two separate occasions in the mid-1990s,

> [Lester] Cole wanted to advocate revenge. I wanted it to be Life itself, a slap across the face, a cry for justice. I know there are blinders on the eyes of the Goddess of Justice, but the blinders slip sometimes and, at least hypothetically, it's possible to eliminate all ills. But revenge, revenge, revenge is a never-ending disaster ... It was 1943. The world was on a blood and fire diet. It was two and a half years before the Nürnberg [sic] Trials. In *None Shall Escape* we invented a name for the asthmatic breathless, thoughtless and impotent League of Nation: 'United Nations'. A moniker of Utopia. Those of us who were singed by

> the fire and hallowed by the blood were craving for justice, it is a vicious circle. Justice or revenge ... *None Shall Escape* was made for justice.[22]

None Shall Escape may well have been made for justice rather than revenge, but the judicial process it depicts, while impressive in its prescience, is naive, occasionally implausible and often ambiguous. As a reviewer in *The Times* of 5 June 1944 noted, 'it is hoped that the methods at the real trials after the war will differ profoundly from those adopted by this particular court'. While the mammoth undertaking that was the IMT would, of course, 'differ profoundly' from this cinematic court, both courtrooms shared the use of film to present evidence of the Nazi plan and atrocities committed against the peoples of Europe. While the IMT would utilize documentary German newsreels and liberation footage, de Toth manufactured his own evidence – including the graphic depiction of the mass murder of a Jewish community – on a Hollywood film-set and presented it as proof through the use of flashback which presented subjective witness testimony as objective truth.

None Shall Escape – a title that, contrary to the suggestive and lascivious imagery of the studio publicity that featured young women in various degrees of undress being molested by uniformed Nazis, referred to the post-war pursuit of the Nazis – is therefore a film that looks back on Nazi crimes and forward to post-war retribution. The opening shot sees a lone swastika hanging from a solitary flagpole atop an unnamed building. The flag is gradually lowered in visual confirmation of the writing which adorned the opening credits: 'The time of this story is the future. The war is over.' An American voice elucidates further as the credits fade: 'Unconditional surrender. The leaders of the Nazi Party are today standing trial in Poland as in the other capitals of Europe.' The camera follows the flag's descent and the image dissolves as we move inside the building to look upon a marbled ceiling and then the reassuring, avuncular face of a middle-aged man (George Lessey), the Presiding Judge of the 'International Tribunal, District of Warsaw'. It is he who has provided the voice-over, and he continues to speak, now looking directly into the camera as, like Judge Kellogg in *Confessions*, he assimilates the audience into the film as judge and jury:

> Today we sit in judgment over those who caused humanity unspeakable miseries. We must be aware of our great responsibility,

> not only to the past but to the future. Throughout the occupation by the Nazis of the invaded countries, a complete record has been kept of the crimes of the Nazis and the Nazi Collaborationists. The names of these criminals were recorded anticipating the day when judgment would be done. This court will decide not only whether the accused are innocent or guilty, but the extent of the crime. This court will determine what penalty the accused must pay.

The camera pans slowly round the semicircular courtroom, showing the diversity of the international tribunal from a position that places the camera – literally and figuratively – at the heart of these proceedings. It halts on a group of seated prisoners who, dressed in uniforms shorn of epaulettes and insignia, are awaiting the opening of the trial.

Although three prisoners can be seen in or beside the dock, *None Shall Escape* is concerned only with the establishment of the guilt or innocence of the first of the accused. He is Wilhelm Grimm (Alexander Knox), the former *Reichscommissioner* of the Western Region of Poland. Grimm is to be charged with 'the wanton extermination of human life ... with the crimes of murder, unlawful detention, degenerate atrocities, and common theft'. These crimes are to be made analogous to those of the Nazi regime as a whole, with evidence provided by a triptych of witnesses who, united as victims of the Nazis, provide in turn the plaintive and plaintiff voices of the Catholic Church, Germany and Poland.

For David Black, any consideration of the law in cinema must recognize that it is dealing with 'the representation of one important cultural practice in the signifying terms of another'. This is made evident for Black, who draws on long-standing debates about the role of law in literature, by the fact that both film and law 'traffic in symbolic representation' at the heart of which is narrative:[23] 'Courtroom scenes – without even trying – give centre stage to the process of the construction of probabilistic narrative; they cannot abstain from referring, in some manner or at some level, to the underpinnings of both filmic and legal narrativity.'[24] The narrative of this film is delivered from the witness stand as oral evidence, but is recreated as a flashback. This prolepsis of the Nuremberg trial is to be unfolded via analepsis as we are 'taken back', as promised, to the scene of the crimes. There is, however, to be no Jewish witness in the witness box, with her/his place being taken by 'courtroom proxies', to borrow Lawrence Douglas's term for the absence of a Jewish voice at Nuremberg.[25]

The first witness is the Reverend Roman Warecki (Henry Travers), the Catholic priest of the small Polish village of Litzbark. In an unlikely preamble to his testimony, Warecki begins with an explanation as to trial's significance:

> The trial of these criminals marks a milestone in human history. It has been argued today that we, having defeated the Nazis, should show tolerance and mercy, that these men are the victims of circumstance and of history, and that they enjoyed no freedom to act in accordance with the dictates of their own consciences. I'd like to relate an incident which occurred many years ago to prove that the accused acted of his own volition and that he had freedom of choice and of will.

His narrative then starts in 'very early in the spring of 1919 following the end of the First World War'. As Warecki speaks, the screen dissolves and we travel back via the conduit of his memory to a bell-tower, and to a bell that bears the inscription 'LITZBARK'. From this vantage point we are afforded an aerial view of the village, a camera angle that is both an establishing shot and an affirmation that, although guided by the subjective mindscreen of Warecki, we are to witness the veracity of the evidence from a privileged position of omniscience.[26]

In the village square below the tower, Warecki and his fellow villagers gather to discuss the Treaty of Versailles and the future of Poland. As they talk, Wilhelm Grimm, the village's German teacher who has been away fighting with the German army, returns to Litzbark. He is warmly received by the villagers, and he shakes hands in greeting with both Warecki and the local rabbi, David Levin (Richard Hale). It soon becomes evident, however, that this is a different man from the one who left the village several years before. It is not that he is an imposter in the sense of the accused in the courtroom of *The Return of Martin Guerre* (France, Daniel Vigne, 1982) or its American remake *Sommersby* (USA, Jon Amiel, 1993), but rather that the war has left him psychologically damaged and physically injured.[27] To make the point clearer, Grimm stutters nervously as he talks to his fiancée, Marja (Marsha Hunt), an involuntary action that betrays the war neurosis from which he suffers, as well as his affection. He – and by extension Germany – has, as Marja later explains when she postpones their wedding, 'changed so inside himself. I don't know him anymore. If I were to marry him now it would be like marrying a stranger.' As the perpetrator becomes the victim, it is war itself that bears the primary responsibility for what follows, although that is not in itself sufficient to excuse or explain Grimm's behaviour.

In post-war Poland, Grimm harbours a resentment of others that has neither restriction nor focus. As he tells Marja:

> You're the only human being in the world that I love; the others I hate, all of them. Not only these village clowns who babble idiotically in the market square, the German people, too. They lost the war not our army. Today the German people babble about freedom and democracy just like the Poles ... The future lies in victory, not in freedom. War will be continued until it's won, that's our destiny ... if we'd won I wouldn't have to spend the rest of my life as a country school teacher, to rot in this village. If we'd won there'd be a German middle Europe, German Lebensraum from Berlin to Baghdad: a colonial empire. I was promised a post in the Ministry of Education ... I'd have had position, responsibility, bring German culture to the barbarians.

In spite of this hatred, Grimm returns to his job at the village school. Six months later, on the day that Marja returns from her self-imposed exile in Warsaw, 'determined to go through with her marriage', Grimm rapes one of his pupils, Anna Oremska (Shirley Mills), who then commits suicide. Arrested by a village lynch mob and placed on trial, Grimm is released for lack of evidence. Impoverished and ostracized, he is compelled to leave Liztbark and, travelling on the financial assistance provided by Warecki and Levin, heads for Germany to, in his own words, 'start my life over again'.

We return to the courtroom as Warecki leaves the stand. He is replaced by the second witness to be called by the tribunal: Karl Grimm (Erik Rolf), 'brother of the accused', whose evidence is again presented as objective flashback,. Karl testifies to Wilhelm's new life in interwar Germany. It is a life that becomes a series of anecdotal episodes that chart the rise of the NSDAP from the Munich 'Beer-Hall' Putsch of November 1923 to the 'Blood Purge' of Ernst Rohm and the SA in June 1934.[28] It is another version of *The Nazi Plan*, but this time personalized and enacted for the camera rather than presented through newsreel footage. In this regime, Wilhelm ascends through the ranks of the SS and in late 1934, after fifteen years of frustration, he is made 'SS *Gruppenführer* and deputy chief of the Uniformed Bureau for Living Space in the Ministry of Education'.

Shortly afterwards, Karl, who with factual referents has threatened to 'write a signed article about ... the Reichstag fire and the Schleicher murder', is arrested and sent to a concentration camp on the orders of his newly promoted brother. He is forced to leave behind his young family, including a son, Willie (Richard Crane), who is thereby delivered into the corrupting tutelage of Wilhelm and the Hitler Youth. His testimony concluded, Karl leaves the stand and retakes his seat in the courtroom.

The third and final witness delivers the most damning evidence, again told through flashbacks as the image continues to be given authority over the word for the cinematic audience. This witness is Marja Paciekowski, the Polish woman to whom Grimm was engaged before the hiatus of the First World War. Unlike the broad narratives of the first two witnesses, which covered a combined total of fifteen years, Marja's narrative, which takes up the greatest on-screen time of the three testimonies, is concentrated on a matter of weeks in September and October 1939. Marja recounts how she arrived back from Nazi-occupied Warsaw in search of refuge on the day that the invading army entered Litzbark under the command of Wilhelm Grimm. Twenty years earlier her return had coincided with the rape and death of Anna; now it heralds the violation of the town. It is during this testimony that we learn of Grimm's and the Nazis' wartime crimes (including the drive for Lebensraum; the debasement of Poland and the Polish people; and the persecution of Polish Jewry); of Polish and Jewish resistance; and of the romance that develops between Marja's daughter, Janina (Dorothy Morris), and Karl's son Willie, now indoctrinated as a lieutenant serving under his uncle. Marja's testimony ends in tragedy when these star-crossed lovers are killed. With Willie's death the flashback ends and the camera returns to the courtroom, back to the future, to hear, one assumes, the verdict and sentencing. And yet, with ambiguity once again – and unusually for a Holocaust trial – there is to be no on-screen resolution: judgment remains for the future – and the audience. As the Presiding Judge sums up in his closing statement: 'Men and women of the United Nations, all of you: You are the jury. It will be up to you to finally judge all criminals and to determine the penalties that shall be meted out to them. For this will only be your war if the final victory brings *you* justice and a true and everlasting people's peace.' The final image is of the courtroom's roof where the lone swastika has been replaced with a row of flags (including the Union Flag alongside both the Stars and Stripes and, in a pro-Soviet gesture, the Hammer and Sickle) of those nations now united by the law promulgated in the courtroom below, suggesting in its final image that the future will be underpinned by justice.[29]

None Shall Escape is, therefore, the story of one man's life, a history of the Nazi Party, and the case against both as it recounts the party's origins; the tainting of the good German; the invasion of Poland; and the various crimes that accompanied the pursuit of Lebensraum. In so doing, it presents a familiar picture of the Nazi proclivity for betrayal, the corruption of youth (that, unusually, is also suggestive of paedophilia) and the abasement of women. What is not so familiar for a film of this period, however, is the focus on the Nazis' persecution of the Jews, the only crime to be referred to directly in the film's dialogue as a 'crime against humanity'.

Patricia Erens has written of the 'persistent archetype of the Jewish Victim' in American cinema that 'begins with Alfred Dreyfus in the 1890s, runs through the Pogrom and Ghetto films of the teens and twenties, recurs in problem films of the forties, which focus on anti-semitism [sic], and continues in the postwar films which treat the aftermath of the Holocaust'.[30] While the Jews of Liztbark conform to this archetype, de Toth is careful to establish for the Jewish community an identity that is individual, religious, cultural and, most strikingly, resistant. From the opening words of Warecki's testimony in which he recalls how he would 'stop to greet my friend the village rabbi', it is apparent that the Jewish community of Litzbark, embodied in the person of Rabbi Levin, is a respected and integrated part of village life, an imagining of post-war life that would become a United Nations ideal. In the villagers' discussion on Poland's future there is talk of Polish nationalism and 'Poland for the Poles', but Levin nods in agreement with such sentiments. Even Wilhelm Grimm, embittered but not yet indoctrinated, volunteers his hand to Rabbi Levin in greeting. It is only with the Nazi invasion of Litzbark in the autumn of 1939 that the Jewish population is singled out. Once the Nazis take control of the village, anti-Semitism becomes an evident feature of village life, one singled out by Marja in her testimony. Firstly Rabbi Levin is told to 'Get out of the line, Jew!' as he is forcibly placed in and then ejected from a food line; and then the village synagogue is desecrated so that it can be converted into stables. Levin (now clearly wearing a Star of David armband) protests, without success, as Jewish cultural and religious artefacts are forcibly removed from the synagogue and burnt in the village square. It is a scene that although exceptional for a Hollywood film was commonplace in towns and cities throughout Poland. Indeed, it is strikingly reminiscent of Lucy

Dawidowicz's account of the manner in which the Jews of Europe were persecuted during the process of German expansion:

> The very moment the Germans entered a town or city, they turned the Jews into outcasts of society. On entering Warsaw, the Germans agreed to distribute soup to the hungry population, having extracted one million zlotys from the municipal administration for that purpose. The agreement stipulated that all the hungry in the city, without exception, were to benefit. Yet immediately the Germans began to eject the Jews from the soup lines, calling upon the Poles to do the same, 'because the Jews deprive the Poles of their spoonful of soup' ... Terror enveloped the Jews. The Germans re-enacted the Kristallnacht in every town and city they invaded and occupied. All over Poland synagogues went up in flames. (Those spared the fire were desecrated, turned into stables, garages and public latrines.)[31]

Although impressive for its willingness to engage with the Nazis' treatment of the Jews, *None Shall Escape*'s narrative is less successful in presenting the reasons behind that persecution as, in the first instance at least, it is presented as a crime of expediency committed solely in the pursuit of victory. As Grimm tells Marja after the ransacking of the synagogue, in an echo of their conversation from twenty years earlier, 'the future is in victory not in freedom, so horses are more important than Jews, that's all'. Similarly, Willie, the naive ingénue, explains to Janina that the expulsion of the Jews from the synagogue is a practical solution, although his explanation is laden with Nazi propaganda and ideology:

> Willie: I really can't understand you Janina. Look, we need horses and horses need stables so we put them in the synagogue. Anyway those weren't people they were Jews. Janina, please don't go, I want to talk to you and I want you to understand. When I was young I felt differently, like you do, and then later I was taught that victory for the German nation was all that matters. Those people mean nothing to you and me.
>
> Janina: Nothing to you I know but they mean very much to me. They're my friends, my neighbours, my schoolmates – older people I've known since I was a child, younger ones who grew up with me. Why do you treat them like animals, worse than animals?

The persecution of the Jews culminates in the mass murder of Liztbark's entire Jewish population under the cover of darkness as they resist deportation on a night train bound for an unknown destination. It is a factual inconsistency – as Bernard Dick points out, 'the rounding up of the Polish Jews ... does not suggest 1939 at all, but 1941–42' – but one which has implications for how the Holocaust is depicted and understood in this film.[32] As we cut to the railway siding, men, women and children – all of whom now wear armbands as we, like the Nazis, identify the Jews of Litzbark as a group and not as individuals – are being lined up and forced into cattle trucks. As a narrative device for the benefit of the audience, Willie asks his uncle to explain what is happening:

Willie: I don't quite understand, Uncle Wilhelm. What's the difference whether they're here or somewhere else?
Grimm: It's not geography, Willie; it's mathematics. There's just so much food at our disposal, there must be fewer mouths to feed. Did I say mathematics? Simple arithmetic.
Willie: Well what's going to happen to them?
Grimm: There's a whole trainload coming from Warsaw, they'll attach these cars to it.
Willie: When?
Grimm: Tomorrow, maybe the next day.
Willie: But without food or water ...
Grimm: I've no doubt that some of them will manage to survive.

Once again Rabbi Levin attempts to intercede on behalf of his people; once again he is unsuccessful. Grimm's sardonic response to the Rabbi is laden with the anti-Semitism that has been his since being reborn as a Nazi:

Levin: I believe you know me, Herr Reichscommissioner.
Warecki: You knew him when he gave you money to escape to Germany twenty years ago.
Grimm: I believe that debt was repaid. Would the Jew demand interest?
Levin: If mercy is interest, yes, I demand it. You must remember what mercy is; you received it from us when you were in need.
Grimm: I merely carry out orders.
Marja: Afraid not to carry out orders.

Warecki:	Before God and man, I protest this crime against humanity.
Grimm:	By all means if it makes you feel any better.
Levin:	May I say a few words to my people before they are taken away?
Grimm:	If he thinks it will stop the noise, yes, let him call for silent prayers.

It is in these 'few words', quoted here in full, that Rabbi Levin warns against tolerance and urges resistance. It is a speech that remains a powerful call-to-arms, although it is also problematic for its pronouncement that this is to be the Jews' 'supreme moment', a statement that can be seen to victimize the Jews and therefore enforce the very identity against which Cole was writing:

> My people, be calm, listen to me. Let us prepare ourselves to face *this supreme moment in our lives*. This is our last journey. It doesn't matter if it's long or short. For centuries we have sought only peace. We have submitted to many degradations believing that we would achieve justice through reason. We have tried to take our place honestly, decently, alongside all mankind to help make a better world, a world in which all men would live as free neighbours. We have hoped and prayed, but now we see that hope was not enough! What good has it done to submit? Submission brought us rare moments in history when we were tolerated. Tolerated! Is there any greater degradation than to be tolerated, to be permitted to exist. We have submitted too long. *If we want equality and justice we must take our place alongside all other oppressed peoples regardless of race or religion. Their fight is ours; ours is theirs.* We haven't much time left, by our actions we will be remembered. This is our last free choice, *our moment in history* and I say to you let us choose to fight! Here! Now![33]

As the villagers run from the trucks to fight hand-to-hand with their guards, Grimm orders his machine-gunners to 'Drive them in!' In a little over two minutes the Jews of Litzbark are annihilated. After the shooting has ceased and the Nazis drive away, the dying Rabbi Levin – shot at close quarters by Grimm – is helped by Warecki to walk to an unmistakably cruciform railway signpost. Leaning first on Warecki and then on the cross for support he begins to say Kaddish, with

Warecki reassuring him: 'You were right, David. We will never die.' It is a short but revealing sentence, one which recalls the 'We Will Never Die' rally held at Madison Square Garden on 9 March 1943 as part of a campaign to increase public awareness of the ongoing persecution of the Jews of Europe.[34] In these four words, therefore, Warecki and the film make a plea for equality, solidarity and action, although as usual de Toth's message is not so straightforward. As the village's 'two servants of God' stand framed in the one shot, the camera pans back to show the shadow cast by the signpost across the ramp and the bodies of the dead. The image fades to black as Rabbi Levin dies, his shadow just visible beside that of the cross as, out of shot, he falls to the ground. Here again the words hint at unity while the image suggests division and culpability, as will be discussed below.

Lester Cole's motive for adding this scene of resistance to the original story was quite simple: 'From my point of view, the story lacked something: the Jews were passive; they went to their deaths without a struggle. True, some did, but others did not. [Burt] Kelly [the film's assistant producer] agreed; passivity was horror but not drama. A climax was required.' And if this hints at dramatic expediency rather than nobility of endeavour, Cole's memory of the scene and description of the thinking behind it are similarly revealing:

> When the train ... came to its destination, the Nazi guards ordered the prisoners down a ramp to waiting trucks that would take them to the gas chambers. The rabbi's moment of decision had arrived. He turned to his fellow victims ... and with what eloquence I could achieve and what passion I already had, I had him exhort them in what might be their last hours not to be herded like cattle to slaughter – but to resist ... Inspired, exalted, the Jews in the film fought, catching the Nazis by surprise, seizing guns, killing some of them, wounding others by throwing stones. They fought and died standing on their feet until the end, and some escaped to join the partisans ... if the Jews did not stand up and fight as I had written it, goddam, they should have, and this picture was showing them in their best light.[35]

Written many years later, this description of events is markedly different from the scene as it played in the film. For example, the train in the siding is not arriving full of prisoners to be unloaded and taken to gas chambers; and neither is there any visual evidence that the Jews killed any of the Nazis or joined the partisans. But it is Cole's insistence on showing the Jews 'in their best light' that is most revealing as to his own agenda and understanding of what happened in Europe.

The impromptu slaughter of the Jews is a brutal scene in which implications of martyrdom, conversion and crucifixion abound. Patricia Erens has noted in respect of *Address Unknown* (1944), one of the few other Hollywood films of this period to 'directly confront' the suffering of the Jews in Europe, that the 'mixing of Jewish and Christian imagery … universalizes the repressive policies of the Nazis, which also affected Catholics, Communists and other non-Jewish groups'.[36] This is, as the Rabbi's speech evinces, an interpretation that also applies to *None Shall Escape*. In having Levin die on the cross, however, there are unavoidable implications of martyrdom, redemption and apostasy. In the third edition of her book *Indelible Shadows*, Annette Insdorf writes that this scene, 'Rather than "Christianizing" the Jewish victims … suggests the ineluctable coexistence of the two religions.'[37] Yet, I would argue, the scene confirms the disruption of the coexistence of the two. In 1919, before the rise of Nazism, the two religions had been almost as one in Litzbark. When Warecki and Levin offer to help Grimm, the Catholic priest's words unite the two religions under God: 'Today you stand before two roads: upon one, humanity walks in brotherly love and human understanding. On the other run wild the forces of destruction. You've started down the wrong road, Grimm, but it's not too late to turn back. Walk with us in the light of God.' Such harmony is being lost by 1939. Although Warecki and Levin appear united in Levin's death scene, their union is disrupted by the physical and metaphorical presence of the cross that splits the frame from top to bottom and isolates them from each other. It is a barrier that does not physically prevent them from touching but visibly comes between them. As if to confirm the point, in the next shot the cruciform signpost is seen to cast its shadow across the bodies of the fallen Jews. But it is not solely Christianity which is implicated. As the Jews are shot down, the camera is aligned predominantly – although not exclusively – with the perpetrator and bystander, implicating the viewer as both.[38] It is this extension of guilt to include the watching audience in which de Toth was specifically interested. Fifty years later he would write: 'Hitler died in the fire he lit himself. Unfortunately, and to our everlasting shame, we just stood by till it was too late and millions went with him in the inferno. We were burned too before the international fire brigade was able to quell the fire.'[39] This complicity is implicit in the camera's point of view, and explicit in the complaisant Doctor Matek (Frank Jaquet), the village burgomaster, who exemplifies the complicity and culpability of tacit compliance and cooperation. Shortly after the Nazi invasion, Matek, Warecki, Marja and Janina gather in the village square on the orders of the Nazis. There they witness the humiliation of Rabbi Levin in the food line. As Warecki moves to intervene he is restrained by Matek, who tells him: 'There's nothing you can do.' Later, when Rabbi Levin asks Father Warecki and Doctor Matek for their help in stopping the deportation, it is again the doctor who is found wanting:

Levin:	Something must be done … Doctor Matek, I beg you to use your influence. There must be someone who can reason with them. *Doctor Matek hesitates.*
Warecki:	Take me down there. I'll talk to Grimm.
Matek:	Don't misunderstand me; I'll do whatever I can.

This question of responsibility is evident, too, in de Toth's use of the Hollywood staple of the polarized good German and bad Nazi. On the surface, the demarcation between the two is unambiguous. It is Karl who represents the 'decent, intelligent people of Germany', those people who, until it was too late, neglected to take the 'hysterical paperhanger and his crowd of hoodlums seriously'. It is Karl who promises to expose the crimes perpetrated by the Nazis against Germany, and it is Karl who is sent away to a concentration camp to 'be made well again'. In contrast, Wilhelm is an arrogant and proud man. He declines to sit down in court and refuses legal aid, insisting that he will act as his own counsel. A sadist, a rapist, a thief and a mass murderer, he is a man for whom no crime is either too big or too small. Yet Grimm, although he is deliberately made into a grotesque Brothers Grimm-style monster, is not a caricature Nazi villain, something evident from the casting of Alexander Knox as well as his on-screen persona. In fact, he and Karl are closer than it at first appears;[40] in Karl's words, he and Wilhelm are

> really more than brothers. We were only fourteen months apart in age and as far back as I can remember we were as close to each other as twins could be: in school, at the university, and all through the first war. I was beside him on the battlefield when he lost his leg. It was I that helped bring him to the base hospital and as is only right and natural it was my blood that was used in the transfusion that saved his life. It was my life too.

As it was Karl's blood – and purity of blood is integral to Nazi ideology – that was used to save Wilhelm's life, then the Grimm who returned to Litzbark after the war had been changed not only by the war, but also by the blood of the 'good' German. The Grimm who becomes the Nazi monster, therefore, is a synthesis of two Germanys, both of which must share the responsibility for the Nazis' crimes.

By 1943, as the 'We Will Never Die' rally and the AJC's request to Lowell Mellett made clear, news was regularly reaching America of the annihilation being carried out against the Jews in Europe. In spite of this abundance of information, for many Americans the Holocaust remained 'beyond belief'.[41] De Toth's film is therefore a precursor to the IMT in its use of film to show the veracity of the reports from Europe as well as to present a history of the Nazi rise and fall in film. The courtroom trope is essential for this endeavour. It is an accepted cinematic conceit that courtroom dramas, particularly ones that foreground the audience's participation as judge or jury, will self-reflexively attest to the veracity of its evidence. This is most commonly achieved via the on-screen swearing of an oath to 'tell the truth, the whole truth, and nothing but the truth'.[42] There is, however, no such moment in *None Shall Escape*, although Karl Grimm does tell the court – rather ambiguously – that he 'want[s] only to tell the truth'. Here it is the use of the flashback and cinematic convention which convinces us that we are being presented with the truth. Each witness's evidence is subjective and yet, as the first shot of Liztbark establishes, the flashback is objective: that is, the evidence becomes proof with our acceptance of the veracity of film. The message is clear: those events capable of being seen in film are incontestable; events unseen by us cannot be taken as proven. Hence it is that Wilhelm Grimm can be released for the rape of Anna – a crime for which there appears little doubt he is responsible – because there is no filmic evidence of his guilt. He may be clearly identified by Anna herself when she tells Marja of how she 'begged him to kill me. He knew I wanted to die. He could have killed me with the long pistols with silver handles. He could have killed me with his walking stick', but the camera never witnesses the rape itself. While in part this is a consequence of the fact that the depiction of rape was strictly taboo in 1940s Hollywood and could only be featured 'by circumlocution', this absence of visual evidence confirms that the only crimes which can be proven are those which can be seen by and recreated for the camera.[43] Twenty-five years on, Grimm can dismiss Warecki's evidence as 'gossip', asking 'Was it ever proven that I molested that young girl? Did the jury dismiss the case for lack of evidence?' There is no such doubt surrounding the murder of the Jews.

None Shall Escape, therefore, pre-empts the IMT in presenting film as proof and establishing the murder of the Jews by virtue of the fact that it can be recreated for and witnessed by the camera. However, in a moment which underlines the ambiguity typical of de Toth, this belief in film as a reliable witness is disrupted by the inclusion of a scene which questions the validity of what we are being shown. Based on de Toth's own wartime experiences, it is a scene which shows how the Nazis and the camera created false footage. As the villagers are forced to queue for food in a breadline, the officer in charge exhorts them to 'smile all of you. Look happy. I want to show smiling, laughing faces.' When the on-screen camera stops rolling, the bread is taken back: the film is a fraud. The affirmation of film as credible evidence is thus denied by this demonstration of film's own artificiality and mediation. By presenting the audience with evidence of the manner in which film can be manipulated, de Toth, a director renowned for introducing uncertainty, succeeds in creating his most ambiguous ambiguity.[44] It is a suspicion of newsreel footage that anticipates Lanzmann by forty years.

According to Lester Cole, when Harry Cohn first viewed the finished film he was shocked by what he saw, and by the scene of Jewish resistance in particular: 'My God, this goddam thing is *controversial!* It would be okay if *goyem* [Gentiles] made it, but for Jews to blow their own horn on how they're standing up to the Nazis is *chutzpah*, absolute *chutzpah*. It ain't true. Where the hell did Jews ever stand up to the Nazis?'[45] But Jews were, of course, standing up to the Nazis all across Europe in the armed forces of the Allies, with more than 500,000 serving with the US troops alone during the Second World War.[46] It was this, Cole recalled, that made the normally obstinate Cohn take notice: 'hundreds of thousands of Jews *were* fighting, in the armies of the USSR. That stopped Cohn, almost. "Them Commies, they're suddenly Jews? Atheists, for crissakes!" Then [Sidney] Buchman [one of Columbia's foremost writers] asked how about the Jews in the US Army fighting Nazis. That finally shut him up.'[47] Further, in camps and ghettos across Europe, there was also Jewish resistance in the form of spiritual and cultural defiance in the face of persecution; elsewhere it was a physical armed resistance similar to that envisaged by Cole. As the *Jewish Chronicle* of 2 June 1944 noted in its review of the film, 'The herding of Jews into the "death trucks" is absolutely horrifying; the vain fight that they make against the fusillade of Nazi machine-gun fire [is] reminiscent of the heroism of the martyrs of the Warsaw ghetto.' In some cinemas in America the audience applauded when the rabbi urged his people to resist; in others – the ethnic German areas of Brooklyn and the Yorkville section of Manhattan, for example – sections of the audience cheered when the Jews were mown down.[48] Anti-Semitism had grown steadily worse across America between 1942 and 1944. In February 1942, 15 percent of the American public believed that 'the Jew' represented the greatest threat to America; by 1944 this had risen to 24 percent, when only 9 percent and 6 percent chose Japan and Germany respectively.[49] As the *Brooklyn Jewish Centre Review* wrote of the anti-Semitic violence seen that summer: 'the streets of New York have become unsafe for Jews and – who knows? – pogroms might be in the making'.[50]

The rise of anti-Semitism in wartime America was also examined in Arthur Miller's novel *Focus*, published in 1945, in which a non-Jewish American, Lawrence Newman, experiences the prejudices of his friends and neighbours first-hand when a new pair of spectacles make him 'look like a Jew'. Near the book's conclusion, Newman sees a film in which, like the contemporary response to *None Shall Escape*, sections of the audience laugh and cheer as a number of Jewish men are hanged by German soldiers. As a pointer for how the Holocaust has been represented and remembered, it is interesting to note that in the recent film version of *Focus* (USA, Neal Slavin, 2001) this film within a film presents a different murder. In this version, the events of the film are discernible only by sound, because the camera's focus is the audience's reaction, not the crime. Although we do not see their death, it is clear how these Jews are going to die, and it is not by hanging. To a constant background of the noise of a slow-moving train, voices from the screen fill the cinema:

Voice 1 (Young Man): What are they going to do with us?
Voice 2 (Older Man): Better we don't know.
A baby cries.
Voice 3 (Young Woman) No, not my child!
Voice 4 (Older Woman): They couldn't kill the children just because they're Jewish.

A man in the audience leaps to his feet to participate in the film's dialogue as he shouts, 'Why not!' before lambasting the 'Ikey' in the audience who stands to complain.[51] In this updated version the hanging of individuals has been replaced with the death of anonymous and unseen groups of Jews who go to their deaths via the cattle-truck journey.

Jews were not the only minority subject to prejudice in 1940s America. A series of OWI interviews conducted in July 1943 'found that 96 percent of the whites surveyed favoured residential segregation, and 76 percent approved of segregation of buses and streetcars. Nine out of ten whites believed white and black soldiers should not train together; three out of four blacks believed they should.'[52] In a deliberate step intended to confront this American prejudice and hypocrisy, de Toth's international tribunal of thirty-two men contains several non-white jurors including black actor Jesse Groves. While not striking today, this was the first time that a 'mixed-race' jury had been seen on the American screen, something about which de Toth was rightly proud.[53] When de Toth first approached producer Jack Cohn, the brother of Harry Cohn, with the idea of placing four black men in the tribunal, the reply was unequivocally negative: 'Do you want to ruin me? ... You're nuts? I couldn't sell the fucking picture in the South with four niggers on an international jury of the United Nations' court. You are out of your fucking mind!' This was a response that was later retold by de Toth to Anthony Slide in greater detail:

> I could hear the voice – speaking from New York, even without a phone – of Jack Cohn, Harry's brother, the head of distribution: 'That son-of-a-bitch is crazy, how the fuck do you expect me to sell the fucking shit in the South with four *Schwartzes* – Bump-bump-bump!!! – four Latinos – Bump-bump-bump-bump!!!! – and four gooks [Asians] on the jury? That bum ... is a Nazi saboteur. Throw the son of a bitch out on his fucking ass.[54]

For de Toth, however, 'Not having blacks on an international jury would be like walking down Hitler's alley. Dirty Jews, jungle bunny blacks, negroes, faggots, discrimination is discrimination, racial prejudice is racial prejudice.' He eventually gained a compromise from Cohn that he would be allowed one black juror: 'I picked the blackest Afro-American ... who stuck out on the jury like a sore thumb ... as silent as Jesse Groves's part was, it represented equality, a judge's and human being's dignity. Blacks, in life and on film, didn't have to be handymen on plantations anymore.' It was a gesture that would be echoed a few years later with Ralph Bunche's appointment as US ambassador to the United Nations, but it would be many years before a similar statement was made in the domestic courts of America. It is also a statement that situated the persecution of the Jews within American racial prejudice, part of a context that went beyond Nazi Germany, and would have added poignancy when black soldiers were among the liberators of the camps.

To summarize, *None Shall Escape* is an anomaly. In featuring the mass murder of the Jews in detail it was unlike any other film produced by Hollywood during the war. In choosing to do so in flashback, it showed itself willing to imagine the crimes being described. Such representations of perpetration would be absent in the post-war period as the Holocaust was established as an event that defied representation and the reality was seen to overwhelm the imagination with the images of liberation seared on the collective consciousness. In the years afterwards, Hollywood would turn to the liberation footage in place of the Jewish witness, for it had authenticity through both its content and context. *None Shall Escape* is also culpable of this negation of the Jewish witness and the absence of a Jewish witness in the courtroom. For the post-war world that absence has been explained as part of the stigmatization of survivors as the world tried to forget the horror of the Holocaust. But in de Toth's film the explanation is different. In this microcosm of the contemporaneous suffering of the Jews in Europe, made during the war as a warning to the future, there is to be no Jewish witness because *None Shall Escape* predicts that if the world continues to watch and take no action then there would be no Jewish survivors.

NOTES

1. André de Toth, cited in Anthony Slide (ed.), *De Toth on De Toth: Putting The Drama In Front of the Camera* (London: Faber & Faber, 1996), p.vii.
2. Ilan Avisar, *Screening the Holocaust: Cinema's Images of the Unimaginable* (Bloomington, IN: Indiana University Press, 1988), pp.90–96, esp. p.92. At the time of writing, this controversy is being replayed in discussions surrounding Ben Urwand's monograph *The Collaboration: Hollywood's Pact with Hitler* (Cambridge, MA: Harvard University Press, 2013).
3. Judith Doneson, *The Holocaust in American Film* (Philadelphia, PA: Jewish Publication Society, 1987), pp.30–32; and Steven Alan Carr, *Hollywood and Anti-Semitism: A Cultural History Up To World War II* (Cambridge: Cambridge University Press, 2001), passim. For an historical overview of the pre-war period of isolationism, see Henry L. Feingold, *The Politics of Rescue: The Roosevelt Administration and the Holocaust, 1938–1945* (New Brunswick, NJ: Rutgers University Press, 1970).
4. H. Mark Glancy, *When Hollywood Loved Britain* (Manchester and New York: Manchester University Press, 1999), pp.51–52. See also Michael E. Birdwell, *Celluloid Soldiers: The Warner Bros Campaign Against Nazism* (New York and London: New York University Press, 1999).

5. Doneson, *Holocaust in American Film*, p.31.
6. Famously, however, even here Chaplin uses artistic licence to parody the camps, a decision which he would come to regret once he became aware of the full horror. Charles Chaplin, *My Autobiography* (Harmondsworth: Penguin Books, 1966), pp.386–411, passim. The background for the period is drawn from Clayton R. Koppes and Gregory D. Black, *Hollywood Goes to War: How Politics, Profits and Propaganda Shaped World War II Movies* (Berkeley, LA: University of California Press, 1987), p.28; Annette Insdorf, *Indelible Shadows: Film and the Holocaust*, 3rd ed. (Cambridge: Cambridge University Press, 2002), pp.59–68; and Avisar, *Screening the Holocaust*, pp.134–48. Again, the complexity of Hollywood's relationship with the Hitler regime has recently been discussed more thoroughly in Urwand, *Collaboration*.
7. Brian Neve, *Film and Politics in America: A Social Tradition* (London and New York: Routledge, 1992), p.74; Richard Maltby, 'Made for Each Other: The Melodrama of Hollywood and the House Committee of Un-American Activities, 1947', in Philip Davies and Brian Neve (eds), *Cinema, Politics and Society in America* (Manchester: Manchester University Press, 1981), p.79. See also Robert Fyne, *The Hollywood Propaganda of World War II* (Metuchen, NJ, and London: Scarecrow Press, 1994); Bernard F. Dick, *The Star-Spangled Screen: The American World War II Film* (Lexington, KT: University Press of Kentucky, 1985); and Koppes and Black, *Hollywood Goes to War*, passim.
8. K.R.M. Short, 'Hollywood Fights Anti-Semitism, 1940–1945', in K.R.M. Short (ed.), *Film and Radio Propaganda in World War II* (London and Canberra: Croom Helm, 1983), p.158. This is not to say that there was no attempt to feature the persecution of the Jews. In one of the many subplots of the Ginger Rogers/Cary Grant romantic comedy *Once Upon a Honeymoon* (USA, Leo McCarey, 1942), for example, Irish-American heroine Katie O'Hara (Rogers) exchanges passports with the Jewish hotel maid Anna so that Anna and her two children, Jacob and Sarah, can escape from Nazi-run Poland. In the ensuing confusion it is O'Hara and reporter Patrick O'Toole (Grant) who are sent to a concentration camp, having been identified as Jewish. While the scenes in the concentration camp make clear the Jewish specificity of the prisoners, the film remains focused on the fate of O'Hara and O'Toole.
9. Short, 'Hollywood Fights Anti-Semitism', pp.157–60; Doneson, *Holocaust in American Film*, pp.44–45.
10. Martin Scorsese, in André de Toth, *Fragments: Portraits from the Inside*, foreword by Martin Scorsese and preface by Bertrand Tavernier (London: Faber & Faber, 1994), p.xii.
11. Patricia Erens, *The Jew in American Cinema* (Bloomington, IN: Indiana University Press, 1984), p.167. See also Ilan Avisar, *Screening the Holocaust: Cinema's Images of the Unimaginable* (Bloomington, IN: Indiana University Press, 1988), p.97; and Dick, *Star-Spangled Screen*, pp.203–05.
12. This is the recollection of Marsha Hunt (who plays Marja in *None Shall Escape*), quoted in Patrick McGilligan and Paul Buhle, *Tender Comrades: A Backstory of the Hollywood Blacklist* (New York: St Martin's Press, 1997), p.310. The post-war trials of the Japanese, the so-called 'forgotten trials', did not make it to the screen even though Hollywood had been particularly damning about the Japanese during the war. *The Purple Heart* (USA, Lewis Milestone, 1944)

featured a war crimes court in Japan during which a prosecutor screens film in evidence, but this was of a Japanese court convened to try American airmen accused of bombing civilian targets. See Thomas Doherty, *Projections of War: Hollywood, American Culture and World War II* (New York: Columbia University Press, 1993), p.31–32.

13. 'Obituaries: André de Toth', *Guardian*, 31 October 2002.
14. Columbia Pictures, *Accessories Catalogue and Campaign Book* (1944) for *None Shall Escape*, p.2.
15. Lester Cole, *Hollywood Red: The Autobiography of Lester Cole* (Palo Alto, CA: Ramparts Press, 1981), p.205; Slide (ed.), *De Toth on de Toth*, pp.32, 41, 47; and de Toth, *Fragments*, pp.vii, 220–23, 262, 310–11.
16. For an introduction to the 'Hollywood Ten' and the Hollywood witch-hunts, see Anthony Slide, *Actors on Red Alert: Career Interviews with Five Actors and Actresses Affected by the Blacklist* (Lanham, MD, and London: Scarecrow Press, 1999); and McGilligan and Buhle, *Tender Comrades*.
17. Cole, *Hollywood Red*, p.202. Contrary to Cohn's expectations, *None Shall Escape* became a moneymaker, and the original story was nominated for an Academy Award. Subsequently Cohn used the film as a 'battle-cry' to his other writers to produce strong films which challenged the industry's regulations. For more on the irrepressible Harry Cohn and Columbia Pictures, see Bob Thomas, *King Cohn: The Life and Times of Hollywood Mogul Harry Cohn* (Beverly Hills: New Millennium Press, 2000); and Neal Gabler, *An Empire of Their Own: How the Jews Invented Hollywood* (London: W.H. Allen, 1989), pp.151–83, 198–202.
18. Slide (ed.), *De Toth on de Toth*, p.41; and Neve, *Film and Politics in America*, p.80.
19. Speeches dated 21 August and 7 October 1942, quoted in Samuel I. Rosenman (ed.), *The Public Papers and Addresses of Franklin D. Roosevelt: Compiled with Special Material and Explanatory Notes by Samuel I. Rosenman. Volume II: Humanity on the Defensive 1942* (New York: Russell & Russell, 1969), pp.329–30, 410.
20. Quoted in Tom Bower, *Blind Eye to Murder: Britain, America and the Purging of Nazi Germany – A Pledge Betrayed* (London: Warner Books, 1997), p.51.
21. The Allied ambivalence towards post-war trials ranged from moral and legal objections to simple uncertainty. See Arieh J. Kochavi, *Prelude to Nuremberg: Allied War Crimes Policy and The Question of Punishment* (Chapel Hill, NC: University of North Carolina Press, 1998); and Bradley Smith, *The Road to Nuremberg* (London: André Deutsch, 1981).
22. De Toth, *Fragments*, p.311; and de Toth, quoted in Slide (ed.), *De Toth on de Toth*, p.47.
23. David A. Black, *Law in Film: Resonance and Representation* (Urbana and Chicago, IL: University of Illinois Press, 1999), pp.2, 13.
24. Ibid., p.73.
25. While many victims of Nazi oppression took to the stand at Nuremberg, there was a relative absence of any Jewish witnesses from the entire proceedings, their place being taken by what Lawrence Douglas has called 'courtroom proxies': non-Jewish witnesses who would attest to the crimes against the Jews. See Lawrence Douglas, *The Memory of Judgment: Making Law and History in the*

2

After Nuremberg, 1946–1961: Film within Film in The Stranger (1946), Sealed Verdict (1948), Verboten! (1959) and Judgment at Nuremberg (1961)

It is generally accepted that in the immediate post-war period the attempted extermination of the Jews of Europe was an event at the periphery of mainstream American life. For some of the 80,000 survivors who arrived in the United States as Displaced Persons between 1945 and 1952, this public disinterest could come as a welcome silence.[1] Some spoke of not wishing to undergo the trauma of remembering; others sought to avoid being labelled as either 'victims' or 'Jewish' at a time when they desired acceptance and integration into American life as Americans. Alan Mintz has summarised this as follows:

> Telling the story of what had happened ... was not something survivors often chose to do even in the family circle, not to mention in public settings ... Survivors themselves were often not held in high esteem but rather viewed as morally tainted by the ordeal they had been forced to undergo. The very term *survivor*, with its intimation of heroism, did not come into wide currency until much later ... Survivors socialized among themselves and formed societies for mutual aid and memorialization, but intercourse with the wider American Jewish community remained limited. There was no invitation offered to draw closer and speak of what had happened 'over there'.[2]

More recent studies have begun to unpack the post-war situation and a fuller picture is slowly emerging, but what previous scholarship has shown is that some survivors who *were* willing to testify to their experiences perceived among both Jewish and non-Jewish communities a reluctance to listen which bordered on pretermission.[3] Henry Greenspan's work, for example, cites the experience of Manny Petchek, a survivor of Auschwitz, for whom there was a direct connection between this disinclination and the exposure to the Nazi atrocities in those newsreels that had become, with such celerity, icons of suffering and salvation: people 'didn't want to listen. No, they said, "We heard about it." Or, "We don't want to hear about it *because* we saw the newsreels."'[4] The newsreels had increased the number of vicarious witnesses to the horrors of Nazi Germany; but they were now assisting in the suppression of dialogue, effectively supplanting the survivor in public discourse, the voice of the victim replaced by the view of the liberator, the reality with the representation, and the memory with the postmemory.

That suspension of engagement with the facts behind the images – and with it any prolonged explanation of the crimes or identification with ith or of the victims – was replicated at the IMT. It would also be found in Hollywood's first post-war courtrooms in which newsreel footage was the primary testimony offered as evidence of the attempted extermination of the Jews of Europe. Even before the IMT had reached its verdict, these images had made their debut as evidence in the faux courtroom of *The Stranger* (USA, Orson Welles, 1946); crime and trial then reappeared together in both *Sealed Verdict* (USA, Lewis Allen, 1948) and *Verboten!* (USA, Sam Fuller, 1959). Finally, two years later, came *Judgment at Nuremberg* (USA, Stanley Kramer, 1961), the all-star vehicle which was released as Eichmann stood trial in Jerusalem.[5] Whereas *None Shall Escape* had used testimony recreated as flashback as evidence of the then ongoing persecution of Europe's Jews, in the films that followed liberation and the IMT's use of the seminal *Nazi Concentration Camps*, witness testimony was secondary to archive footage. That is, after 1945, after the impact of the images of liberation, after the IMT at Nuremberg, and after the convergence of the two in the prosecution's evidence *Nazi Concentration Camps*, film-makers who strove for authenticity presented as evidence those images which had already featured in a real-life trial, using them as apodeictic proof of a crime many still could not comprehend and did not wish to countenance. It was evidence of a loyalty to the authenticity of the courtroom while simultaneously affirming by default that this was a crime which could not be articulated and was beyond the realm of language and the imagination.

The Stranger (1945)

The *LA Examiner* had surely felt confident in its prediction of early 1944 that *None Shall Escape* was simply the 'forerunner of a cycle that will hit the screen; it is a neat, compact and interesting film dealing with the problem of retribution'.[6] However, the reality was never as straightforward. By 1946 it had become increasingly apparent that the machinations of the germinal Cold War would affect the western attitude to the post-war trials of the Nazis, the sentences passed, and the pursuit of suspected war criminals. The swift rehabilitation of Germany took precedence over its punishment. As renowned Nazi-hunter Simon Wiesenthal would later recall being told, 'Yesterday's allies just aren't allies any longer. You'll see how quickly things change. The Germans are needed against the Russians. Good Germans alone are too few.'[7] Instead of pursuing the Nazi criminal, Hollywood reflected the neuroses of war as film noir's often bleak version of life began to dominate.[8] One film, however, attempted to marry the war-induced paranoia and insularity of film noir with the desire for retribution. Although Orson Welles's *The Stranger*, a film made contemporaneous to the establishment of the IMT, is neither a courtroom drama nor a film that ventures into the courtroom proper at any point, it is the first post-war fiction film to integrate liberation footage, projected in the quasi-courtroom of the home of a Supreme Court Justice. Here it is used as evidence of genocide, although its purpose is to trigger guilt in a bystander rather than establish the guilt of the perpetrator.

A production of Sam Spiegel's International Pictures, *The Stranger* was filmed in late 1945 and released in May 1946. It was the only one of director Orson Welles's films to make a profit on its initial release, a fact that suggests that until the end of the IMT at least, the public retained an interest in bringing the Nazis to justice.[9] Written by John Huston and Anthony Veiller from an Oscar-nominated story by Hungarian émigré Victor Trivas, *The Stranger* recounts the hunt for a Nazi war criminal 'gone to ground' in the United States in late 1945. Edward G. Robinson, previously seen pursuing the insidious Nazi in *Confessions of a Nazi Spy*, plays Mr Wilson, a member of the Allied Commission for the Punishment of War Criminals. On Wilson's instructions, Konrad Meinike (Konstantin Shayne), the 'commander-in-charge of one of the more efficient concentration camps', is permitted to escape from confinement in Europe in the hope that he will lead Wilson to Franz Kindler (Orson Welles), 'one of the most brilliant of the younger minds from the Nazi Party' and an 'obscenity who must be destroyed'.

Wilson follows Meinike to the United States and to the small town of Harper, Connecticut, where Kindler is hiding under the alias of Charles Rankin, a popular and respected college professor.[10] On the very evening that the two new strangers arrive in town, Rankin is to cement his place in the community through his marriage to Mary Longstreet (Loretta Young), the daughter of Supreme Court Justice Adam Longstreet (Philip Merivale). It is, as Rankin tells Meinike when they meet, 'the perfect camouflage'. Alarmed at being discovered by his former underling, Rankin murders Meinike, initiating a sequence of events that culminates with his own death. In the film's famous finale, whilst being pursued by Wilson and Mary through the town church's clock-tower, Rankin falls to his death, having first been impaled on the sword of justice held by the clock's figure of the avenging angel.

Whilst later films would question the identity and identification of the suspected war criminal, using that uncertainty to generate tension, for the audience there is never any doubt that Rankin is Kindler. Instead, *The Stranger*'s tension and suspense is generated through the audience's participation in watching Wilson struggle to identify and then capture Kindler. As a recent arrival in Harper who shares Kindler's interest in horology (the only fact Wilson knows about Kindler is his passion for clocks), Rankin is soon Wilson's prime suspect. However, Wilson declares Rankin to be 'above suspicion' when the latter argues that the world's solution to the problem of recurrent German aggression is 'annihilation ... down to the last babe in arms'. Wilson considers this as proof that Rankin *cannot* be Kindler: he is too anti-German to *be* a German. It is only when Wilson's subconscious remembers Rankin's subsequent assertion that 'Marx wasn't a German. Marx was a Jew', that Wilson realizes his error. For this war crimes investigator, therefore, it is not Rankin's advocacy of genocide that is conspicuous in small-town America – even though it was Kindler who 'conceived the theory of genocide' – but the anti-Jewish focus of his prejudices. It is anti-Semitism and not mass murder which marks him out as an imposter.

Although the audience knows that Rankin and Kindler are the same man, Wilson does not yet have his proof. For this he requires the cooperation of Mary, Rankin's new bride, the only person who knows that Meinike came to Harper to meet Rankin. Rankin has already confessed to Mary that it was he who killed the mysterious stranger, but Mary knows only part of the story. She does not know 'the truth' about why they met, her husband's past or his real identity; she believes that he killed to guarantee their future happiness together and therefore she agrees to remain silent. It is a guilty silence of misplaced loyalty; as Wilson tells her in words that have an additional resonance in respect of the Nazis' crimes against the Jews of Europe: 'In failing to speak you become part of the crime.' The task that faces Wilson is, in the words of David Thomson, 'to persuade Mary that her man is the devil'.[11]

Neither Mary nor the audience is aware of what is to come when, soon afterwards, she visits her father at his home. As Mary enters she finds her father and Wilson watching an unseen film. Wilson stops the projector and with little delay accuses her of 'shielding a murderer', a charge she denies. He then produces a photograph of the recently deceased Meinike, to 'refresh [her] memory'. When this also fails to elicit an admission from Mary, Wilson seeks her cooperation in a different way. 'I've been showing your father some films', he tells her, 'and I'd like you to see them too.'

Although this marks the footage's Hollywood debut, the images themselves are on-screen for only twenty-six seconds of the two minutes and fifty seconds that Mary is made to watch. That is, just as the first reports from the IMT of the showing of *Nazi Concentration Camps* focused on the reaction of the defendants, so too it is Mary's response with which the camera will now be concerned. As the projector is turned on, the light emitted physically illuminates those in the room; it is a precursor to the intellectual enlightenment that will follow as Mary learns 'the truth' via this newsreel footage.

From this medium close-up of Mary and the projector, the camera cuts to a reverse shot, now showing us the screen from Mary's point of view. There are two important things to note here. Firstly, with the film being projected against the backdrop of the judge's luxuriant curtains, the mise en scène recalls the newsreels' recent appearance in cinemas across the country, making Mary and the audience witness the Nazi crimes once again. Moreover, staged within the setting of the judge's house, the curtains recall the IMT's use of film in a similar way. Secondly, there is the image itself. It is an indistinct image of a pile of bodies which shocks rather than explains, with the blurred shot mirroring the uncertainty of the contemporary understanding of what is being seen. There is no narration to accompany this image, the only sound being the mechanics of the projector. A further reverse shot of Mary shows how she feels compelled to look at these abhorrent images while also clearly wishing to turn away, mirroring the reaction of the first audiences to the films of liberation.

As Mary's eyes are drawn back towards the screen, she guides the camera to the interior of a large barn-like structure; it is Wilson who explains what is (not quite) being seen: 'A gas chamber, Mrs Rankin. The candidates were first given hot showers so their pores would be open and the gas would act that much more quickly.' The camera returns to look at Mary, its focus and clarity restored as it lingers on her discomfort, now confident in what is being seen and being shown.

The next images show American liberators gesturing for a Nazi to enter into a shed. Wilson's shadow falls across the screen as fact and fiction merge, simultaneously suggesting that he was one of the liberators, that his spectre continues to haunt the camps, and that he, in turn, continues to be haunted by the experience and the memory. But the specific content of the image itself is overlooked in his commentary: 'And this is a lime pit, in which hundreds of men, women and children were buried alive.' The camera then cuts to focus on Wilson as a large cudgel is seen being brandished in the footage behind him, now transferring to him the identity of victim.[12]

A close-up of Mary follows, her anguish both caused and witnessed by the camera. 'Why do you want me to look at these horrors?' she asks Wilson. He explains while standing between her and the screen, images of the dead now being projected onto his face as he now speaks for them, a gesture with a hidden meaning for the Jewish-Romanian Edward G. Robinson, who had been born Emanuel Goldenberg and participated in the 'We Shall Never Die' pageant of March 1943:[13]

> All this you see, it's all the product of one mind, the mind of a man named … Franz Kindler … It was Kindler who conceived the theory of genocide, mass depopulation of conquered countries so that regardless of who won the war Germany would emerge as the strongest nation in Western Europe – biologically speaking. Unlike Himmler, Goebbels and the rest of them, Kindler had a passion for anonymity. The newspapers carried no pictures of him, oh no, and just before he disappeared he destroyed every evidence that might link him to his past, down to the last fingerprint.

As Wilson describes 'the theory of genocide', the camera cuts back to the film for the final time. An emaciated man is seen clasping his hands together in a gesture of thanks, pain and prayer, as he is placed on a stretcher by Allied troops.[14] The images from the screen are not shown again, the camera choosing instead to focus on the interplay between Wilson and Mary Rankin.

Mary's initial response is that of denial, not to the crimes but to the true identity of her husband. 'My Charles is not a Nazi', she tells Wilson as she stands to leave. According to Wilson, 'She has the facts now but she won't accept them; they're too horrible for her to acknowledge.' But what facts does she have? Certainly none concerning her husband's direct involvement in such atrocities, and very few concerning the images she has been shown. While she may have been told more than the audience at Nuremberg, what she has been told is barely sufficient. Barbie Zelizer has noted in respect of photographs of liberation that any 'lack of accreditation, wrong or misleading captions, or a questionable relationship with words faded in importance alongside the success of photos in depicting the atrocities. Not surprisingly, people hailed the image's role in bearing witness and its ability to support a broad story about Nazi atrocity.'[15] It is a germane summation of Wilson's use of the newsreels which do not prove that Rankin is Kindler, or establish Kindler's role in the horrors that are being seen. In fact, the details of these images appear to be unimportant: there is no effort made to identify the 'gas chamber' or 'lime pit' that are shown, or to explain that not all who died did so in this way. Furthermore, there is nothing explicit in Wilson's narrative or the images themselves to identify the victims as Jewish. The description of genocide does not include explicit reference to the Jewish identity of the victims even though it can be inferred from the visual and had been crucial to Wilson's thinking. These are little more than symbolic cadavers: a pile of corpses that embodies the atrocity yet fails to inform the viewer as to the facts behind the pictures. Rather than presenting 'the truth', these images are gratuitous, inserted for their contemporary resonance and not as a didactic tool. It is a warning as to the perils inherent in misappropriating such images and one that both points to future films and recalls the use of film at Nuremberg. Mary is horrified by what she sees, but the images without appropriate exposition are a surfeit of horrors that lose their power to stimulate and educate. 'Mr Wilson was there', she later tells her husband. 'He tried to tell me that you were a Nazi and I was supposed to believe it. Imagine you being an escaped Nazi. Oh, he thinks he's very clever that Mr Wilson. His idea was to horrify me into telling him about the little man.' She concludes, 'He made it all up just to trick me.'

Like Edward G. Robinson, many Jewish actors would naturalize their names so as to avoid highlighting their Jewish roots. Likewise, many of Hollywood's post-war films that featured Jewish characters began 'to Americanize, to democratize Jewish history' as the image of the Jew moved from stereotyped foreigner to assimilated American.[16] In films such as *Crossfire* (USA, Edward Dmytryk, 1947), *Gentleman's Agreement* (USA, Elia Kazan, 1947) and *Open Secret* (USA, John Reinhardt, 1948) Hollywood finally focused on American anti-Semitism, a subject it had avoided for so long, including in *The Stranger*. The specificity of the Holocaust, however, was little in evidence, and even deliberately exorcized. In *The Search* (USA, Fred Zinnemann, 1948), for example, the first American film to be shot on location in the US-controlled zone of Germany, numerous implicit references are made to the Holocaust (including the stigmatizing of the tattoo; an erroneous reference to fully-functional gas chambers at Dachau; a Jewish child adopting a non-Jewish identity through fear of prejudice; and the embarkation of Jewish children to the new state of Israel), but all direct references to Hitler's 'Final Solution' were removed at an early stage.[17] In the same year as *The Search* and *Open Secret*, however, the persecution of the Jews of Europe was to be found in Lewis Allen's *Sealed Verdict*, the first film since *The Stranger* to evoke war crimes trials and the first to create the courtroom. It does so far more directly, using newsreel footage of the IMT to link the narrative of the film to the contemporary concerns.

Sealed Verdict (1948)

Paramount's *Sealed Verdict*, directed by Lewis Allen from the novel of the same name by Lionel Shapiro, is a mixture of rubble-film, romance and courtroom drama. Set in the fictional town of Reschweiler, in the American-occupied zone of Germany, the film places at its heart the post-war trial of seven Nazi war criminals before an American military tribunal. While the persecution of the Jews of Europe is not cited as one of the crimes in the courtroom and, indeed, the words 'Jew' or 'Jewish' remain absent from the film, the treatment of the Jews by the Nazis plays an important part in the film's narrative.

The film begins by 'attest[ing] to its [own] authenticity' with the opening credits noting that the exterior scenes were filmed on location in Europe.[18] This foregrounding of its realism and factual origins continues after the credits with scenes of the Nuremberg courthouse and then footage of Justice Robert Jackson's opening address at the IMT on 21 November 1945:

> This inquest represents the practical effort of four of the most mighty of nations, with the support of 15 more, to utilize international law to meet the greatest menace of our times – aggressive war. These prisoners represent sinister influences that will lurk in the world long after their bodies have returned to dust ... [They are the] living symbols of racial hatreds, of terrorism and violence, and of the arrogance and cruelty of power.[19]

As Lawrence Baron has noted, the camera then 'pulls back to reveal that this is a newsreel film being screened to United States Army lawyers' in an unidentified courtroom.[20] These lawyers will spend the next year prosecuting lower-ranking Nazis, with 'the legal procedure [they] establish in western Germany as representatives of the Judge Advocate General's office'. The procedure will 'just as surely become a part of international law' as that of the IMT; and it is law, the officer-in-charge tells the trainees, that is to be 'civilisation's only hope against war in the future'.

At the end of the introductory passage the camera focuses on one of the lawyers, Major Robert Lawson (Ray Milland), a former New York attorney and soon to be the lead prosecutor in the trial that follows. It is a trial in which, according to a newspaper article seen on-screen as the desire for realism and authenticity continues, seven Nazi war-criminals are accused of 'brutal crimes against humanity'. The most prominent of the accused is General Otto Steigmann (John Hoyt), former Military Governor of Bohemia and the so-called '"Scarface" mass murderer' who is 'reputed to have been guilty of the Leemrach atrocity', a massacre which Baron has identified as 'modelled on the Nazi massacre of Czechs at Lidice'.

The next phase of the film begins with the camera entering the courtroom. There is to be no explanatory introduction as seen at the commencement of *None Shall Escape*; instead, the trial is already in session. Inside the court the camera focuses on Steigmann as the prosecution's opening address accuses him of being directly responsible for the order that resulted in the death of 'all but one of the sixty hostages' in the Leemrach massacre. To prove this, Lawson provides documentary evidence (the first evidence is exhibit no. 132 'an order signed by Otto Steigmann which proves he was military governor of the area at the time'), but the case relies on testimony from eyewitnesses Maria Romanek (Patricia Miller) and 'modern Lazarus' Slava Rodal (Norbert Schiller), the lone survivor of Leemrach. There is no oath or flashback here as the film relies on the spoken word of the two witnesses. In a move that foreshadows the trial in *Music Box*, which will be discussed in Chapter 4, Rodal is also asked to confirm that Steigmann was the man who gave the order to fire. 'I never forget. As long as I live', he tells the court, pointing at Steigmann.

After Rodal's testimony the camera fades out, returning to the proceedings one week later. The prosecution has now given way to the defence, whose case relies on discrediting the human witnesses: 'The real problem of this court is to separate the valid documentary evidence from the oral evidence, which may have been distorted by hatred, by malice, or by a burning desire for vengeance. Much of the testimony which has been given is suspect, by reason of one or more of these very things.' Yet the defence's case also rests on oral evidence that is never confirmed in film, in particular the testimony of Themis DeLisle (Florence Marly), a young French woman who testifies to the role Steigmann played in rescuing her father from the Nazis in Paris. In trying to undermine DeLisle's evidence, Lawson suggests that Steigmann's motives for helping her father were sexual rather than altruistic, implying that she and Steigmann had a relationship that was tantamount to collaboration. It is an accusation dismissed as 'unfounded' and 'prejudicial' by the defence, a view shared by the judge who sustains the objection.

In his summing-up Lawson reveals that the case against the accused has included evidence of 'prison camps, the gas chambers, the crematory ovens, the mass graves heaped high with corpses, but all this, damning as it all is, fades into insignificance beside the pitiful stories of the victims'.[21] But these crimes have been neither seen nor discussed. Instead the focus has been on Steigmann's case, the evidence of Rodal and the human witness: 'the starved, diseased, maimed, deranged, survivors of history's blackest page'.

Steigmann is sentenced to hang, but in the trial's aftermath Lawson becomes increasingly uncertain as to whether the law has been served by the verdict: the case 'didn't really produce any really incriminating documents' and in particular there was no evidence of Steigmann being the man who ordered the first Nacht und Nabel (Night and Fog) decree, as has been claimed.[22] Lawson's doubts are not helped by

Rodal's subsequent confession that his testimony was what was needed, rather than what was necessarily true.

As Lawson's doubts grow he discovers that Steigmann's mother might possess the missing evidence. She has been living in the town throughout the trial, staying with Rabbi Jacob Meyersohn (Ludwig Donath), an old family friend. When Lawson visits Meyersohn, the Rabbi explains that he finds nothing odd in harbouring Frau Steigmann: 'I'm old. Hate is gone from me. I have only pity for those who persecuted me and my people.' Again there is no explicit use of the word 'Jew', and even 'Rabbi' appears to be a nickname and a signifier for both the townsfolk and audience rather than an accurate description. Meyersohn recounts how, after liberation from the camps, he returned to Rechsweiler and waited for news of his family, eventually learning that his wife died of starvation in Belsen and his three daughters were killed at Buchenwald. At Meyersohn's home, Frau Steigmann tells Lawson that her son is innocent: he is simply a soldier, a member of a Junker family that has 'believed only in Germany' and never been political. Rodal, however, tells Lawson that Frau Steigmann is concealing evidence which proves her son's guilt. (He has been blackmailing Steigmann's mother, believing that he is entitled to the money as compensation for his suffering.) In the scenes that follow, Frau Steigmann exposes her true feelings for Meyersohn, 'erupting in an anti-Semitic tirade, beginning in English but ending in German: "You meddle too much – you and all of your filthy kind, filthy (then slipping into German expressing what she had been suppressing), dirty, dirty pigs. Next time we will exterminate you."'[23]

The kind of explicit tirade and warning found in *Sealed Verdict* was unusual for post-war American cinema, where the Holocaust tended to have a more tangential presence. In *The House on Telegraph Hill* (USA, Robert Wise, 1951), for example, a film noir murder mystery, the Polish, non-Jewish heroine is a former inmate of Belsen, a camp which in this version of history is liberated by the Americans. But, again, this is not to suggest that there were no films that confronted the fate of the Jews of Europe both during and after the Second World War. In *The Juggler* (USA, Edward Dymytrk, 1953), the first American film to be shot in Israel, Kirk Douglas played Hans Muller, a German-Jewish survivor haunted by his past; or more widely known is *The Young Lions* (USA, Edward Dymytrk, 1958), a film that restaged and recreated liberation and could be said to begin the movement away from the use of newsreels as evidence.[24] It was not until 1959 and the release of *The Diary of Anne Frank* (USA, George Stevens, 1959), a film which 'has long been the most important landmark in the Americanization of the Holocaust', that American cinema began to take an overt interest in the Holocaust and its victims, albeit in a heavily sanitized form.[25] One week after the premiere of *The Diary of Anne Frank*, the camera returned to Nuremberg and to the evidence of liberation footage in Sam Fuller's *Verboten!*, a film that focused on collective rather than individual guilt but recalled some of the other themes of *Sealed Verdict*, in particular the forbidden relationship between an American soldier and a German woman.

Verboten! (1959)

Sam Fuller, as his autobiography *A Third Face* makes clear, 'was one of the most prolific and independent writer-producers in Hollywood', with his films intending 'to capture the truth of war, racism, and human frailties, and incorporate some of his own experiences'.[26] That personal experience influenced both what he represented and how, much as it had for de Toth fifteen years before. In May 1945, Fuller had been a member of the US 1st Infantry and had been present at the liberation of Falkenau, a sub-camp of Flossenburg situated near the Czech-German border. It was an experience the fledgling film-maker would record in a twenty-minute 16 mm film:

> My captain wanted a record of what happened there. I shot it all. The German officers loading the bodies of their victims onto the wagons, pulling them through the town. My captain wanted these townspeople to see it, put their noses in it, to look at what they claimed they didn't know anything about. The camps, the ovens, the dead. I shot many rolls of that stuff.[27]

Fourteen years later he would return to the camps and the by then unfashionable question of German guilt, becoming the first American film-maker to recreate the trial of the Nazi leaders in a fictive film. He would do so by intercutting staged scenes of the viewing gallery at Nuremberg with newsreel footage of the trial and images of liberation, forcing ordinary Germans to 'look at what they claimed they didn't know', now explicitly naming the victims as he did so.

Verboten! begins as the story of the forbidden love between an American GI and a German woman in Nazi Germany in the spring of 1945. The film's protagonist is Sergeant David Brent (James Best), the senior member of an advanced patrol whose responsibility it is to 'flush out' German snipers. Near the end of the war, advancing to the accompaniment of Beethoven's Fifth Symphony (a piece of music that by 1945 was Allied shorthand for 'Victory'), Brent is injured in attempting to secure the town of Rothbach. He is rescued and nursed back to health by Helga Schiller (Susan Cummings), a German woman with anti-Nazi sympathies who wants to show him that 'There is a difference between a Nazi and a German.' Like Karl Grimm in *None Shall Escape*, Helga regrets that she remained silent until it was too late for her country. 'And why didn't you Germans open your big mouths when he started throwing people in the gas chambers?' Brent asks. 'We are *all* guilty for not opening our big mouths', she replies, a candid condemnation that had been only suggested of the Polish in *None Shall Escape* fifteen years before but was now explicit and extended to include the Allies. As the German troops retreat, the soon to be repatriated Brent writes a letter of recommendation addressed to the incoming American Military Government (AMG), in which he swears that Helga and her family were never Nazis. 'This oughta give them the idea that you're kosher', he tells her, a comment that almost playfully confirms his complicity in forgetting the Nazi past while acknowledging her guilt and suggesting that she is to masquerade as Jewish to ensure her safety in the post-war denazification of Germany.

After the war, Brent returns to Rothbach. He now walks with the aim of a walking stick, a visual reminder of the damage caused by the war and a scene that recalls the return of Wilhelm Grimm in *None Shall Escape*. But Brent is not embittered. Now a civilian, he has come to work as a liaison officer with the AMG. Stock footage of post-war Germany depicts the destruction wrought by the Allied bombers. Shots of food lines and crumbling cities segue to a re-establishing shot of an Americanized Rothbach, with the 'Stars and Stripes' hanging from the municipal building (now the AMG's headquarters) where once there flew a swastika. The feeling is of transition and confusion as temporary signposts in English point the way to such unfamiliar landmarks as 'DP CAMP VIII', 'WATER POINT', 'FIELD HOSPITAL', 'US ARMY PRO STATION'.

Amid the desolation, Helga and Brent are reunited and then married, their union for her a pragmatic alliance of necessity that only later blossoms into true affection. It is an unsubtle analogy for the American/German relationship, even if it becomes less straightforward if one recalls the fate of the wounded nation in *None Shall Escape*. As the newly-weds enjoy a honeymoon cruise, a different picture of Germany emerges as the ship's radio reports of the arrangements in place for the imminent start of the trial of the Nazi leaders where 'Herman Göring and twenty-one major war criminals will be charged with Crimes against Peace, War Crimes, and Crimes against Humanity. Martin Bormann, still missing, will be charged in absentia.' A short while later, the townsfolk of Rothbach assemble in the central square outside the AMG to listen to a radio bulletin of the trial's opening day. This outlines the crimes of which the Nazi leaders stand accused, including 'wholesale murders, beatings, tortures, concentration camp gassings, genocidal eradication of whole communities, and the killings of surrendered allied soldiers. They claim ignorance of their campaign of annoyance, brutality and annihilation such as the world has not witnessed since the pre-Christian age.'

Verboten! does not suggest that the guilt for these crimes rests solely with the accused in the dock, or indeed that all the Nazis are now in captivity. Inside the AMG building, one wall bears the banner: 'WANTED WAR CRIMINALS'. On the right are clipboards under the headings: 'MASS and ISOLATED ATROCITIES'; 'SLAVE LABOUR'; 'GESTAPO'; two for 'MEDICAL EXPERIMENTATION IN CONCENTRATION CAMPS'; then the 'SS' (Schutzstaffel) and finally the 'SD' (Sicherheitsdienst). The wanted men are identified by headshots of five real-life fugitives along with a description of their crimes: 'SS LT-GEN RICHARD GLUECKS, HEAD OF CONCENTRATION CAMP', the officer who in February 1940 reported to Himmler that Auschwitz was suitable to be used as a concentration camp; and, adjacent to him, 'SS BRIG-GEN WERNER BLANKENBERG, HEAD OF SECRET EUTHANASIA, OFFICE IN HITLER'S CHANCELLERY', an officer under Philip Bouhler, the head of Hitler's Chancellery responsible for the euthanasia crimes of *Aktion* T4. Next in the list of wanted men, and making his screen debut, is an unrecognizable 'SS LT-COL KARL EICHMANN, BOASTED OF 5 MILLION MURDERS. GESTAPO.'

As a consequence of the infamy and publicity of his trial, Eichmann or his image need little introduction today, and yet his prominence on the wall is an anachronism, for it was only at the IMT that the extent of his responsibility and involvement in the murder of Europe's Jews became apparent. After Nuremberg, as journalist Moshe Pearlman would write in 1963, Eichmann was 'Suddenly … the name on everyone's lips, an unknown, revealed by the central spotlight as the star player in a stark tragedy.'[28] In particular, it was the testimony of Dieter Wisliceny, Eichmann's deputy in Department IV-B-4 of the RHSA (Reichssicherheitshauptamt, the Reich Security

Head Office) that brought Eichmann to the world's attention. At Nuremberg, Wisliceny stated that he had last seen Eichmann towards the end of February 1945 in Berlin. 'At that time', Wisliceny continued, Eichmann had said that 'he would leap laughing into the grave because the feeling that he had 5,000,000 people on his conscience would be, for him, a source of extraordinary satisfaction'.[29] *Verboten!* evinces, therefore, that even as late as 1959 Eichmann remained a relatively anonymous figure even if his crimes were better known, referred to here by his first Christian name, Karl, rather than the more familiar Adolf. Perhaps most striking is the headshot used of Eichmann. Today one of the most iconic of Nazi war criminals, Eichmann, like Franz Kindler in *The Stranger*, had tried to conceal his identity during the war and regularly refused to be photographed. The image used here, with moustache and staring eyes, bears no similarity to face of the man in the glass booth.[30] After Eichmann comes 'HEINZ KAMMLER' the architect of the concentration camps; and then 'MARTIN BORMANN, LAST SEEN ALIVE MAY 2, 1945, CHIEF OF PARTY OFFICE'. To these names and faces is added the fictitious 'OTTO HEIDEN, ESCAPED FROM WAR CRIMINALS' CAMP, 'WEREWOLF' ORGANIZATION CHIEF', a man who murdered his son-in-law 'because of some non-Aryan strain' and was responsible for the murder of ' seventy-one American prisoners at Malmedy', the war crime which had galvanized the US commitment to post-war trials.[31]

In Rothbach, home to Heiden's son Eric (Sasha Harden), the Werewolves are described by the town's mayor (Steven Geray) as a group of 'fearless delinquents', a thinly veiled articulation of the contemporary American apprehension towards youth as seen more famously in *Rebel without a Cause* (USA, Nicholas Ray, 1955) and *Blackboard Jungle* (USA, Richard Brooks, 1955). The Werewolves are a threat whose numbers are growing under the leadership of Bruno Eckhart (Tom Pittmann), an old friend of Helga's who also works for the AMG. In a parallel to Fuller's earlier use of Beethoven, Wagner's 'Ride of the Valkyries' from *Die Walküre*, later used to such powerful effect in *Apocalypse Now* (USA, Francis Ford Coppola, 1976), accompanies a montage of Werewolf crimes in which archive footage of the denazification of Germany is assembled together with fresh images shot by Fuller. One of the identifiable Werewolves is Franz Schiller (Harold Daye), Helga's younger brother who, in a reversal of the more familiar portrayal of collective guilt, has hated all Americans since losing the use of an arm in an American air raid. When Helga learns of Franz's allegiance to the Werewolf cause, she is quick to condemn him, not because of the new loyalties of her marriage but because such behaviour is 'anti-German':

> Helga: Franz, the first to suffer under Hitler were the Germans ... The first to be thrown in camps were anti-Nazi Germans.
>
> Franz: He only put the Jews in there! The Jews and Poles, and all the enemies who started the war against us.
>
> Helga: He killed German Catholics, German Protestants ... German Lutherans, German priests, German old men; German old women; German cripples, German sick, German insane ... If I can prove to you what the Nazis did will you believe me[?] ... If I am wrong I will help you fight the Americans.

As soon as Helga has finished her sentence a drum-roll transports us from Rothbach to stock footage of the destroyed city of Nuremberg, and the interior and exterior of the imposing Palace of Justice. Spliced with this footage is a sentry post through which Franz and Helga pass as they enter into a small room that resembles a church interior but is in fact a reconstruction of the visitors' gallery at the IMT. In the complicated montage sequence that follows, fact and fiction continue to merge as documentary images of the IMT are intercut with shots of Franz and Helga as they experience the whole trial in one day (including events that have already happened, according to the previous scenes and radio bulletins).

Fuller's version of the IMT begins with an archive shot of the four judges and their alternates entering the courtroom. The images that follow show the accused in the dock as both a group and as individuals. These pictures are accompanied again by Fuller's own voice-over which lists the accused 'individually, and as members of ... [the] groups or organizations to which they respectively belong'. The camera then cuts to footage of Justice Robert Jackson standing by the speaker's stand on what purports to be the trial's opening day (although this is not the case, as Göering is clearly visible in the witness box and Kaltenbrunner in the dock). Fuller's narration, now assuming the role of Jackson, continues to guide the audience: 'Justice Robert H. Jackson, the chief American prosecutor, makes the opening statement for the prosecution: "The privilege of opening the first trial in history for crimes against the peace of the world imposes a grave responsibility. In the prisoners' dock sit 20-odd broken men, reproached by the humiliation by those they had led – ".' The camera cuts back to the dock, to a panning shot that moves across the prisoners from left to right. We then return to the gallery, now moving from right to left in imitation of the left to right pan across the dock seen the moment before. The symmetry of the camerawork unites both sets of observers in culpability and guilt, a parallel between the ordinary Germans, like Helga, and the Nazi leaders now seated in the dock. It is a unifying moment that is confirmed in the doppelgängers of Von Papen, Streicher and Speer, who are watching the trial alongside Helga and Franz.

The commentary continues: ' – almost as bitterly by the desolation of those they have attacked. What makes this inquest significant is that these prisoners represent sinister influences that will lurk in the world long after their bodies have returned to dust. They are the living symbols of arrogance, power, racial hatred, terrorism and violence.' Franz sits watching and listening intently, as yet uncertain as to what it is he has been brought here to see. A head-on close-up shows that although captivated by what he is seeing, he is also as yet unmoved. In contrast to the reaction of Mary Rankin in *The Stranger,* here it is as if Franz is confronting the camera's evidence, challenging it to produce something that will convince him of the truth of his sister's words; and yet at the same time he is also increasingly hypnotized by the words and images: 'The United States of America presents count one of the indictment that all the defendants participated as organizers or accomplices in a common plan or conspiracy to commit Crimes against Peace, War Crimes, and Crimes against Humanity. We will show you the defendants' own film, you will see their own conduct.' This last sentence is spoken over a re-establishing shot of the courtroom in which the viewing screen is now clearly visible. Brief clips from the films shown by the Americans at the IMT (and some which were not) are then played as an integral part of the IMT's proceedings. They begin with the image of a man being dragged backwards across a street as evidence of how the Nazis abused Europe's population

> in the course of the conspiracy. Its history is the history of the Nazi Party that grew from the brawling streets of Munich in the 20s. Their aim was the highest degree of control over the German community. 'Give me five years. Today: Germany; tomorrow the world. The Nazi party alone has the right to rule Germany and the right to destroy the enemy.'

In the gallery we return to a head-on close-up of Franz. An image of the Werewolf leader Bruno is superimposed over this face as Franz makes the connection between the horrors of Hitler's Germany and the actions of the Werewolves.

The voice-over continues with a photograph of Martin Bormann: 'Martin Bormann, last seen alive May 2, 1945, fate unknown, tried in absentia, said "The enemy is to work for us and as far as we don't need them, they must die."' The screen cuts to another close-up of Franz with an image of Bruno superimposed as the Werewolf leader repeats Bormann's words.[32] Newsreel images of a number of the Nazis' different victims are then shown, with the dialogue offering more explanation: 'German anti-Nazis were the first victims. Medical experiments were standard procedure at many concentration camps for Germans who did not agree with Hitler. Defendant Frick, as Minister of the Interior, directed the Nazi program aimed at the aged, insane, crippled, or incurable Germans. The so-called "useless eaters".' At this, the camera returns to the gallery, to a close-up of Helga and Franz; the latter's breathing now laboured, his brow glistening with sweat as he learns, as Helga had promised he would, of how it was Germany that suffered under Hitler:

> Thousands were committed to special institutions. Few of the German anti-Nazis ever returned. Evidence proved they were murdered because they were useless to Hitler's plan. A most intense drive was directed by Hitler and his Nazis against German Protestants, Lutherans, Catholics. Pastor Niemöller was sent to a concentration camp; Bishop Gräbe was beaten up. Hitler inspired vandalism against church property. Nazi teaching was inconsistent with the Christian faith. It was the Nazi plan to suppress the Christian church completely after the war.

We then cut back from the archive footage to the viewing gallery, following what is now an established pattern. This time a headshot of Bruno is superimposed over Franz as Franz remembers Bruno's condemnation of the 'old Christian era [that] lasted 2000 years and is a failure'. More archive footage follows, but now of desolation and poverty in occupied Europe as the narrative, redolent of the narrative path adopted by *The Nazi Plan*, moves to a consideration of the effects of Nazi expansion in a film montage which conflates all of the American films used at the IMT: 'But with the war the number of victims swelled to include citizens of all the nations in Europe.

Included among the executed and the burned were citizens from Holland, France, Belgium, Poland, Hungary, Czechoslovakia, Greece and other countries.' The footage then turns to the familiar images from the camps, particularly Belsen, as the film moves from a geographical analysis of the victims to a specific consideration of the crimes against the Jews for which the abasement of Christian teaching is given in explanation:

> But perhaps the greatest crime against humanity the Nazis committed was against the Jews whom they used as a scapegoat to camouflage their plan to make Hitler god and to make *Mein Kampf* the Bible. Goebbels was Hitler's trumpet. Goebbels catered to children, filled them with campaign cries that went to the heart of the Nazi movement – Hate was the Nazis' religion; hate was their battle cry; hate was their god.

Once more it is the memory of liberation which illustrates this explanation, although here it is the liberation of Auschwitz filmed by the Soviet troops. This includes the now familiar images of children displaying their tattooed arms to the camera. As these pictures fill the screen, the voice-over explains: 'Children of tender years were invariably exterminated since they were unable to work. The Nazis endeavoured to fool them into thinking they were going through a delousing process.' The reference to 'delousing' then triggers a cut to the killing process itself. Rather than the Zyklon B that a modern audience might expect, it is at first an image of an SS gassing van, before the camera moves to the interior and a hand opening a valve:

> A thousand years will pass and this guilt of the Hitler gang will still not be erased. It took from three to fifteen minutes to kill the people in the gas chamber depending on the climatic conditions. The Nazis knew when the people were dead because the screaming stopped.
>
> After the bodies were removed special Hitler commandos took off the rings and extracted the gold from the teeth of the corpses. Much of this loot was then transferred to secret vaults of the Reichsbank at Frankfurt am Main.

The pictures of the Reichsbank as used in the case against Funk – pictures that are known to be of dubious use as evidence but are authentic in the courtroom context – are shown only briefly before the camera cuts back to Franz who finally closes his eyes.

Brought to Nuremberg to witness that the Nazis crimes were directed firstly against Germans, it is the footage of the crimes against the Jews, universalized into an example of genocide, that forces him to acknowledge the Nazis' crimes and Germany's guilt: 'This was genocide, the premeditated destruction of entire peoples. Genocide – the direct result of the Nazi belief that they have the right to destroy Hitler's opposition. Tomorrow the world: dead or alive.' The footage concludes with the now infamous scenes from the liberation of Belsen, and two female Nazi guards burying the dead in a mass grave. We return to the gallery, where Helga, Franz and the other visitors remain seated. Franz is distraught, his head bent down towards his feet as he repeatedly mouths the word 'No'. Helga takes hold of his chin and in a symbolic gesture forces him to look up so that he too may bear witness:

Helga:	Franz, I want you to look ... You've got to look. We will look together. This is something we should see. Everyone should see. The whole world should see, Franz. You didn't believe it, did you? Franz, look!'
Franz:	I didn't know. I didn't know. I didn't know.

It is an image and a message that implores the world to remember the atrocities committed in the name of Germany.

The scene fades to be replaced with the image of Franz, now back in Rothbach, seeking out Brent to tell him what he has seen and learnt. The IMT has been a didactic experience triggered not simply by attending the trial but specifically by seeing the films:

Franz:	She took me to Nuremberg today, I saw the trials.
Brent:	She took you to the trials ... You saw Göring?
Franz:	I saw Göring. I saw film. I didn't know.

Because of this experience Franz betrays Bruno to the AMG. In the film's closing scene, the railway carriage that had been the Werewolf headquarters is engulfed in flame, the recently written words 'HITLER VERBOTEN!' clearly visible through the conflagration that seeks to cleanse Germany of its past. *Verboten!* links the image and the narrative, utilizing the camera as witness in both past and present, a pedagogic strategy which is aimed at both the diegetic and non-diegetic audiences. It is also notable for the explicit naming of the Nazis' victims and definition of the murder of the Jews as the 'greatest crime against humanity the Nazis committed'. Moreover, unlike *The Stranger* fourteen years before, *Verboten!* acknowledges that the German people also suffered under Hitler. If the earlier film was about facing up to the past, then this new film was about looking to the future. It is not surprising, therefore, that Fuller's movie is also impressive for its refusal to depict the Nazis and the Allies as opposites. Both are victims and perpetrators of war crimes, even if only one nation is on trial. These same issues would resurface within two years in *Judgment at Nuremberg*, probably the most famous of all Holocaust-related courtroom dramas, in which the Jewish voice continued to be absent as once again the Holocaust was represented through liberation footage only.

Judgment at Nuremberg (1961)

On 23 May 1960, David Ben Gurion announced to the Knesset and the world that Adolf Eichmann had been captured and was to stand trial in Israel for his crimes against the Jewish people. For the first time, the attempted annihilation of the Jews of Europe was to be the focus 'of a court action of international significance'.[33] In West Berlin on 14 December 1961, the day before Eichmann was to be sentenced to death, Stanley Kramer premiered *Judgment at Nuremberg*, his all-star courtroom drama featuring, amongst others, Spencer Tracy, Burt Lancaster, Marlene Dietrich, Montgomery Clift and Judy Garland. For the first time, the release of a Holocaust-related courtroom drama was to be a major international event. According to the souvenir programme produced to commemorate and publicize the film's opening:

> Probably no picture in Hollywood history aroused as much world wide interest as 'Judgment at Nuremberg.' During the course of production, newspapermen from 38 different countries visited the set, among them a team of photographers flown over from Germany for a special four-page layout on the Kramer production that deals with one of the blackest pages in German history.[34]

The premiere was a 'public relations bonanza' spread over several days at an estimated cost of USD 200,000.[35] A reception for 450 guests at the Grand Ballroom of the Hilton Hotel on the first day was followed by prearranged interviews with the stars on the second. The first screening the next day in Berlin's Kongresshalle was attended by 1,500 people, including Willy Brandt, the mayor of West Berlin and future West German Chancellor. For Brandt, this necessary reminder of Germany's malfeasance was 'an important political event' – recognition, as it had been for the fictional characters Karl Grimm and Helga Schiller, that 'the roots of the present position of our people, country and city lie in the fact that we did not prevent right from being trampled underfoot during the time of Nazi power'. He continued: 'We may like or dislike or disagree with many things but here it is.'[36] It was not a widespread attitude. In spite of the pre-release publicity, for Stanley Kramer all that could be seen in 1961 was Germany's desire to forget: 'The picture opened and closed that night and was not released in Germany until twenty years later after [the 1978 miniseries] *Holocaust* was a hit on German television, and even then it was a disaster.'[37]

The film made its American debut in New York five days later, going on to become the eleventh most popular picture of 1962 and the most successful American 'Holocaust film' in the United States until *Schindler's List*. In total it grossed USD 5,000,000, a fraction of the box office takings of United Artists' biggest hit of 1961 *West Side Story* (Robert Wise, gross USD 25,000,000) and Kramer's 1963 comedy *It's a Mad, Mad, Mad, Mad World* (USD 19,300,000), but the same as Sergio Leone's classic western of four years later *The Good, the Bad and the Ugly* (1967) and Kramer's own *On the Beach* (1959).[38] This, however, represented only a small net profit – the result, according to Kramer (and at odds with the publicity brochure's optimism), of the continued apathy felt by the American public towards war crimes and war crimes trials that had hampered the film since its inception: 'United Artists, my usual source of financing, would have preferred to film a group of people having their hair cut rather than pay the bills for a picture about war crimes trials. War guilt, people in ovens, and crooked German judges did not put them in mind of jingling coins at the box office.'[39] In fact, like the IMT before it, Kramer's film was criticized more for its length and lack of action rather than because of its subject matter per se. Even if, as Kramer asserted, the film's subject matter were unlikely to guarantee commercial success, it would certainly ensure critical success, for, as Pauline Kael would note caustically, critics 'knew that if they didn't like the film, they were as bad as Nazis'.[40]

Although intentionally released amid the media glare of Eichmann's trial, *Judgment at Nuremberg* had originally been presented on CBS's *Playhouse 90* on 16 April 1959, a month before the premiere of the film version of *The Diary of Anne Frank*, and over a year before Eichmann's capture was announced. Author Abby Mann had started work on the teleplay in autumn 1957, long before Eichmann was back in the headlines and at which time, he would later recall, to mention German guilt was considered a 'breach of good manners'.[41] '*Judgment at Nuremberg*, unlike the other films already discussed, is a painstakingly researched and recreated - but ultimately fictionalized and simplified – depiction of the so-called 'Justice Trial', the third of the twelve 'Subsequent Proceedings' held by the Americans in Germany from October 1946 to April 1949..[42]During the 'Justice Trial', held from March to December 1947, sixteen former members of the Reich Ministry of Justice or People's (*Volksgerichtshof*) and Special (*Sondergerichte)* Courts stood accused of having 'participated in a Common Design or Conspiracy to commit and did commit War crimes and Crimes against humanity as defined in Control Council Law 10' as enacted by the Allied Control Council on 20 December 1945.[43] On 3–4 December 1947 the verdicts were heard and sentences passed down. Ten of the sixteen were convicted, with four receiving life sentences and the remaining six sentenced to between five and ten years' imprisonment.[44] There was little homogeneity among the accused as individuals, even among those who shared the same sentence. The 72-year-old Franz Schlegelberger, for example, had served at the Ministry of Justice from 1931 to 1942, firstly as Secretary of State under Franz Guertner, and then as acting Minister of Justice upon Guertner's death in January 1942. He resigned from the ministry in August 1942 when the astringent Otto Thierack was appointed as the new minister. Schlegelberger argued that he had served the Nazi regime only reluctantly (although that did not prevent him from accepting a retirement gift of RM 100,000) and that by remaining in power he had ameliorated conditions in the Reich. The tribunal dismissed his reasoning and sentenced him to life imprisonment, concluding: 'We are under no misapprehension. Schlegelberger is a tragic character. He loved the life of intellect, the work of the scholar. We believe that he loathed the evil that he did, but he sold that intellect and that scholarship to Hitler for a mess of political pottage and for the vain hope of personal security.'[45] In comparison, another defendant, Oswald Rothaug, was a far less sympathetic character. Born in 1897, he had been appointed Senior Public Prosecutor in Nuremberg in June 1933, and from April 1937 to May 1943 was the Director of the District Court. The tribunal's judgment against Rothaug found no mitigating circumstances, as he too was sentenced to life.

In their abridged version of the 'Justice Trial', Kramer and Mann reduced the number of defendants from sixteen to just four in order to 'amplify' the issues. In Mann's screenplay each defendant is ascribed with a different character to represent the heterogeneity of the Nazi judiciary: Emil Hahn (Werner Klemperer), based on Rothaug, is abrupt and ill-mannered, staring around him 'as though he were the accuser instead of the accused'; Friedrich Hofstetter (Martin Brandt) is 'courteous, straightforward and sincere'; Werner Lammpe (Torben Meyer) is confused and tremulous; and, finally, Ernst Janning (Burt Lancaster), based on Schlegelberger, is the enigmatic representative of Germany's intelligentsia.[46] Individually distinct, all four face the same charge, 'called to account for murder, brutalities, torture, atrocities' and other 'crimes committed in the names of the law'. For Defence Counsel Hans Rolfe (the Oscar-winning Maximilian Schell), the 'avowed purpose of this Tribunal is broader than the visiting of retribution on a few men. It is dedicated to the re-consecration of the Temple of Justice.' Lawyers and, by extension, judges are often romantically portrayed as 'some idealized notion of … the personification of truth and justice embodied within the framework of the law'.[47] Here, however, it is the judges and the law who are on trial. As the US Chief Prosecutor Colonel Lawson (Richard Widmark), based partly on Telford Taylor, the United States Chief Counsel for War Crimes at Nuremberg, explains: 'The case is unusual in that the defendants are charged with crimes committed in the names of the law. These men … are the embodiment of what passed for justice during the Third Reich … [They] distorted and they perverted and they destroyed justice and law in Germany … Here they will receive the justice they denied others.'

Present at Nuremberg to 'judge the judges' and in the process reassert the law's integrity are three American civilian judges. The Presiding Judge and the film's protagonist is Dan Haywood (Spencer Tracy), an educated, mature man who cannot comprehend how men of obvious intelligence – and, in Janning's case at least, morality – came to enforce these immoral laws. It will be for Haywood and his two colleagues to sit 'in judgment of [the] judges in the dock. This is how it should be. For only a judge knows how much more a court is than a courtroom … It is the House of Law.'

According to Lawson, the responsibility for such crimes lies with the individual and not the process of law. It is an exculpation of the law that is only to be expected from a man who has devoted his life to – and indeed is a son of – the law. However, for Rolfe, if one is to assert that the guilt is that of the individual, then

> certain implications must arise. A judge does not make the laws. He carries out the laws of his country. The statement, 'My country right or wrong', was expressed by a great American patriot. It is no less true for a German patriot. Should Ernst Janning have carried out the laws of his country? Or should he have refused to carry them out and become a traitor ... The defence is as dedicated to finding responsibility as is the prosecution. For it is not only Ernst Janning who is on trial here. It is the German people.

The placing of the German people as a whole on trial had already been implied in both *None Shall Escape* and *Verboten!*, yet it had been carefully avoided by Jackson and the American prosecution at the IMT:

> We would also make clear that we have no purpose to incriminate the whole German people. We know that the Nazi Party was not put in power by a majority of the German vote. We know it came to power by an evil alliance between the most extreme of the Nazi revolutionists, the most unrestrained of the German reactionaries, and the most aggressive of the German militarists ... The Nazi nightmare has given the German name a new and sinister significance throughout the world which will retard Germany a century. The German, no less than the non-German world, has accounts to settle with these defendants.[48]

In being permitted to argue Janning's case in this way, Rolfe uses the courtroom as the forum for a more general exculpation of the German people. It is a corollary that is allowed to go unchallenged in the courtroom – as, indeed, does Rolfe's use of Carl Schurz's 'My country, right or wrong' dictum, a statement originally made before the US Senate on 29 February 1872. Rolfe fails to point out that Schurz, a German émigré born near Cologne in 1829, continued: 'if right, to be kept right; if wrong to be set right!' In using the abbreviated form, Rolfe exposes his knowledge of the darker side of Germany's recent past because these words, translated into German as 'Recht oder Unrecht mein Vaterland', were to be found on prominent display at Buchenwald.

Judgment at Nuremberg foregrounds the Nazi abuse of the rule of law, so as to be able to reassert the process of law and allow for a more general examination of the challenges that exist in trying to assess collective and individual guilt. It is a conventional courtroom drama in that it relies primarily on dialogue for its narrative and tension. The flashbacks of *None Shall Escape* are replaced, with one notable exception, by the oral testimony of German witnesses. The first witness is Doctor Karl Wieck (John Wengraf), Ernst Janning's mentor, who testifies to the corruption of the law under the Nazis. Next to offer testimony is Rudolph Petersen (Montgomery Clift), a man who had been forcibly sterilized on the orders of the defendant Hoftstetter by the authority of Ernst Janning. The third witness, Doctor Heinrich Geuter (Karl Swenson), was the defence lawyer in the 'notorious' Feldenstein Case, a travesty of justice that had been prosecuted by Emil Hahn.[49] In this case an elderly Jewish man, Lehmann Feldenstein, had been executed for 'racial pollution' under the Nuremberg Laws of 1935, having been found guilty of having 'intimate relations' with a young German girl, Irene Hoffmann. It is Irene Hoffmann herself (Judy Garland) who then takes to the stand to provide evidence for the prosecution. She is followed by Elsa Lindnow (Olga Fabian), a former cleaner to Mr Feldenstein, who is questioned as a witness for the defence. Irene Hoffman then returns to the stand to be cross-examined. The final witness is Ernst Janning, his testimony a confession that acknowledges Germany's guilt and concludes the trial.

Once again, therefore, there is no Jewish witness to bear witness to the crimes against the Jews for although Janning's Jewish physician, Doctor Alexander Cohn, is called to testify in the published script, he fails to make it to the screen.[50] The only witness to these crimes from a non-German perspective is the liberation footage introduced into evidence by Colonel Lawson at the conclusion of the prosecution's case. Unlike the introduction of newsreel to galvanize individual awareness as seen in *The Stranger*, this is intended as proof of collective Nazi brutality and specifically of the Holocaust, even though it again fails to explain or identify the victims as Jews..[51] Rather than evidence of a widening understanding of the Holocaust, the inclusion of the footage affirms that sixteen years after liberation, American memory of what was now 'the Holocaust' continued to be drawn from the documentary footage shot by the liberators. It is testament to the efficacy of the original film in the formation of memory and meaning, and of Hollywood's continued reluctance to let the victims tell their own stories.

On the stand, Colonel Lawson attests under oath that he was present during the filming of the images which are about to be shown. It is a statement that replaces the IMT's use of written affidavits, and the use of film on its own as 'the truth' that had been seen from 1944 until 1959. It is a problematic assertion for, as will be seen, Lawson's films contain pictures taken at the liberation of Auschwitz and Belsen, camps that were not liberated by the Americans and at which Colonel Lawson would not have been present. We (the non-diegetic camera and audience) focus on the accused as the footage begins to play to the silent courtroom. They are a group united in their collective guilt, but their reactions betray their individuality: Hahn looks straight ahead at the judges; Hoftstetter looks down; Lamppe looks at the screen; and Janning gazes away disinterestedly.

Clearly modelled on *Nazi Concentration Camps* – and with an attempt at replication and authenticity which exceeds the previous films within films – this compilation begins, as did its factual antecedent, with a map showing the camps' locations throughout Europe.[52] We are then taken on a tour of Buchenwald, Dachau and Belsen, western camps liberated by the western Allies and all found in the original film; they are now names which are familiar to an American audience and synonyms for horror, although what they show continues to be under-explained.

This new film begins in Buchenwald, with Lawson's narrative associating the three sections of the Buchenwald motto with three different images: 'Break the body' he intones as a naked, emaciated man is shown; 'Break the spirit', as the film cuts to a close-up of the face of a different prisoner; and then 'Break the heart', as the camera cuts to an image of a child. Lawson then turns to a consideration of the disposal of the bodies in ovens. A reverse shot of the defendants reveals that Lamppe has been compelled by Lawson's words to look at the screen. There follows a close-up of the manufacturer's nameplate on the ovens, and a montage of images of 'by-products': toothbrushes, shaving brushes, shoes, spectacles, gold from teeth, a lampshade, skin being used for painting, and the infamous shrunken heads. Following the precedent established in previous films, the camera alternates between reaction in the court and shots of the footage, noting that when Lawson presents the shrunken heads, Janning looks towards the screen for the first time.

The camera moves from 'by-products' to victims. By implication we are still looking at pictures from Buchenwald, but the footage now shown – which comprises many of the same images used in

Verboten! – is that shot by the Soviet film crew that liberated Auschwitz. As Lawson describes 'children who'd been tattooed to mark them for eventual extermination', the children, already used in *Verboten!*, are seen again, now seemingly being encouraged to roll up their sleeves and show their tattooed arms to the camera. The factual error as to the children's location obscures the distinction between Auschwitz and Buchenwald, between the different types of camp and their inmates, and between western and Soviet liberation, all of which are thus synthesized in the public memory as simply one camp and one experience. It is a distortion of the evidence in order to heighten the audience's shock, but the composite feels strangely out of place in a film which is as much about the Cold War as it is about the Nazi past.

From Buchenwald the footage moves to Dachau. Previously, Lawson's narration has been simultaneous with the images; for the shot of the bodies, however, there is only silence. After three seconds, Lawson explains the images: 'The bodies of those who had come in box-cars without food, without air, who hadn't survived the journey to Dachau.' He then provides an explanation of the killing process in the gas chambers and a demographic breakdown, country by country, of those killed. Numerous images of bodies are intercut with audience reaction to both the numerical and visual horror. There are close-ups of Hahn (who continues to look directly ahead at the judges), a horrified Hofstetter, a confused Lamppe, and Janning. Then Rolfe, Judge Ives (Ray Teal) and Haywood. The section concludes with Lawson, the camera showing him looking at the defendants as he introduces the footage of 'what was filmed when British troops liberated Belsen Concentration Camp'. The now familiar image of two female guards disposing of a body into a mass grave (again, already used in *Verboten!* as well as at the IMT) is followed by one of the most iconic of liberation images, that of a bulldozer disposing of bodies for 'sanitary reasons'. A close-up of the bulldozer's scoop is without narration. Again, there are no words that Lawson feels he can provide to supplement the images.

Lawson next moves to a description of Dachau's gas chambers that were, he tells the court, disguised as showers. Conditioned by the demand for authenticity, he confirms that this description is drawn from a statement made by an anonymous witness 'at one of the executions'. Again the images are familiar, their use a form of ritual and memorialization: 'Inmates were made to leave their clothing on a rack. They were told they were gonna take baths. Then the doors were locked. Tins of Zyklon B were released through the specially constructed apertures. You could hear the groaning and whimpering inside. After two or three minutes, all was quiet.' It is a statement that suggests that the gas chambers were regularly used as a tool for mass murder, but, as has been noted already, the chambers at Dachau were only experimental facilities. The confusion as to what we are actually seeing is augmented in the reverse shot that follows of Haywood's reaction to the footage. Haywood covers his mouth in horror as Lawson describes the release of the gas and the subsequent 'groaning and whimpering'. The clear implication is that Haywood is watching images of a gassing in action, but no footage of such a moment is known to exist, and it certainly could not have been filmed by liberating troops.[53] Kramer therefore uses the suggestion of an unseen and unseeable image to generate in the cinematic audience's imagination a picture of an unimaginable crime.

After the film has ended, these images continue to reverberate outside the courtroom. None of the accused has an appetite that evening, not even the recalcitrant Hahn. 'How dare they show us those films?' he asks. 'We're not executioners. We're judges.' Seated beside the accused is Oswald Pohl (Otto Waldis) as once again fact and fiction combine to buttress each other. During the war, Lamppe informs us, Pohl and Eichmann (surprisingly his only mention in an updated script) had been in charge of the concentration camps. How could such a large-scale slaughter have been possible, Lamppe asks. Pohl replies, while casually continuing to eat his food, that the real problem was the disposal of the bodies and not the killing. Across Nuremberg, Judge Haywood is also without an appetite as he dines with Mrs Bertholt (Marlene Dietrich), the widow of a senior German officer executed by the Americans for his part in the murder of American prisoners of war at Malmedy. She condemns Lawson's use of 'those pictures' before attempting to convince Haywood that her husband did not know about such things, much as Franz had claimed ignorance in *Verboten!* two years before: 'He didn't know! I tell you he didn't know! (*pause*) It was Himmler. It was Goebbels. The SS knew what happened. We didn't know.' Similarly, in court the next day, Rolfe acknowledges that he was 'ashamed that such things could have taken place in my country' but he protests that 'Very few Germans knew what was going on. None of us knew what was happening in the places in these films. None of us.' Although none of the American prosecution challenges him, for the non-diegetic audience Rolfe's words have already been exposed as courtroom rhetoric by the confession of the Halbestadts (Virginia Christine and Ben Wright), Haywood's housekeepers:

Mrs Halbestadt: Hitler did some good things … We won't say he didn't do some good things. But the things – the things they say he did to the Jews and the rest. Well we knew nothing about that. Very few Germans knew.

Mr Halbestadt: And if we did know, what could we do?

And then later, this time in court, Rolfe's words are again denied, now in Ernst Janning's mea culpa that places responsibility for Hitler before the German people:

> My defence would have you believe that we were not aware of concentration camps. Not aware? Where were we? Where were we when Hitler began shrieking his hate in the Reichstag? …
>
> My counsel says we were not aware of the extermination of millions. He would give you the excuse we were only aware of the extermination of hundreds. Does that make us any less guilty? Maybe we didn't know the details. But if we didn't know, it was because we didn't want to know.

Although Janning makes this comment as an individual, his admission is, to quote Primo Levi, for all those Germans who 'delud[ed] themselves that not seeing was a way of not knowing' and also those who believed 'that not knowing relieved them of their complicity and connivance'.[54] It was an assessment that Levi would also consider in the afterword to the 1987 edition of *If This Is A Man*, one of the outstanding Holocaust memoirs and a book that was first published in English in 1960:

> in spite of the varied possibilities for information, most Germans didn't know because they didn't want to know. Because, indeed, they wanted ***not*** to know … In Hitler's Germany a particular code was widespread: those who knew did not talk; those who did not know did not ask questions; those who did not ask questions received no answers. In this way the typical German citizen won and defended his ignorance, which seemed to him sufficient justification of his adherence to Nazism. Shutting his mouth, his eyes and his ears, he built for himself the illusion of not knowing, hence not being an accomplice to the things taking place in front of his very door.[55]

Judgment at Nuremberg is a film, therefore, that seeks to establish beyond any doubt that knowledge of the Holocaust was widespread across Germany and not reserved for those in power. It also offers an explanation for how such horrors came to take place in a civilized country. As Judge Haywood tells Ernst Janning in the film's closing moments: 'It came to that [mass murder] the first time you sentenced a man to death you knew to be innocent.' In placing the responsibility on the individual, *Judgment at Nuremberg*, like *None Shall Escape* and *The Stranger* before it, 'simplifies the question of establishing a connection between mass atrocity and individual responsibility'.[56] But in placing the wider responsibility on the judiciary and the Nazi abuse of the law, Kramer's film offers an easy and effective solution. By offering the corruption of the law as the genesis of the genocide, *Judgment at Nuremberg* offers the restoration of the law as a solution. As early as 1945, Simon Wiesenthal, working as a staff member of the 'Office of War Crimes', was told by his immediate superior, Captain Taracusio, a professor of international law, that 'Only the law can be our answer to an age of lawlessness', but this was not an age of lawlessness; rather, it was the law itself which had failed.[57] The simple return to law combined with an acknowledgment of its failure was not the solution, for the law had been culpable and, as Lawrence Langer has argued, 'Admission of guilt neither restores decency ... nor explains its perversion.' As he continued:

> with its concluding irony that by July 1949 none of the ninety-nine sentenced to prison at the last of the second series of trials was still behind bars, [this film] renders a judgment *of* Nuremberg, of Nazism, and of the contemporary world that it probably never wished to impose: that uncorrupted justice, the highest expression of law, order, morality, and civilization, is only a charade in the presence of atrocities literally embodied by the mounds of twisted corpses in mass graves at Belsen.[58]

Conclusion

The use of film as evidence in each of the films discussed in this chapter attests to the importance of newsreel footage for the audience both on-screen and off. It also confirms the impact that liberation footage had on the public imagination. Having been used at the IMT as credible proof of incredible crimes, and swiftly assimilated into public memory as evidence of the worst crimes of the Nazis, the liberation footage had historical authenticity in respect of both the crimes and the process of justice. In electing to use this as the pre-eminent evidence and representation of the murder of the Jews of Europe, the four films reveal their allegiance to the representation of the process of retribution. This unconsciously prioritizes the act of witnessing justice over the process of explanation and thereby silences the voice of the victim in favour of celebrating and reliving liberation, a moment of redemption as well as revelation for the American audience. And yet, in spite of its power as evidence, the documentary footage seen in *The Stranger*, *Sealed Verdict*, *Verboten!* and *Judgment at Nuremberg* was used primarily not for its historical value as evidence but for the effect it could be seen to have on both diegetic and non-diegetic audience. This was not a straightforward relationship: the two audiences were watching and reacting with different knowledge and experiences – they saw the same images but the meaning was changing with every viewing and new context. The reliance on liberation footage also meant the continued absence of the Jewish victim, a situation which would continue until after 1961 when, prompted by the new precedent and new paradigm of the Eichmann trial, the cinematic courtroom would finally turn to a Jewish voice. It was a change which reflected the rising cachet of the survivor and the questioning of the veracity of the documentary image.

NOTES

1. For an analysis of the background to this period, see Alan Mintz, *Popular Culture and the Shaping of Holocaust Memory* (Seattle, WA: University of Washington Press, 2001), pp.3–21; Peter Novick, *The Holocaust in American Life*, pp.62–123; Leon A. Jick, 'The Holocaust: Its Use and Abuse Within the American Public', *Yad Vashem Studies*, 14 (1981), p.303; and Leonard Dinnerstein, *America and the Survivors of the Holocaust* (New York: Columbia University Press, 1982).
2. Mintz, *Popular Culture*, pp.8–9.
3. For a different evaluation of the films in question and their meaning, see Lawrence Baron, 'Trial by Audience: Bringing Nazi War criminals to Justice in Hollywood Films, 1944–1959', in David Cesarani and Eric J. Sundquist (eds), *After the Holocaust: Challenging the Myth of Silence* (London: Routledge, 2012), pp.158.
4. My emphasis. Cited in Henry Greenspan, 'Imagining Survivors: Testimony and the Rise of Holocaust Consciousness', in Hilene Flanzbaum (ed.), *The Americanization of the Holocaust* (Baltimore, MD, and London: Johns Hopkins University Press, 1999), pp.45–67, esp. pp.50–51.
5. A similar use of film within film to explore individual and collective German guilt can also be seen in Ealing Studios *Frieda* (GB, Basil Deardon, 1947).

6. Cited in Lester Cole, *Hollywood Red: The Autobiography of Lester Cole* (Palo Alto, CA: Ramparts Press, 1981), pp.205–06.
7. Simon Wiesenthal, *Justice Not Vengeance*, trans. Edward Osers (London: Mandarin Paperbacks, 1990), p.49.
8. Judith Doneson, *The Holocaust in American Film* (Philadelphia, PA: Jewish Publication Society, 1987), p.50.
9. David Thomson, *Rosebud: The Story of Orson Welles* (London: Abacus Books, 1997), p.268. See also Natasha Fraser-Cavassoni, *Sam Spiegel* (London: Time Warner 2003), pp.91–100 passim.
10. Against Welles' wishes, *The Stranger* was subject to extensive cutting by producer Spiegel. See James Naremore, *The Magic World of Orson Welles* (Dallas, TX: Southern Methodist University Press, 1989), pp.269–72.
11. Thomson, *Rosebud*, p.267.
12. The cudgel image was taken at Buchenwald, and the 'lime pit' is the infamous woodshed found during the liberation of Ohrdruf, a sub-camp of Buchenwald in April 1945 in which layers of lime-covered bodies were found. The local townsfolk were made to enter the shed by the US troops so that they could see what had been perpetrated in Germany's name. Both images featured in *Nazi Concentration Camps* and other newsreel compilations of the period.
13. For more on the life of Robinson, see Rudy Belhmer (ed.), *Inside Warner Brothers (1935–1951)* (New York: Viking Press, 1985); Robert K. Carr, *The House Committee on Un-American Activities* (Ithaca, NY: Cornell University Press, 1985); Frank Donner, *The Un-Americans (1935–1951)* (New York: Ballantine Books, 1961); Charles Higham, *Warner Brothers* (New York: Scribner, 1975); Clive Hirschhorn, *The Warner Bros Story* (New York: Crown, 1979); Edward G. Robinson, *All My Yesterdays: An Autobiography* (New York: Hawthorn Books, 1973); Edward G. Robinson, Jr, *My Father, My Son* (New York: Frederick Fell, 1958); and James Robert Parish and Alvin H. Marill, *The Cinema of Edward G. Robinson* (Cranbury, NJ: A.S. Barnes, 1972).
14. This image was taken at Nordhausen slave labour camp, liberated by the 3rd Armoured Division in April 1945. Again, this image featured in *Nazi Concentration Camps* and other newsreels.
15. Barbie Zelizer, *Remembering to Forget: Holocaust Memory Through the Camera's Eye* (Chicago, IL, and London: University of Chicago Press, 1998), p.148.
16. Doneson, *Holocaust in American Film*, p.10–11.
17. Pat McGilligan (ed.), *Backstory 2: Interviews with Screenwriters of the 1940s and 1950s* (Berkeley, CA, and London: University of California Press, 1997). *The Search* tells of an American GI, Ralph 'Steve' Stevenson (Montgomery Clift), who befriends a small Czech boy, Karel Malik (Ivan Jandl), a former inmate of Auschwitz who has been separated from his mother, Hanna (Jarmila Novotna). See Patricia Bosworth, *Montgomery Clift: A Biography* (London: Bantam Books, 1979), p.127; and Brain C. Etheridge, 'In Search of Germans: Contested Germany in the Production of *The Search*', *Journal of Popular Film & Television*, 34, 1 (Spring 2006), pp.34–45.
18. The exterior scenes were shot in Strasbourg because of its resemblance to Reschweiler as described in Shapiro's novel. *Sealed Verdict* press book, British Film Institute Library, London.

19. The images shown are not all of the opening day of the IMT and the meaning of his speech altered by editing. A scene included to foreground the film's authenticity does therefore demonstrate film's ability to be manipulated as a witness and in tuen manipulate its audience.
20. Baron, 'Trial by Audience', p.158.
21. Ibid., p.159.
22. A brief introduction to the Nacht un Nabel can be found at http://www.ushmm.org/wlc/en/article.php?ModuleId=10007465.
23. Ibid., p.159.
24. Ibid., *passim*.
25. Flanzbaum, in Flanzbaum (ed.), *Americanization of the Holocaust*, p.1. See also Doneson, Judith E., 'The American History of Anne Frank's Diary', *Holocaust and Genocide Studies*, 2, 1 (1987), pp.149–60.
26. Samuel Fuller, *A Third Face: My Tale of Writing, Fighting, and Filmmaking* (New York: Alfred A. Knopf, 2002), back cover. Marsha Orgeron provides an excellent summary of the background to the film and the choices Fuller faced in bringing his experiences to the screen in ' "The Most Profound Shock": Traces of the Holocaust in Sam Fuller's *Verboten!* (1959) and *The Big Red One* (1980)', *Historical Journal of Film, Radio and Television*, 27, 4 (October 2007), pp.471–96.
27. Lee Server, *Film is a Battleground: A Critical Study, with Interviews, a Filmography and a Bibliography* (Jefferson, NC: McFarland, 1994), p.22. Forty-three years later Fuller's experiences of liberation would be an integral part of Emil Weiss's documentary, *Falkenau, Vision of the Impossible: Samuel Fuller Bears Witness* (France, Emil Weiss, 1988). See Annette Insdorf, *Indelible Shadows: Film and the Holocaust*, 3rd ed. (Cambridge: Cambridge University Press, 2002), p.201. It was an experience that Fuller himself would finally attempt to recreate in *Big Red One* (USA, Sam Fuller, 1981), a film intended to be his chef-d'oeuvre.
28. Moshe Pearlman, *The Capture and Trial of Adolf Eichmann* (London: Weidenfeld & Nicolson, 1963), p.9.
29. Dieter Wisliceny at Nuremberg, 3 January 1946, cited in *IMT*, vol. 3, p.289.
30. Wiesenthal, *Justice Not Vengeance*, p.82.
31. Although Heiden is fictitious, the 'Werewolf', the collective name given to guerrilla resistance units that carried out subversive raids on Allied troops in occupied Germany, is not. For more on the Werewolf, see Perry Biddiscombe, *The Last Nazis: SS Werewolf Guerrilla Resistance in Europe, 1944–1947* (Stroud: Tempus, 2000). The 'Werewolf' units were also the subject of Lars von Trier's *Europa* (Denmark, 1991).
32. In one of the more unusual of war criminal references, Martin Boorman's photograph is used to represent the fraudulent winner (living in Paraguay) of the fifth golden ticket in *Willy Wonka and the Chocolate Factory* (USA, Mel Stuart, 1971).
33. Lawrence Douglas, *The Memory of Judgment: Making Law and History in the Trials of the Holocaust* (New Haven, CT, and London: Yale University Press, 2001), p.98.
34. Al Horwits (ed.), *Stanley Kramer's Judgment at Nuremberg Souvenir Program* (London: Classics Illustrated, 1961), p.3. See also John Gillett, 'Judgment at Nuremberg', *Sight and Sound*, 31, 1 (Winter 1961–62), p.41.

35. Gary Fishgall, *Against Type: The Biography of Burt Lancaster* (New York: Scribner, 1995), p.207.
36. Cited in ibid., p.212. See also Tino Balio, *United Artists: The Company That Changed the Film Industry* (Madison, WI: University of Wisconsin Press, 1987), p.145; and Maurice Leonard, *Montgomery Clift* (London: Sceptre, 1997), p.263.
37. Stephen Bach, *Marlene Dietrich: Life and Legend* (London: Harper Collins, 1992), p.410.
38. Michael Munn, *Burt Lancaster: The Terrible-Tempered Charmer* (London: Robson Books, 1995), pp.141, 143; Fishgall, *Against Type*, p.212; and Balio, *United Artists*, p.138.
39. Stanley Kramer, with Tomas M. Coffey, *A Mad, Mad, Mad, Mad World: A Life in Hollywood* (London: Aurum Press, 1998), p.179.
40. Kael, 'Intentions of Stanley Kramer'.
41. Foreword to Abby Mann, *Judgment at Nuremberg: The Script of the Film* (London: Cassell, 1961), p.v. See also the novelisation Abby Mann, *Judgment at Nuremberg* (New York: Signet Books, 1961).
42. At the subsequent proceedings, 177 individuals (charged as individuals and as members of the SS, SA (Sturmabteilung), SD, Gestapo, civil servants, industrialists and German ministries) were called to account as war criminals. See University of Southampton archive collection, MS 200, Papers of the International Military Tribunal and the Nuremberg Military Tribunals, 1945–49. The twelve separate cases may be found under the references MS 200/1 to MS 200/12. These are indexed in K. Robson, *MS 200: Papers of the International Military Tribunal and the Nuremberg Military Tribunals, 1945–9* (Southampton: University of Southampton, 1993). For more on the Nazi judiciary, see Jackson, 26 July 1946, *IMT*, vol. 19, pp.400–01. See also J. Walter Jones, *The Nazi Conception of Law* (Oxford: Clarendon Press, 1939); Donald M. McKale, *The Nazi Party Courts: Hitler's Management of Conflict in his Movement, 1921–1945* (Lawrence, KS: University Press of Kansas, 1974); and particularly Ingo Muller, *Hitler's Justice: The Courts of the Third Reich*, trans. Deborah Lucas Schneider (London: I.B. Tauris, 1991).
43. University of Southampton Archive, Papers of the International Military Tribunal and the Nuremberg Military Tribunals, 1945–49, MS 200/3/25/3, pp.10608–09.
44. Of the remaining accused, four were acquitted, one died before the trial began and one was subject to a mistrial due to ill-health.
45. University of Southampton Archive, Papers of the International Military Tribunal and the Nuremberg Military Tribunals, 1945–49, MS 200/3/25/3, pp.10608–09.
46. The descriptions are taken from Mann, *Judgment at Nuremberg*, pp.15–16.
47. Steve Greenfield and Guy Osborn, 'Where Cultures Collide: The Characterization of Law and Lawyers in Film', *International Journal of the Sociology of Law*, 23, 1995, p.120.
48. Jackson, 21 November 1945, *IMT*, vol. 2, pp.102. This view was not held unanimously. The French, for example, were 'not prepared to make a rigid distinction between the Nazis and the German people as sharing responsibility for Nazi war crimes'. See 17 January 1946, *IMT*, vol. 5, passim; and Ann Tusa and John Tusa, *The Nuremberg Trial* (London: BBC Books, 1985), p.189.

49. As has been widely noted, the Feldenstein Case is based on that brought against Lehmann Katzenberger, chief of the Jewish community in Nuremberg and prosecuted by Oswald Rothaug. See Raul Hilberg, *The Destruction of the European Jews*, with a new postscript by the author (1961; New York: Harper Colophon Books, 1979), pp.109–11.
50. See Mann, *Judgment at Nuremberg*, pp.128–29. Thomas Harris, in an otherwise excellent examination of the issues raised by the film, mistakenly identifies Judy Garland's character as 'a Jewish woman named Irene Hoffman'. Similarly, in his biography of Montgomery Clift, Maurice Leonard reveals how Clift's father, 'a man who approved of neither blacks nor Jews', was outraged to discover that Clift was to play 'Rudolph Peterson, a retarded Jew who was sterilized by the Nazis in their genocide programme'. Both Clift and Garland were portrayed contemporaneously in the media as tragic 'victims': Clift had been stigmatized as 'a drunken homosexual', a man struggling to rebuild his life after a severe car crash; and Garland had been given less than five years to live following yet another period of hospitalization, on this occasion with severe hepatitis as the result of alcoholism. I suggest that in a confusion of fact and fiction, both authors identify the character's role with the actor's circumstances: both were victims and, even in the 1990s, victims were often understood to be Jews. See Thomas J. Harris, *Courtroom's Finest Hour in American Cinema* (Metuchen, NJ, and London: Scarecrow Press, 1987), p.136; Leonard, *Montgomery Clift*, pp.206–07, 246–49; and David Shipman, *Judy Garland* (London: Fourth Estate, 1992), pp.383–85.
51. Lawrence Douglas, 'Film as Witness: Screening *Nazi Concentration Camps* Before the Nuremberg Tribunal', *Yale Law Journal*, 105 (1995), p.478.
52. Seeing the map is made easier by the fact that unlike Mr Wilson in *The Stranger*, Lawson does not cast a shadow or become a screen, even though he stands directly in front of the camera.
53. The filming of the death throes is one of the few images to remain taboo and it is seldom created. A notable exception was the gassing of the Jews in the same year's *Operation Eichmann*, discussed in Chapter 3.
54. Primo Levi, *The Drowned and the Saved*, translated by Raymond Rosenthal (London: Michael Joseph, 1988), p.65.
55. Primo Levi, *If This Is A Man/The Truce*, trans. Stuart Woolf (1958/1963; London: Sphere Books 1987), p.386. Emphasis in original.
56. Lawrence Langer, *Admitting the Holocaust: Collected Essays* (Oxford: Oxford University Press, 1996), p.170.
57. Wiesenthal, *Justice Not Vengeance*, p.17.
58. Langer, *Admitting the Holocaust*, pp.170, 173. Emphasis in original.

Part Two

After The Watershed

The trial of former *Obersturmbannführer* Adolf Eichmann that began in a specially converted public theatre in western Jerusalem on 11 April 1961 has long been regarded as the watershed for the world's interest in the Holocaust. Unlike the IMT, Eichmann's trial foregrounded the mass murder of the Jews of Europe, with four of the fifteen counts under which Eichmann was indicted accusing him of crimes committed specifically 'against the Jewish People'. It had been evident from the trial's outset that the legal proceedings which followed were intended to convey more than simply the guilt of the man in the dock. The trial was, as Tim Cole has noted, 'a self-conscious attempt to bring awareness of the massacre of six million European Jews to both native-born Israeli youth and the wider world'.[1] A significant component in the successful completion of this objective was the coverage afforded to the trial each day by the world's media, including the daily-videotaped recordings made by the New York-based Cities Broadcasting Corporation. It was these images of the trial, edited and broadcast via television directly into people's homes, that 'presented [the Holocaust] to the American public as an entity within its own right' for the first time. That is, a generation after the IMT and the revelations of the liberation newsreels which had done so much to promote horror but discourage enquiry, moving pictures of this Jerusalem courtroom – pictures which, although they told the story of the Holocaust in an often dramatic and emotive form, still offered a mollified, distanced version of events that was contained within the controlled courtroom setting which represented the intersection of civilization, law and order – helped to inform and invigorate interest in what was soon 'popularly recognised' as the Holocaust.[2]

The decision taken by the three sitting judges on 10 March 1961 to allow cameras into the courtroom is placed prominently at the front of the official transcript of the trial. The judges write: 'We have satisfied ourselves that these machines stand concealed behind netted apertures, and that the persons operating them are likewise concealed; the machines record pictures by the ordinary lighting in the room and make no noise whatsoever.'[3] Robert Servatius, Eichmann's defence counsel, protested against the introduction of the cameras, regardless of their lack of cognizable physical presence, on the basis that the cameras would exert a psychological influence. This, reasoned Servatius, was potentially injurious to the process of justice because the 'knowledge that the proceedings are being recorded for television and the cinema may induce the witnesses not to give evidence truthfully'. Further, he argued, the broadcasting of the trial in an incomplete, edited format was 'apt to lead to a distorted representation of the proceedings'. In reaching their decision, the judges set out in some detail their reasons for consenting to the recording of the forthcoming trial 'on videotape films with soundtracks, for the purpose of television broadcasts and cinema showings in Israel and abroad' and reaffirmed the court's impartiality: 'Needless to say that the Court will see to it that the fact that the proceedings before it are published by television and cinema does not in any way alter the manner of conducting the trial, and we do not doubt that the representatives of the parties will conduct themselves accordingly.'[4]

As has been seen in the preceding chapters, at the IMT the American prosecution had intentionally relied upon extensive documentary evidence to present the case against the Nazi leaders, believing it to be the most credible and enduring of proof. One crucial element to this was the inclusion for the first time of film as witness, an innovation that would have a long-lasting influence on American film's subsequent attempts at representation of the Holocaust and specifically on the presentation of authentic testimony in the filmic courtroom.. As has been seen in Chapter 2, the first post-war films turned regularly to the use of film within film to depict the crimes of the Nazis. It was a decision intended to garner authenticity, accuracy and authority in terms of both crime and retribution. In so doing they replicated the silencing of the voice of the victim, relying on the power of the image over that of the word. The Eichmann trial, in contrast, situated the witness at the heart of its proceedings. Whereas only fifteen years previously the IMT had stultified, Eichmann's trial excited and horrified as the succession of survivors took to the stand to tell their stories to the watching world.[5]

In terms of the argument of this book, however, what is of note is that even with this new focus on the victims' stories and assurance on the integrity of language, Eichmann's trial also featured the use of film footage as evidence. This was no longer because of the credibility of the evidence provided in this way, but because the power of these images had already been established in popular memory. At the IMT the French, Americans and Russians had each presented film as evidence, in the process maintaining a distance between those camps liberated by the western and eastern Allies. During Eichmann's trial the Israeli prosecution amalgamated this footage into one film. This would now support rather than supplant the voice of the Jewish witness as, in a reversal of roles, nine 'identification witnesses' were used, each to 'identif[y] a portion of the pictures [in turn], and hence, in this way, [authenticate] the entire screening'.[6] The manner of its projection, the contents and responses again all pave the way for what was to follow as the courtroom began to put its faith in the victims' stories and not the ability of the camera.

The new compilation of archive film was shown in one sitting on 8 June 1961 to a darkened and, for security reasons, near-deserted courtroom. No longer simply evidence of Nazi barbarity or meant to give a sense of what the concentration camp meant, the images were presented specifically as evidence of the crimes against the Jews. These images began with pictures of an Einsatzgruppen execution in a movement away from the presentation of the camps as the sole or primary method of annihilation. The images continued, in the words of Israeli Attorney General Gideon Hausner, who provided the court with an accompanying narration to what were silent images, with 'a number of fragments. Firstly, the train from Westerbork to Auschwitz ... next ... will be Birkenau. Next, Mauthausen, and after that Strasbourg.' As for the following section, that would deal 'with the camps in the American sector. It will show the United States forces entering the camps, General Eisenhower visiting the camps, the surviving remnants of all kinds.' The concluding segment would then show an extract from the iconic footage of the liberation of Bergen-Belsen.[7]

Before the films were shown, Servatius, who had also been present at Nuremberg, had queried the authenticity of the images they were about to see. His objections recalled the problematic use of the Reichsbank footage at Nuremberg, and highlighted the increased anxiety and uncertainty in using film as witness:

> Firstly, we see the actions of an operational group – to that I have no objection. But, immediately thereafter, comes a scene of a pile

> of corpses, a burning pile. *I have the feeling that this scene was prepared after the event* ... Subsequently, there is a scene showing decapitated bodies, and the heads in a separate receptacle. *I assume that both the scenes of the corpses and those of the heads are genuine. But I have the impression that it was put together for the purpose of reports that were made. Thereafter, we are shown some rectangular objects, and it is said that this was soap made from these bodies. I request that, in this instance, too, the text be examined.*
>
> The last aspect to which I want to draw the Court's attention is the concluding scene depicting the disposal of the bodies [at Belsen]. I believe that this is more like a photographic report. There, the bodies are collected and gathered together and brought by a bulldozer into a pit. *My feeling is that whoever prepared the report aimed less at a factual description than at the impression made*, and I ask that this, too, should be examined.[8]

A similar discussion had taken place two days before when, in response to Hausner's request to show films, Servatius had informed the judges that, while he had no objection 'in principle' to any such screening, he 'would want to know ... when and where they were made'. In response, an almost insouciant Hausner informed Servatius and the court that

> with regard to some of the films, we know that they were taken immediately after the end of the War by the liberating armies, and they depict the camps in the same condition as the liberation armies found them. In the case of others, it followed from the contents that they were actually taken at the time of the events shown. We are unable to say when, exactly. *But we shall only exhibit a film in a case where some witness or other will be able to appear and swear that what he saw with his own eyes at a particular place and at a particular time looked as the film shows.*
>
> We have a short film of an execution by the Einsatzgruppen. I do not know who filmed it, and I do not know when it was taken. *But we shall produce a witness who will swear that this was what the execution looked like.* We have a film which was apparently taken at the time of a deportation to the Westerbork camp. *We shall bring a witness who will swear that when people were deported, the scene looked like that, and this will illustrate the testimonies heard.*[9]

Hausner had already made repeated reference to the source of the films' authority on 26 May 1961 when he had interrupted the presentation of evidence concerned with the destruction of the Jewish community in Hungary 'to request the directives and the guidance of the Court in a matter which is to take place next week':

> It is our intention to exhibit in Court a number of documentary films in order to illustrate certain events about which evidence had already been led, and other events on which evidence will be produced next week. Naturally we will ensure suitable authentication of the incidents contained in these films. *We shall produce witnesses who will be asked to testify under oath that this is how matters looked in fact.*[10]

As he outlined the content of these films for the court, Hausner was careful to stress how these films were to be authenticated:

> One film is about Auschwitz after the liberation – showing the appearance of the survivors. One film which we will also show ... concerns the Warsaw Ghetto ... There is one film dealing with the transport of Jews to Ravensbruck. There is another one showing scenes of the Mauthausen camp ... There is one scene, really apocalyptic, of thousands of people standing at a roll-call, naked, which was certainly shot at the precise moment when it took place. *And there will be a witness who will testify that this is indeed what it looked like.*[11]

As for the film of the transportation to Ravensbruck, 'We are not aware of the origin. I cannot tell the Court with certainty who photographed it. We have our assumptions, but I do not want to deal with assumptions. *At any rate we shall not exhibit anything which cannot be substantiated by witnesses.*'[12] Even in respect of those parts of the film that already been used by the prosecution at the IMT, Hausner would rely on survivor verification:

> According to the record of proceedings at Nuremberg, there was some authentication on behalf of the Allied military authorities at the beginning of the film. This authentication does not appear in the films in our possession, and hence we shall require a different method of authentication. There is also a film which the German television prepared towards this trial ... It is a film which

> we do not propose showing to the Court in its entirety, because it adopts a moralizing tone in order to arrive at certain conclusions and clearly it would not be proper for us to ask the Court to view all of it. But it contains sections on the operations of the *Einsatzgruppen*, which were apparently filmed at the time they were taking place, and *these, too, will be verified by witnesses.*[13]

What these extensive and repetitive quotes illustrate is that at Eichmann's trial, archive film, only fifteen years before being used as the most credible of evidence, supported with signed affidavits, was now reliant upon survivor memory for its formal authority as the image became subservient to the spoken word. It was not that the Eichmann trial was the first time that the victim's story had been heard – there are many examples of the victim being heard prior to Eichmann, with the success of *The Diary of Anne Frank* as a book, play and film being perhaps the most famous example from 1950s America, but the capture and trial of Eichmann focused the public's attention on the specificity of the crime being described by human witnesses, Jewish victims of the Nazi genocide who would soon become 'Holocaust survivors'. This rise of the survivor coincided with increased uncertainty around the use of film, with film evidence used only to supplement rather than supplant the oral testimony of the survivor. Once again it would be a factual precedent that would be followed in the filmic courtroom as, over the next fifteen years, the use of film within film to represent the murder of the Jews of Europe would gradually disappear, firstly from the courtroom scenes and then the film entirely, even if the memory of the films continued to exert an influence on how the Holocaust was referenced. In these next films the Jewish survivor gained firstly a voice and finally a physical presence in the courtroom as American film-makers gained fresh interest in the Holocaust and its victims.

NOTES

1. Tim Cole, *Images of the Holocaust: The Myth of the* 'Shoah *Business*' (London: Duckworth, 1999), pp.7, 58.
2. Novick, *The Holocaust in American Life*, p.133; Jeffrey Shandler, *While America Watches: Televising the Holocaust* (New York and Oxford: Oxford University Press, 1999), p.xix; and Tony Kushner, 'Who Do You Think You Are Kidding, Mr Sawoniuk? British Memory of the Holocaust and Kosovo, Spring 1999', in Peter Gray and Kendrick Oliver (eds), *The Memory of Catastrophe* (Manchester: Manchester University Press, 2001), pp.205-21.

3. A copy of this memorandum can be found in State of Israel Ministry of Justice, *The Trial of Adolf Eichmann: Record of Proceedings in the District Court of Jerusalem* (Jerusalem: Trust for the Publication of the Proceedings of the Eichmann Trial, 1992–95) [hereafter *AET*], vol. 1, p.ix.
4. Ibid.
5. Lawrence Douglas, *The Memory of Judgment: Making Law and History in the Trials of the Holocaust* (New Haven, CT, and London: Yale University Press, 2001), pp.104–05.
6. 8 June 1961, *AET*, vol. 3, pp.1283–85.
7 Ibid.
8. My emphasis. Ibid.
9. My emphasis. 6 June 1961, *AET*, vol. 3, pp.1196–97. Survivors were used therefore to authenticate films that had been shot by the perpetrator and/or liberator. This creates a tension between what was seen and what was being authenticated that was disregarded by Hausner and requires further analysis.
10. My emphasis. 26 May 1961, *AET*, vol. 3, pp.990–91.
11. My emphasis. Ibid.
12. My emphasis. Ibid.
13. My emphasis. Ibid.

3

From Out of the Shadows: Operation Eichmann (1961), QB VII (1974) and The Man in the Glass Booth (1975)

On 15 March 1961, almost exactly one month before Eichmann's trial opened, Allied Artists Pictures' *Operation Eichmann* (USA, R.G. Springsteen, 1961) recreated the life and dramatic 'shanghaiing' of the accused. Written by *None Shall Escape*'s author Lester Cole (credited under the pseudonym of Lewis Copley because of the Hollywood blacklist), this small-budget film had been produced subsequent to Eichmann's capture to meet, in the words of one reviewer, 'the demands of urgent topicality'.[1] Although released before *Judgment at Nuremberg*, it had been written four years after Abby Mann's original script for the latter film. While *Operation Eichmann* reveals similar misconceptions about the killing process to those depicted contemporaneously in *Judgment at Nuremberg* – errors no doubt exacerbated by the haste with which the film was made – it offers a strikingly different engagement with and representation of the Holocaust. Told in retrospect by a survivor – but without the courtroom structure and not from the witness stand - the film suggests itself as evidence in the forthcoming trial and includes a taboo-breaking graphic recreation of the final moments inside a gas chamber.

Operation Eichmann (1961)

Operation Eichmann, like *The Stranger* before it, is not a conventional courtroom drama, but the film does open in a stylised courtroom and, as an extended conceit, one can interpret everything that follows as evidence. In the opening prologue, a lone figure (Eichmann, played by Werner Klemperer, later that year to be seen as Emil Hahn in *Judgment at Nuremberg* before going on to play the far more benign and popular Colonel Klink in the popular television series *Hogan's Heroes*) stands in a distant dock, his shape picked out by a single spotlight in a long shot of a darkened, cavernous room. In this highly stylized representation of how Eichmann's trial is imagined, this barely discernible figure harangues the camera (and with it the cinematic audience) with a combination of defiance, disbelief and foreboding:

> Justice! Justice! Who are you to speak of Justice? All of you out there, staring at me as if I were an inhuman monster, a grotesque beast. You there, smug and self-satisfied now that I have been captured, you will learn of true justice and you will get it – from us! Even now, at this moment, while I stand here, forced to perform in your circus, your travesty of a trial, we are rising again, once more growing in strength in Germany, in Argentina, in America. You will put me to death but you will stop nothing. Hang me, but watch as you spring the trap on the gallows. Look at my dangling feet and you will see them dancing about the myriads I have sent to their graves. Heil Hitler!

The isolated Nazi, at this point still identifiable as Eichmann only by the audience's non-diegetic knowledge, then salutes the camera. It is a speech which is stylistically reminiscent of Rabbi Levin's speech in *None Shall Escape*, although the intentions are clearly different.

After a brief caesura for the opening credits, the film's narrative recommences with documentary footage of Buchenwald. Significantly, however, these are not images of the dead and dying found by the Americans at liberation, but rather pictures taken at the camp in 1961, as *Operation Eichmann* recognizes that the Holocaust is now part of both the past as history and the present as an aspect of memory and memorialization. The number of visitors present at the camp is testament to the burgeoning interest in the past and the nascent dark tourism. The images themselves are significant, with the shots of the 'Street of All Nations' and the close-up of Fritz Cremer's *Revolt of the Prisoners* projecting a specifically international message of remembrance and resistance.

A different voice accompanies these images, providing an opposing and measured but disembodied voice of the survivor to counter Eichmann's tirade:

> My name is David. I am one of the survivors of the hell and holocaust that was Nazism. These memorials will stand for all time in memory of its victims. Even now, so many years later, I still must remind myself that Adolf Eichmann was not only a beast, a grotesque monster, but the final end product of a political process. Eichmann was a Nazi.

Empowered by articulation, it is David (Donald Buka) – both cipher and metonym for a specifically Israeli survivor – who narrates the story of Eichmann's life from the end of 1941 to his capture in Buenos Aires in 1960. As with *None Shall Escape*, this testimony dissolves to tell the story as objective flashback, although significantly this is not evidence delivered from the witness stand within a proper courtroom. In this harbinger of Eichmann's trial, the 'holocaust that was Nazism' (the murder of the Jews of Europe cannot as yet be encapsulated in the capitalized singularity of the one word 'Holocaust', but this is drawing ever closer) comes to the fore in a story that concerns itself with the Jewish victims and their struggle for retribution and justice.

Eichmann may be identified as the 'end product of a political process', but he is also demonized and caricatured as an individual and one who is directly responsible for the Nazi crimes. As the story of his life begins it is Eichmann who, in the latter half of 1941, hosts a meeting for 'concentration camp' commandants, including a corpulent and sybaritic (almost Göring-esque) Rudolf Höss (John Banner), the commandant of Auschwitz. In this parody of Wannsee, Eichmann relays to them the instructions he has received directly from Hitler: 'I have been honoured by the Fuhrer with the responsibility for our supreme task: the Final Solution of the Jewish Problem … Auschwitz is ideally suited … we will also develop facilities for extermination in Dachau, Bergen-Belsen and Buchenwald. Our first experiments will take place in Auschwitz.' *Operation Eichmann* is full of such factual references that are also inaccuracies, the distinction between fact and fiction blurred by the framing of the fictive within a factual precedent, as the structure and content of Eichmann's speech is borrowed from Himmler's words to Rudolf Höss, words that Höss had repeated to the IMT on 15 April 1946:

> In the summer of 1941 I was summoned to Berlin to *Reichsfuehrer SS* Himmler to receive personal orders. He told me something to the effect – I do not remember the exact words – that the Fuehrer had given the order for a final solution of the Jewish question …

> He had chosen Auschwitz on account of its easy access by rail and also because the extensive site offered space for measures ensuring isolation.[2]

In this dramatization, Eichmann has a seemingly permanent presence at Auschwitz, from where he oversees the killing process. This he quite literally does in one particularly ghoulish scene in which he witnesses a group of Jewish men, women and children being put to death in the gas chamber. The horror of the scene is exacerbated by the camera point of view for it marks the breaking of the taboo of viewing the interior of the gas chamber. It is a gratuitous and meretricious scene that adds nothing to our understanding of the man or his crimes, and is a scene which, in using liquid Zyklon B, again misinforms as to the minutiae of the killing process. It is also a scene that resurrects the dead so that they may be violated again, now apparently for the satisfaction of the camera and Eichmann. Once again the scene is ripe with ambiguity in terms of meaning and is a direct descendant of *None Shall Escape*'s slaughter in the railway siding. Here, as there, the camera even forces the audience to share the perspective and potentially, therefore, the voyeurism of the perpetrator – this time Eichmann, who watches the death throes of the victims from the window in the door. On other occasions the camera is clearly situated within the chamber, its focus shifting between the victims and Eichmann as it acts as witness but also bystander, a passive presence able to record but not act. It is a moment that demonstrates the powerlessness of witnessing and at the same time reveals the inadequacy of liberation footage as a representation of the Holocaust's perpetration.

In this version of the past, Eichmann also participates directly in the murder process, something that the prosecution would strive to prove shortly afterwards at the real-life trial. It is he who takes personal responsibility for driving a group of Jewish prisoners onwards to Dachau when the order comes to evacuate Auschwitz, and it is he who orders and then leads the shooting of these prisoners when it becomes evident that they will be unable to reach their destination. Again there are clear parallels here with *None Shall Escape*, as it is a scene that visually recalls the murder of the Jews of Litzbark, with the personal culpability of Grimm being replaced by that of Eichmann.

The similarity between the two men, the two scenes and the two films, although this is clearly influenced by the fact that they share a common author, suggests that after seventeen years the conclusion is the same: regardless of whether the Jews of Europe chose to resist or to comply, they would all share a common fate. It was an observation that would shortly be the subject of historical debate, as Raul Hilberg's *The Destruction of the European Jews* (1961) and Hannah Arendt's *Eichmann in Jerusalem: A Report on the Banality of Evil* (1963) both raised unwelcome questions of alleged Jewish passivity, collaboration and compliance.[3] In 1944 all the potential Jewish witnesses were murdered; but in 1961, mirroring the events of the Jeruslaem courtroom, there are survivors left to tell the tale.

Operation Eichmann is, therefore, a film that tells the story of the perpetrator through the narration of the survivor, as for the first time in one of the films under discussion, the Jewish victim is given not only a voice, but also agency. It is also a film that includes some important changes in how the past is presented, even if it also relies on the written and visual connections to *None Shall Escape*. Soon the survivor would tell his/her own story, and not only in the Jerusalem courtroom. In his review of Eugene Heimler's *Concentration Camp* (1961), Lord Russell of Liverpool, Britain's former Deputy Judge Advocate General and one of the first commentators to write at length on Eichmann's trial, noted: 'This book deserves a place of its own in the literature of Nazi horrors as it deals with these events from an unusual aspect – the effects upon the victims themselves.'[4] It was an assessment that would soon appear archaic as, in the wake of Eichmann's capture and trial, the cachet of the Holocaust and Holocaust survivor rose exponentially. Works such as Rudolf Vrba's *I Cannot Forgive* (1963), Alexander Donat's *The Holocaust Kingdom: A Memoir* (1963), and Judith S. Newman's *In the Hell of Auschwitz* (1964) were published, as survivors found both a voice and – more significantly – a general market for their suffering as the murder of the Jews of Europe began to be not only conceptualized but also commodified as 'the Holocaust'.[5] Hollywood, too, began to recognize the increasing potential of the Holocaust, and soon the stories of its victims, although they had never been totally absent, could be seen foregrounded in films such as *The Pawnbroker* (USA, Sidney Lumet, 1964) and *Ship of Fools* (USA, Stanley Kramer, 1965), even if the reference to genocide was normally used to connote general moral and social problems at the heart of American society, rather than focusing on the Holocaust in particular.[6]

In early 1965, writer Sterling Silliphant and producer Herbert Brodkin, later a co-producer of *Holocaust*, had attempted to raise public debate about American involvement in Vietnam in their proposal for a motion picture to be called *Groundswell* (after a book by Siliphant). This was to be a courtroom drama of a different kind in which Vietcong troops would kidnap the US Joint Chiefs of Staff and place them on trial for war crimes. The film was never made but, by the close of the decade, private concerns about morality in the continuing war in Vietnam, particularly in the light of the trial of Lieutenant William Calley, were becoming increasingly public. How could a country responsible for a massacre 'where some 200 Vietnamese civilians were killed by [an American] force ... acting on the principle that one dead gook was as good as another' continue to consider itself the paradigm of justice?[7] As Telford Taylor, former Chief Counsel at Nuremberg for the American prosecution, wrote in 1970 in the introduction to his book *Nuremberg and Vietnam*:

> In the United States, far from being forgotten, the Nuremberg trials are invoked today, not in connection with a war that is ancient history to everyone under 50, but as part of the seething, anguished debate over the war in Vietnam, which is shaking our society to its foundations ... [The] wheel has spun full circle, and the fingers of accusation are pointed not at others for whom we have felt scorn and contempt, but at ourselves.[8]

By 1967–68, prompted in part by this self-doubt over its actions in Vietnam, the implications about America's own role in the Holocaust were being analysed by academics in Arthur Morse's *While Six Million Died* (1968), 'the first important study of American bystanders' and David Wyman's *Paper Walls: America and the Refugee Crisis* (1968), works which in turn stimulated an entire genre of writing on the Holocaust and America.[9] More significantly for the next film to be discussed in this volume, 1967 was also the year of the Six Day War, the first of two particular wars within a six-year period – the other being the Yom Kippur War of 1973 – that focused American attention – and particularly American-Jewish attention – on contemporary events in the Middle East.[10]

Israel had long been a part of American representations of the Holocaust. In *The Search* (Fred Zinnemann, Switzerland/USA, 1948), the orphaned Jewish child survivors are taken to Israel to start new lives in a new country. And thirteen years on it is notable that in *Operation Eichmann* the only people to escape alive from the camps are the children, with the boy David (Jim Baird) leading his fellow survivors to Israel to bring an end to the diaspora and begin a new dynasty. In the words of the adult David:

> The land was rocky and arid; water was scarce, the heat intense, but for the first time in two thousand years we had a homeland: Israel. From the holocaust of Europe we had arrived a decimated people, old and young, sick and wounded, deeply scarred in body and heart to build a nation. In a few short years we left behind for ever the despair and hopelessness that had been our heritage.

A similarly strong Zionist message, perhaps first encountered post-war in Kirk Douglas's *The Juggler* in 1953, was evident in *Exodus* (USA, Otto Preminger, 1960), *Judith* (USA/Israel, Daniel Mann, 1965) and *Cast a Giant Shadow* (USA, Melville Shavelson, 1965), all films in which the Holocaust formed the backdrop to – and is, in fact, often suggested as the raison d'être for – the creation of the state of Israel. The best known of these remains *Exodus*, the film of the international bestseller written by Leon Uris that had had an 'immense effect on public perceptions of Israel'.[11] For Sara Horowitz, *Exodus* is 'representative of popular American representations of Jewish history that, in depicting the state of Israel as the culmination and redemption of the *Shoah*, conflate the American and the Israeli Jew'. This 'working out [of] Jewish American identity', continues Horowitz, 'is even more explicit' in *QB VII*, a made-for-television miniseries and courtroom drama that was also based on a novel by Leon Uris. As Horowitz concludes, 'If in *Exodus* the birth of the state of Israel cannot be told without reference to the Holocaust, in *QB VII* the story of the Holocaust cannot be told without reference to Israel.'[12] It is a film that conflates not only the American and the Israeli Jew, but wartime America with present day Israel.

QB VII (1974)

QB VII is noteworthy as a Holocaust-related courtroom drama for a number of reasons. It was the first courtroom film to tackle the Holocaust after the Eichmann trial; the first to be made in colour; and the first to be made for television as a serial, reflecting both the growth of the medium and the Holocaust's appeal. It also marks a point of departure from its predecessors in that for the first time the war criminal brought to the courtroom is neither a Nazi nor a German; nor is he the defendant, for this is not a 'war crimes' trial, although war crimes are an integral part of the case.[13] Most significantly in respect of this book, it sees the screen debut of Jewish survivors returning to the courtroom to be seen delivering testimony in person from the witness box – witnesses who in some cases were also played by survivors.

Like *Judgment at Nuremberg*, *QB VII* is the fictionalized account of a factual trial, but it is also based on a book which had already fictionalized the trial and been a bestseller. In a passage of *Exodus* in which he had detailed the medical experiments carried out at Auschwitz, author Leon Uris had written: 'Here in Block X, Dr Wirthe used women as guinea pigs and Dr Schumann sterilized by castration and X-ray and Clauberg removed ovaries and Dr Dehring [sic] performed 17,000 "experiments" in surgery without anaesthetics.'[14] In June 1962, amid the renewed interest in war crimes and the mass murder of the Jews of Europe generated by the trial and recent execution of Eichmann, Doctor Wladyslaw Dering, a former inmate and doctor at Auschwitz, brought a libel action against Uris, his publishers and printers. Dering did not deny that he had been a surgeon in Auschwitz, only that he was guilty of any such impropriety. He had, in fact, already been cleared of being a war criminal in January 1947 when the English authorities established that no prima facie case against him existed. Seventeen years later, from 13 April to 6 May 1964, after eighteen days in court and in a famously pyrrhic victory, the jury found in Dering's favour, but awarded him only one halfpenny in damages.

This was the trial that brought 'Auschwitz to England' and, like the Eichmann trial, encouraged engagement with the past. Indeed author Anne Karpf, the daughter of Holocaust survivors, has noted that this 'was much more significant [than the Eichmann trial] ... At last it appeared that a smattering of what had been contained in the home had spilled out. It was an odd feeling, as if some family secret had now been shared, and this critical experience of my parents was now receiving a smidgeon of public acknowledgement.'[15] In his introduction to *Auschwitz in England*, Mavis M. Hill and L. Norman Williams's 1965 book on the Dering trial, journalist Alan Schwartz wrote: 'No book, no play, no motion picture I know approaches this factual account of a libel case in communicating the extent and meaning of this unspeakable blot on our past.'[16] It is a statement that acknowledges both the limitations of artistic representation and the lack of interest in the Holocaust found prior to this period. Within ten years, however, there would be both book and film of a fictional version of this trial as the Holocaust pervaded deeper into American life.

Adapted for television by screenwriter Edward Anhalt, *QB VII* (USA, Tom Gries, 1974) was broadcast in April 1974 as the first of

ABC's 'Novel for Television' series. A transatlantic production filmed in America, Europe (including scenes shot in Belgium at the former concentration camp Breendonk) and Israel, *QB VII* took three years to make, featured over 160 speaking parts and was edited down to under six hours in length from a total of eighty-eight hours of recorded film. Adhering to the basic facts behind the Dering case, but with the significant alteration that the proceedings are updated from 1964 to 1973, *QB VII* tells of how noted physician Sir Adam Kelno (Anthony Hopkins) sues American-Jewish author Abraham Cady (Ben Gazzara) for libel in Queen's Bench VII, a courtroom of the Royal Courts of Justice in London.

Cady has alleged in his international bestseller *The Holocaust* that while a prisoner in the fictional Jadwiga concentration camp, Kelno 'carried out a thousand or more experiments on Jews without the use of anaesthetic using them as human guinea pigs'. In extensive courtroom scenes, witnesses testify to their suffering in the camp yet, because of the death of a crucial witness, it is Kelno who emerges victorious. He is, however, awarded only one halfpenny in damages and leaves the court in silence. It is Cady who is surrounded by the world's press. In an earnest close-up of the type favoured by Hollywood he concludes with the trial's ultimately universal message that brings genocide into the present:

> Am I satisfied? It's a word that can't be used in connection with the issues this trial has touched upon because what happened between 1939 and 1945 in Europe is still happening in half a dozen countries across the world, and will continue to happen as long as evil men remain organized and good and gentle men are deceived, and put upon, and paralysed by them.

Dering's libel action had come to court in 1964 when the events being described were still new to the majority of observers. The trial in Uris's novel *QB VII*, originally published in 1970, took place, however, in 1967, by which time the Holocaust had gained widespread attention. In the miniseries the proceedings were again updated, now to 1973, as the attempted annihilation of the Jewish people was brought into the present, moving from the post-Eichmann period of awakening Holocaust awareness, through the summer of the Six Day War to the winter of the Yom Kippur War. It was, therefore, a movement from forgetting to remembering; from suppressing the past with screen memories to the oral articulation in the present. In *Operation*

Eichmann, the central character David and his wife Sara (Barbara Turner) had discussed the consequences of continuing to pursue Eichmann. 'Please', Sara says to her husband, 'I don't want to remember.' His reply, pre-empting Claude Lanzmann's interrogation of Abraham Bomba in *Shoah*, points to the imminent transition that would lead many survivors to speak of their experiences for the first time: 'You must remember', he tells her. 'We must all remember.' Similarly in 1964, Lord Denning, the Master of the Rolls, could reflect when writing about the Dering case that 'While the trial was in progress, many thought: "All this is too horrible. Let us turn over this page of history and forget it." '[17] By the time of the trial's novelization six years later, Leon Uris would have Abraham Cady implore the assembled survivor witnesses:

> Our side of this case begins tomorrow. I know and you know the terrible ordeal before you. But we are here because we can never let the world forget what they did to us. When you are in the witness box remember all of you, the pyramids of bones and ashes of the Jewish people. And remember when you speak, you are speaking for six million who can no longer speak ... remember that.[18]

Across the Atlantic in *QB VII*'s representation of Beverly Hills in the mid-1960s, it is Abraham Cady who wishes to forget – not only what happened to the Jews of Europe, but also that he is Jewish. He is the all-American hero who lives fast, loves and fights for his country, and has little time for the lessons of the past or his Jewish heritage. This attitude earns him the disapproval of his father, Morris (Joseph Wiseman), someone who cannot conceal his disappointment that his son, a successful screenwriter and winner of two Academy Awards, has not yet written 'one word about [his] own people'. If nothing else, Morris implores him, tell your own son:

> Morris: [H]e should know what they did to his father's people and nobody lifted a finger.
> Cady: The concentration camps were long ago. Why should we lay it on his generation? Best we forget about it.
> Morris: If we forget about it, it could happen again.

Cady is unmoved and continues to live the life of the playboy while his father moves to Israel. It is only when Cady himself travels to Israel in September 1973 to be with his terminally ill father that his position alters. Previously determined to define himself as an American and not a Jew, the death of his father and his presence in Israel amid the tension leading up to the Yom Kippur War see him reassess his primary self-identity.

At his father's funeral in Jerusalem, Cady invites his companion, the philo-Semitic WASP (White Anglo-Saxon Protestant) Lady Margaret Alexander (Lee Remick), to travel with him to visit Yad Vashem. 'It's the memorial', says Cady, reflecting the contemporary American understanding of the Holocaust, 'to all the Jews who died in Concentration Camps. My father always wanted me to go there.' Their visit ends at Ohel Yizkor, the Hall of Remembrance, where the name 'Jadwiga' has been added to the floor as another site of genocide and memory. It is an image that simultaneously gives authenticity to the suffering of the fictional inmates of Jadwiga while blurring the boundaries between fact and fiction, pulling Jadwiga into a wider referential realm. It also takes the act of witnessing beyond the courtroom.

Before visiting the memorial flame in the Hall of Remembrance, Cady and Lady Margaret, a Jewish/non-Jewish partnership, take a tour of the memorial's many photographs, concluding with a viewing of a brief compilation of moving images that includes a montage of liberation footage. Significantly, this is not part of the courtroom evidence but an aspect of the memorialization that had been started in Buchenwald in *Operation Eichmann*, with Cady and Lady Margaret being just two of many visitors to Yad Vashem. The film begins with a shot of a mass grave. Merging fact with fiction once more, a diegetic voice-over – in English but with a heavy generic Russian/Eastern European accent – explains how in 1945 the Soviets overran the 'most dreaded concentration camps, those of Auschwitz and Jadwiga'. Next come images of tiered bunks and emaciated women and children. A fictitious commentary is then added to the documentary images to enhance the film's authenticity: 'In Barracks 1 to 5 at Jadwiga the Nazis had been conducting secret physical experiments on prisoners ... How fast and efficiently can a Jew be castrated with minimum anaesthetic? ... How many times can a child's legs be broken and set before they can no longer be healed ... ?' Finally, there is the seemingly ubiquitous footage first shown by the Russians at the IMT of children at Auschwitz holding their arms to the camera. The camera comes to rest on one child in particular. It is by now a familiar image which has been seen many times, and yet this is also a new image as *QB VII* openly manipulates the evidence, doctoring the image (and with it the memory) for a new audience and new purpose. The blurred tattoo on the child's arm has been removed and replaced with a more distinct image, the camera now able to read the number on the child's arm. It is, therefore. an image included to enhance authenticity but one which has the opposite effect, foregrounding instead the film-maker's propensity for manipulation.

The reaction from Lady Margaret (even now the reaction is as important as the content) is immediate and universal: 'My God', she cries, it 'makes you ashamed to be a member of the human race'. Cady weeps. If his presence in Israel, the threat of war, and the death of his father have precipitated the rediscovery of his Jewishness, then it is the films which provide the final catalyst for the writing of the book in which he will marry the creation and continued existence of the Jewish state to the Holocaust:

> I know what to write now. I want to do the testing of the Jewish people by the lord God of Israel and I want to take them from the ovens of Jadwiga to Sinai and Suez. I want the reader to be there when they hoist the Star of David over Jerusalem and rekindle the Eternal Flame. I pray that God gives me the talent to do it.

After thirty years it is a book that can be entitled simply *The Holocaust*.

Although the footage of liberation – hitherto at the trials in *Verboten!* and *Judgment at Nuremberg* the filmic courtroom's evidential epiphany with regard to the Holocaust – continues to be used as the necessary referent to trigger feelings of sympathy, shared suffering, guilt and outrage, it is replaced in the courtroom by survivor testimony. Again this has a basis in fact. At the Dering trial, survivor witnesses, many of whom were Greek and spoke no English, gave evidence for the defence. In contrast, the six survivors in the witness box of *QB VII* are all English-speaking Israelis, a collective identity that adds another layer to the film's conclusions about the Jewish state and the Holocaust. The six witnesses have been brought to London by Doctor Parmentier (Edith Evans), a non-Jew who, now a consultant psychiatrist at Hadassah Hospital in Jerusalem, was once a doctor in Jadwiga. For Doctor Parmentier the decision to travel to the courtroom is a journey symbolic of the movement towards remembering, not only for the victims, but also the rest of the world. Like Cady senior, this is a conscious move for she does not want to forget the horrors she has seen: 'I do not want anyone to forget ever – otherwise in another country with other people it might happen again.'

The six survivors, some of whom are played by survivors, enter the courtroom simultaneously, their entrance greeted with an expectant murmur from the gallery and to a soundtrack of synthetic screams.[19] In conformation of a collective identity, they are seated in a line facing the judge as they all listen to each other's testimony, taking it in turns to provide evidence. The first witness, Bella Shulman (Hana-Maria Pravda), is introduced by a close-up of the number tattooed on her arm.[20] She continues to hold her arm upturned as she tells of the psychological and physical torment she underwent in Jadwiga. Once more this had a basis in fact. A key piece of evidence in the case against Dering was the several volumes of the Auschwitz Prison Hospital Operation Register. Each day the ledgers were brought to the courtroom and the witnesses would then show their arm and tattoo to the court, permitting identification when cross-referenced with the details in the register.[21] In the film, however, the ledgers are missing, and the search for them forms a significant subplot, one which allows the camera to move beyond the courtroom. The use of Mrs Shulman's arm in this way is indicative of the symbolic value now attached to the tattoo as a signifier. It is also an image that suggests an extended jump cut from here to the footage of Auschwitz and Jadwiga as seen at Yad Vashem. The two tattoos, apparently written by the same hand, connect the two images and the two survivors. Once again it is a contrivance intended to accrete authenticity that highlights the camera's increasing ability to manipulate the images of the past.

The witnesses who follow Mrs Shulman also testify to their suffering in Jadwiga, the camera often choosing to focus in close-up on the witness's face. Mrs Cohen (Miki Iveria) recalls being struck and abused as a 'damned Jewess' by a camp doctor; Moshe Bartov (George Pravda) in turn remembers being given his testicle with the words 'Here is your egg, Jew. Enjoy the other one because that goes next.' The testimony of the fourth witness, Mrs Gold (Isabelle Telezynska), introduces the question of the frailty of memory that would return to the filmic Holocaust courtroom in subsequent years. After having listened to her damning testimony, Kelno's lawyer, Sir Robert Highsmith (Robert Stephens), argues that Mrs Gold 'remember[s] because [she] want[s] to remember'. Her response, made directly to Highsmith's face as she walks through the courtroom, reinforces an idea already seen in *Operation Eichmann* that if the attempt made by many survivors to forget in the immediate post-war period was deliberate, then the pain of remembering was always obligatory: 'Mister Counsel, I want to tell you something. You don't forget anything the day you are fixed like a cat or dog at sixteen.'

In the previous chapters we have seen how the first films after 1945 utilized liberation footage as courtroom evidence for three reasons: to satisfy the desire for authenticity; to present a familiar and ostensibly explained horror; and to provide a recognizable catalyst for (predominantly German) contrition and guilt. *QB VII* marks a movement away from the use of this documentary footage as evidence in favour of the contemporary articulation of memory by survivors in a manner reminiscent of *Operation Eichmann* but now with a physical, visible presence in the courtroom. The following year, more tortured memories were to be found in *The Man in the Glass Booth* (USA, Arthur Hiller, 1975), another Edward Anhalt-penned adaptation that brought the Holocaust back into the courtroom and onto American screens. Like *QB VII* this film would have its origins in events of the early 1960s, be updated for the 1970s and conclude by universalizing the Holocaust, making a 'dramatic statement about common humanity – its ironies, weaknesses and general involvement in guilt'.[22] The manner in which this point is made, however, is markedly different as, made consequent to the Yom Kippur War, it is far more circumspect in its treatment of Israel: Anhalt's script for *QB VII* had presented the American and Israeli Jews as sharing a common identity and heritage, and had equated the Arabs with the Nazis. A year later it is both an American Jew and the Israelis who are accused of being Nazis. After thirty years it would be the first American courtroom film to replicate the Holocaust without the use of liberation or any other newsreel footage.

The Man in the Glass Booth (1975)

At Eichmann's trial the apparent normality and mundane appearance of the defendant made it difficult for many observers to reconcile the man before them with the horror and enormity of the crimes of which he was accused. This reaction had been anticipated. Before the trial, Simon Wiesenthal for one had 'suggest[ed] – without success – that Eichmann should be dressed in an SS uniform for his courthouse appearances. That way he would look like a murderer (and less like one of us).'[23] In 1975 a uniformed Nazi war criminal, 'brushed and pressed' with 'jack-boots gleaming' would finally be placed in the dock in Arthur Hiller's film *The Man in the Glass Booth*, a title and story with obvious allusions to Eichmann and to Hannah Arendt's evaluation of his trial.[24] Although the accused now looked like the public preconception of an SS murderer, he was in fact a German-Jewish survivor. *The Man in the Glass Booth* does literally, therefore, what many felt Hannah Arendt had done metaphorically in her analysis of the Eichmann trial, as the Holocaust survivor is placed in the dock.

Based on the 1967 novel and later play of the same name by actor Robert Shaw, *The Man in the Glass Booth*, a production of Ely Landau's American Film Theatre (AFT), remains one of the more extraordinary of American films on the Holocaust.[25] The AFT, America's first 'National Theatre-on-Film', adapted notable works of contemporary theatre for nationwide cinematic release. As founder Ely Landau explained to *HBO Magazine* in March 1976: 'No live theatre group could possibly present productions of this scope or quality in a single season or afford to employ such an array of great artists and creative talent. [The AFT] solves the logistic and financial problems which have prevented all but a handful of people from seeing theatre at its best and most professional.'[26] *The Man in the Glass Booth* was one of five plays released as films in the AFT's second and final season of 1974–75. Whereas *QB VII* took several years to film, *The Man in the Glass Booth* – working to the budget and time constraints of an independent production – was shot in just a month: five days on location in New York in an apartment overlooking Central Park West, and twenty-two on the set at the 20th Century Fox studios in Hollywood.

Actor Robert Shaw had spoken on British television in 1970 about his relationship to the Holocaust and his reasons for writing the original novel. He had, he remembered, been

> most affected in my life, for some reason or other, by what happened to the Jews in Germany, possibly because it happened when I was a boy, it was the first dreadful thing that really went into me … Also in my own family, my grandmother, for example, was anti-Semitic and I resented it and didn't really know why. Secondly though I've a curious iconoclastic sense of justice and I thought that when the Jews took Eichmann and killed him, which was terribly understandable, somehow or other, because they had suffered so much themselves, they should have tried or behaved better than anybody else. I think they should have taken Eichmann and tried him and proved that what he did, and then let the monster free, wander, anywhere, in the desert, whatever. But … not kill him.

Shaw had written the novel in response to a suggestion from his friend, the playwright Leo Lehman, who had asked Shaw what the trial would be like 'if the Jews got the wrong man'. The idea had lain dormant with Shaw until, travelling to New York in 1964, he heard John Heuss, vicar of Trinity Wall Street, argue that England was the sickest country in Europe. Shaw became fascinated by Heuss and it was while waiting to see him for a tour of the parish that he heard the announcement from the Second Vatican Council that the Pope 'was kind enough to forgive the Jews of the death of Jesus Christ' [sic]. Shaw shared the news with his friend, 'a Jewish tailor ... called Mordie Sills ... and Mordie said, who needs it!'[27]

Set in New York and Israel in 1974, the film tells the story of Arthur Goldman (Maximilian Schell), Holocaust survivor turned successful businessman of almost limitless wealth. As the film opens, Goldman is in a state of flux, prone to constantly changing moods and opinions. At one moment he appears to be a confused fantasist who speaks in anti-Semitic platitudes; the next a quick-witted raconteur and bon viveur. Regardless of which aspect of this dual personality he exhibits, all of Goldman's conversations invariably return to the subject of Hitler and the Holocaust, for Goldman remains mired in the horror of his past. He is a man of antithetical perspectives, so affected by his experiences that, for him, Hieronymous Bosch is 'a draughtsman, a photographer'. 'That's reality, Charlie', he says to his personal assistant Charlie Cohn (Lawrence Pressman) as they look at the 'Hell' panel of Bosch's *Garden of Earthly Delights* triptych.

Goldman's confused state of mind is illustrated when the camera shares and presents his subjectivity when he looks through a telescope on top of the penthouse where he lives. From this vantage point he sees an Orthodox Jew standing by a pretzel cart on the street corner below. Shouts of 'Achtung!' and 'Raus!' suddenly fill the air, shouts that by their reverberation are recognizably subjective. These incongruous cries are given meaning as Goldman identifies the pedlar as his father and then continues: 'Nobody's going to say: Mr Goldman your father was murdered in a shower in Auschwitz in 1943 at the age of 70 so he couldn't be pushing a pretzel cart on Fifth Avenue?' When he next looks through the telescope, however, he sees a man dressed in full Nazi uniform, an image accompanied with shouting and the stamp of marching jackboots. Like the character of Sol Nazerman (Rod Steiger), the damaged survivor at the heart of Sidney Lumet's *The Pawnbroker* (1964), Arthur Goldman's memories continue to draw him back into himself and into the past.[28] And, as with *The Pawnbroker*, these memories manifest themselves through the aural soundscape as well as the visual flashbacks. Sound provides a subjective and internalized remembrance in which we are, in Goldman's own words to his doctor, 'sucked into the logic of the mad'. It enables us to witness both cause and effect simultaneously, although the meaning of this is not always straightforward.

This aural/visual convergence of past and present is repeated when the camera goes with Goldman beyond the symbolic threshold of a locked door in his penthouse. In this physical manifestation of his mind, Goldman maintains a shrine to his hidden past. To continue with the uncomfortable conflation of Judaeo-Christian imagery which foreshadows the confusion of identity within the courtroom, this room is Goldman's purgatory, the holding point where he remains until the necessary purification.[29] Indeed for this modern-day Dorian Gray it is the repository for all of his worst memories. Here he keeps the striped uniforms of the camps; a menorah and other recognizable articles of Jewish heritage; piles of eyeglasses and shoes, creating his own private museum and a physical representation of the psychological confusion he feels. These are the visual fragments that keep the past in the present as he relives his past.

One evening Goldman secludes himself in this room as he withdraws into himself. He places a yarmulke on his head and, with deliberate messianic imagery, walks on bandaged feet across to a trunk which contains more memories in the form of clothes and photographs. As he looks at this collection of camp ephemera we slip into his mind: the memories start with the sound of children playing – then a bicycle bell – children shouting and the sound of a marching band – then drums and jackboots – thunder – Hitler shouting orders – marching boots – Shouts of 'Sieg Heil!' – ambulance sirens – shouts of 'raus!' – knocking on a door – a door being kicked in – a woman's screams – more excerpts of Hitler – a train whistle – train wheels and whistle – 'Raus!' again – a baby crying – a man shouting – dogs – screams – cries of 'Fatherland', 'Achtung' and 'Fire!' It concludes with the noise of machine guns. It is, it appears, a sequence that allows us to piece together through sound the life of Arthur Goldman, from a period of happiness to the death of his family and his own terror in the camps. As Goldman remembers his past he holds a lighted candle beneath his armpit in an apparent act of catharsis.

One aspect of Goldman's paranoia is that he believes himself to be under constant surveillance. 'Are they Germans?' Charlie Cohn asks. 'They are trying', replies Goldman. It soon becomes evident that this is not paranoia. Goldman is being watched by members of the Israeli secret service, for it transpires that Goldman is really Adolf Dorff, a former colonel in the Einsatzgruppen. His memories are those of the perpetrator, the candle held beneath the arm an attempt at removing the evidence of an SS tattoo. Firstly placed under house arrest by the Israeli agents, Goldman, forsaking his rights as an American citizen, permits himself to be taken voluntarily to Jerusalem where he will be placed on trial in a glass booth for crimes committed against the Jewish people.

The Israeli courtroom of *The Man in the Glass Booth* is clearly modelled on the Eichmann trial. Three judges sit in front of the Israeli flag and a symbolic menorah. Opposite them are the audience and counsel benches. Alongside the counsel sits Dorff in his glass booth. The booth is equipped, the Presiding Judge explains, with listening devices and a microphone. There is also a switch with which to cut him off, 'should your testimony or response become irrelevant'. Dorff is impressed.[30] Such a device would have 'saved a lot of embarrassment' at the Reichstag Fire trials, he remarks.

The prosecution case begins with a public statement on behalf of the government of Israel to justify the necessity and cost of such a trial thirty years on. 'My statement is addressed to the non-Jewish world', begins Miriam Rosen (Lois Nettleton), the state prosecutor. 'Certainly no Jew requires an explanation', she continues. Although there is, says Rosen a legal precedent for Israel's actions 'if the non-Jewish world demands it', they also have a moral right to try Dorff which transcends man's law. Once more Dorff is impressed: 'To bypass the niceties of international law – shaky at best – ... [and to place it all] under the umbrella of the big Jew in the sky' is, he declares, both 'brilliant' and 'safe'.

During the course of the trial the man in the glass booth revels in the attention he is being afforded by the spectacle of the trial. He uses it as a forum to ridicule the dead and the living, to glory in murder and to praise Hitler. As the trial nears its conclusion, however, it is suddenly revealed that the court and the audience has been misled: Goldman is not Dorff. Arthur Goldman has deliberately falsified evidence so that he may be placed on trial. Revealed to the court as an imposter, Dorff slips into catatonia before recovering briefly to remove the emblematic uniform. It is now Arthur Goldman who disintegrates within the booth until he becomes, like the shoes, spectacles or glasses seen within similar cases in Holocaust museums the world over, a poignant presence and remnant of what was once a human being; a fragmentary reminder of what has been lost. He slides slowly towards the floor of the booth, his shirt now hanging from his arm as a death shroud. He comes to rest halfway down, arms outstretched, cruciform, as he moves towards the martyrdom that he desires – a redemption, he hopes, not only for himself but for all of those Jewish victims of the Nazis who have been accused over the past forty years of having gone to their deaths meekly and without resisting.

At the trial's conclusion the Presiding Judge (Luther Adler) asks: 'Why did you do it, Mr Goldman? Why did you assume the identity of Colonel Dorff? Why did you want to degrade yourself? Why do you want to take all this guilt upon yourself? Why, Mr Goldman, why?' The answers to such questions change according to the identity of the man in the booth. By assuming the identity of Dorff, Goldmann can place an unrepentant Nazi in the dock to counter both the exoneration of guilt as suggested in *Judgment at Nuremberg*, and the denial of guilt seen elsewhere since the war. While Dorff presents the familiar argument that he acted out of a sense of duty, he does not deny his crimes or show repentance. 'I'm no clerk like Eichmann', he tells Miriam Rosen in a pretrial interview, for he has participated willingly and directly in mass murder. It is a position he maintains in the courtroom as from within his glass booth he takes pleasure in recounting his deeds, including a description of the murder of the Jews of Dubno that is taken almost verbatim from the affidavit of Hermann Graebe which was read into the evidenceat Nuremberg. In this narrative, therefore, the IMT and the Eichmann trials converge in a fictional construct, creating a third trial and a composite memory.[31]

While Dorff may willingly admit to being a Nazi, he does not plead guilty. 'How can you plead not guilty when you … accept our proof?' asks Miriam Rosen during a pre-trial meeting with Dorff. He answers while urinating: 'You charged me with genocide which is not correct. I killed criminals under the laws of Germany.' Their crime? 'Being Jewish.' Later he tells the doctor (Lloyd Bochner) who has come to assess his mental health: 'If I'm psychotic then 80 million Germans were psychotic, and half the Gentiles, all the Muslims, the black activists and protestant members in the United States were psychotic, and even you won't say that … These were socially approved acts and socially approved, particularly when they are committed by a whole nation, ain't psychotic. You people just aren't popular, Doc.'

In contrast, Arthur Goldman, the man in the glass booth, submits to the degradation of the trial for two different reasons. Firstly, it is an attempt to assuage the guilt he feels for having survived. On the penthouse rooftop, having seen his father and then the unidentified

Nazi through the telescope, Goldman reels away and collapses, gulping for breath, tapping his chest and whispering 'mea culpa … mea maxima culpa'. He starts to cry, asking 'God, why do I live?' In 1964, the year that Rolf Hocchuth's controversial play *The Deputy* – later filmed as *Amen* (Costa-Gavras, 2002) – was translated into English and transferred to Broadway, the Second Vatican Council in Rome was working on the wording of the *Nostra Aetate*, a declaration that would include a statement 'repudiating antisemitism and absolving Jews of culpability in the death of Jesus'.[32] Although the formal declaration was not made until October 1965, it was the reporting of the Council's deliberations that was the impetus for Shaw to write the novel, and in the film it is the catalyst for Goldman. Like the Catholic Church, Goldman wishes to exonerate the responsibility he feels, but, unlike the Church, he finds little solace in his gesture of remorse.

Secondly, Goldman places himself on the stand to allow for an exploration of the accusations of acquiescence, cooperation and meekness that were levied at the Jews of Europe at Eichmann's trial and after. Goldman recites his own version of 'Dies Irae', the opening to the Catholic Requiem Mass, in which he combines the Christian hymn of the Final Judgment with Wilfred Owen's 'Anthem for Doomed Youth', a combination of the folly of war, redemption and sacrifice as well as a further reference to the accusations of Jews dying as sheep

> What bells will ring for those who died like sheep?
> *Dies Irae, Dies Illa*
> *Solvet saeclum in favilla,*
> What bells will ring for those who died in excrement?
> Rest eternal grant them
> Light eternal shine upon them.

Later, to ensure that the audience knows what drives Goldman on, he strikes Charlie Cohn about the face 'as a test', but it is unclear who is being tested. 'Why did you do that, Mr Goldman?' asks Charlie. 'Because I couldn't resist', he replies.

The success of this often complicated narrative rests on a compelling performance from Maximilian Schell, an actor previously seen as the idealistic young German lawyer Rolfe in *Judgment at Nuremberg* and more recently as the former SS captain Eduard Roschmann, pursued and shot by journalist Peter Miller (Jon Voight) in *The Odessa File* (UK, Ronald Neame, 1974).[33] Goldman's pivotal status is established physically in the film's opening tracking shot of a crenellated Manhattan rooftop overlooking Central Park West. As the camera moves right, across one of the wealthier skyline views of New York, we see an elderly man, Arthur Goldman, standing beside a memorial in a rooftop garden. The camera continues its panorama, moving from outside to inside, into a luxurious penthouse apartment which is packed with works of art and expensive antiques. Photographer Sam Leavitt described this movement from exterior to interior:

> The camera moves on into the room and swings around to follow the action of Maximilian Schell and the other actors, until it is eventually facing back toward the doors through which it came in. So, what you have, in effect, is an almost 360 turn from the outside to the inside and all around the room – but it is actually a composite of the location exterior and the studio interior butted together to look like a single shot.[34]

There is in this opening shot, therefore, the sense of movement around Goldman, and the almost imperceptible transition of perspective which mirrors his unfolding mental breakdown. In looking from the inside out, and outside in, the camera offers a replicated subjectivity of the dual perspectives of Goldman as he vacillates between survivor, wracked by guilt and beset by demons, and his alter ego Colonel Dorff, the Einsatzgruppen colonel who exalts in killing. As Hiller explained, Arthur Goldman is 'very back and forth [and the film is] designed to show the paranoia that he feels about having survived the concentration camps when nobody else did, and to show his way of trying to redeem himself, to get rid of that guilt he's feeling'.[35]

In the freeform courtroom of Goldman's trial, the case against the accused is made neither by newsreel footage nor flashback but by a succession of witnesses who offer graphic testimony of horrific crimes, the words now taking precedence as evidence.[36] The first witness, Charlotte Levi, remembers Dorff from when she was a prisoner at Mauthausen in 1941. Dorff ridicules her suffering, remembering that the forced labour was pointless, except in that it kept him and his fellow officers away from the front line. He outrages the audience (prompting some of them to attack the booth) by reminding the court that he was not concerned with fatalities because 'after all we had six million to draw on'. The second witness, Joachim Berger, was once a cinematographer in the Ministry of Information under Goebbels.

Berger foregrounds film's artificiality as he tells the court how in October 1943, in the Polish town of Talnia, he photographed a 'punitive operation by the counter-insurgency section of the SS' involving the defenestration of the town's Jewish men under 13 and over 60 (all the other men having already been deported to the camps). The SS, Berger recalls, held back from throwing all of the men from the windows so that some could be photographed from a different angle and provide close-ups. The finished film was then shown in Polish theatres as a warning to 'Obey the German occupiers or this will happen to your town.' For Dorff, such films provided evidence of a counter-insurgency operation. This meant the assumption at headquarters of an insurgency, even though there was none. This, he tells the court, 'keeps you looting and raping in style behind the lines ... I understand the Americans developed it to a fine point in Vietnam. The My Lai massacre was a classic.' It was a reference that would resurface in *Music Box* fifteen years later, although not explicitly in the film itself.

The final prosecution witness, Samuel Weinberg (Leonidas Ossettynski), begins his testimony even before he reaches the stand, such is his desire to tell his own story. Weinberg begins by telling the court of his dreams, dreams that are full of vengeance, before describing the SS system of 'depersonalization and dehumanization' that humiliated the Jewish population and made the Holocaust possible. The Presiding Judge asks Weinberg why, in such circumstances, the Jews did not rebel. Surely by 1944 they knew their fate? It was, explains Weinberg, because 'our fate was beyond our imagination'. Even now, thirty years on, he adds, there are some who still do not believe.

Weinberg's conclusion points to the question at the heart of so much that is written on the Holocaust as an event beyond the limits of the imagination, but what is increasingly evident is that film-makers were prepared to try, even when the film's setting was the courtroom. *Operation Eichmann* may have been rushed and have a B-movie quality to it, but it looks forward rather than back, and that once again allows for a degree of freedom. Moreover, by having a new trial and a new precedent to anticipate, it could be imaginative, moving beyond the constraints of Nuremberg in a film which parodied Eichmann and the Nazis more generally. *QB VII*, on the other hand, while tied to a transcript, had its own freedom because the series was more adaptation than recreation – based that is, more on Uris's book than on the trial which preceded it. Significantly, this film refers to the attempted murder of the Jews of Europe as 'the Holocaust'. Moreover, while there is liberation footage used within the film, it is shown outside the courtroom and is not used as evidence for the trial, foregrounding instead how it has also become part of popular memory in another very different, formalized and sacral setting – the memorial museum. In contrast, *The Man in the Glass Booth* uses sound rather than image to denote the worst memories, using the absence of the visual to suggest the confusion of the mind of Arthur Goldman. And yet even here the film reverts to the IMT to provide sources for some of its testimony, combining fact with fiction, appearance and reality, blurring the lines between the two.

QB VII and *The Man in the Glass Booth* therefore mark the completion of the movement away from the use of film footage as the pre-eminent evidence of the Holocaust. In coming out of the shadow of a precedent which had become stifling, all of these films created a forum for survivors to tell their own stories to the camera, stories which included the imagination. In contrast to the earlier films, these are also detailing contemporary trials, inspired by events in or around 1964, but firmly placed in the present, updated to reflect current issues and concerns, acknowledging that the Holocaust was not only part of the past. This is how the relationship between the Holocaust and the courtroom drama would continue to develop, as the next films would continue to use the survivor to provide witness testimony but also look increasingly to consider the implications for America rather than the Holocaust. As will be seen in the next chapter, when Hollywood looked once again towards the courtroom, it was memory, not honesty or sincerity, which would be questioned.

NOTES

1. *Jewish Chronicle*, 14 April 1961, p.30. See also *The Times*, 11 April 1961.
2. *IMT*, vol. 11, pp.396–97. See Robert Jan Van Pelt and Debórah Dwork, *Auschwitz 1270 to the Present* (New Haven, CT, and London: Yale University Press, 1996), pp.276–306, passim. Höss's testimony was itself flawed, making claims as to dates and places that could not possibly have been correct.
3. David Cesarani, *Justice Delayed* (London: Mandarin Paperbacks, 1992), p.187.
4. Cited on the cover of Eugene Heimler, *Concentration Camp* (1961; London: Corgi Books, 1979).
5. Rudolf Vrba, *I Cannot Forgive* (London, Sidgwick & Jackson, 1963); Alexander Donat, *The Holocaust Kingdom: A Memoir* (1963; London, Secker & Warburg, 1965); and Judith S. Newman, *In the Hell of Auschwitz* (Fort Lauderdale, FL: Exposition-Phoenix Press, 1964).
6. Sara R. Horowitz, 'The Cinematic Triangulation of Jewish American Identity: Israel, America and the Holocaust', in Hilene Flanzbaum (ed.), *The Americanization of the Holocaust* (Baltimore, MD, and London: Johns Hopkins University Press, 1999), p.153.

7. Hugh Brogan, *The Penguin History of the United States of America* (Harmondsworth: Penguin, 1985), p.377. For a detailed consideration, see Michal R. Belknap, *The Vietnam War on Trial: The My Lai Massacre and the Court Martial of Lieutenant Calley* (Lawrence, KS: University Press of Kansas, 2002); and Kendrick Oliver, *The My Lai Massacre in American History and Memory* (Manchester: Manchester University Press, 2005).
8. Telford Taylor, *Nuremberg and Vietnam: An American Tragedy* (New York, Bantam Books, 1971), pp.11–12. The comparison between crimes against humanity committed during the Holocaust and in Vietnam would converge in film most noticeably in 1976 in Marcel Ophuls' seldom shown film *The Memory of Justice*, an extensive treatise on the hypocrisy of nations who commit crimes they condemn in others.
9. Michael R. Marrus, *The Holocaust in History* (London: Penguin Books, 1993), p.5.
10. Peter Novick, *The Holocaust in American Life*, p.148.
11. Chris Godat, 'Leon Uris' in David Mote (ed.), *Contemporary Popular Writers* (New York and London: St James Press, 1997), p.405.
12. Horowitz, 'Cinematic Triangulation of Jewish American Identity', p.156.
13. The cover of the 1966 US paperback edition of *Auschwitz in England*, for example, even advertised the book as 'the stunning courtroom drama of England's only "war crimes" trial'. See Mavis M. Hill and L. Norman Williams, *Auschwitz in England: A Record of a Libel Action* (New York: Ballantine Books, 1966).
14. Leon Uris, *Exodus* (London: William Kimber, 1959), p.155. This passage was based on a similar paragraph in Joseph Tenenbaum's *Underground: The Story of a People* (New York: Philosophical Library, 1952), one of the few texts of the early 1950s to be translated into English and published in America which contained an extended consideration of such matters. See also D.D. Guttenplan, *The Holocaust on Trial* (London: Granta Books, 2001), pp.9–10. For a history of the impact of *Exodus*, see M.M. Silver, *Our Exodus: Leon Uris and the Americanization of Israel's Founding Story* (Detroit, MI: Wayne State University Press, 2010).
15. Anne Karpf, *The War After: Living with the Holocaust* (London, Minerva Books, 1997), p.206.
16. Alan U. Schwartz, introduction to Hill and Williams, *Auschwitz in England*, p.xi.
17. Lord Denning in Hill and Williams, *Auschwitz in England*, p.xv.
18. Leon Uris, *QB VII* (New York: Doubleday, 1970), p.292.
19. Anthony Hopkins was initially unsure as to whether to play Kelno. According to Hopkins, he decided to commit to the role after having met the survivors in the cast and having read Miklos Nyiszli, *Auschwitz: A Doctor's Eyewitness Account* (1960; London: Grafton Books, 1978). See Michael Feeney Callan, *Anthony Hopkins: In Darkness and Light* (London: Sidgwick & Jackson, 1993), p.175.
20. For more on Pravda's experiences see Hana Pravda, *I Was Writing this Diary for You, Sasha* (Oxford: Day Books, 2000).
21. Hill and Williams, *Auschwitz in England*, pp.31, 142.
22. David Hammond, 'Behind The Camera on 'The Man in the Glass Booth', *American Cinematographer*, 56, 6 (June 1975), p.664.

23. Tim Cole, *Images of the Holocaust: The Myth of the 'Shoah' Buisness* (London: Duckworth, 1999), p.48.
24. Robert Shaw, 'The Man in the Glass Booth', in J.C. Trewin (ed.), *Plays of the Year, Volume 34, 1967–1968* (London: Elek, 1968), p.161; Hannah Arendt, *Eichmann in Jerusalem: A Report on the Banality of Evil*, rev. and enlarged ed. (1963; London: Penguin Books, 1994), p.5.
25. The novel was published in January 1967 and reviewed in *The Times*, 12 January 1967. The play premiered in July 1967 at St Martin's Theatre in London and transferred to Broadway the following year. See *The Times*, 28 July 1967.
26. Hammond, 'Behind the Camera', p.665.
27. *Omnibus*, 'Robert Shaw: The Actor as Novelist', BBC1, tx. 21 November 1971.
28. Maureen Turim, *Flashbacks in Film: Memory and History* (New York and London: Routledge, 1989), passim.
29. For more on the subject of the survivor's body and mind see Julian Levinson, 'The Maimed Body and the Tortured Soul: Holocaust Survivors in American Film', *Yale Journal of Criticism*, 17, 1 (Spring 2004), pp.141–60. This use of audio and visual to represent simultaneously the trauma of the past and its memory in the present can also be found in QBVII when Cady visits Jadwiga.
30. Although it transpires that the man in the booth is Goldman throughout, to facilitate comprehension I will refer to him as Dorff when he assumes that role.
31. Affidavit of Hermann Graebe dated 10 November 1945 (USA494, 2992-PS), see *IMT*, vol. 1, pp.236, 251; vol. 4, p.253; vol. 19, p.507; vol. 20, p.203; and vol. 22, pp.24, 479.
32. Rolf Hocchuth, *The Deputy* (1963; New York, Grove Press, 1964); Novick, *Holocaust in American Life*, p.182.
33. When the idea of making Shaw's book into a film was first mooted, George C. Scott was to play Arthur Goldman. Subsequent suggestions included that the film be a serious role for comedian Sid Caesar. Shaw was unhappy with Anhalt's script and the final film. He insisted that his name be removed from the titles. See John French, *Robert Shaw: The Price of Success* (London: Nick Hern Books, 1993), pp.150, 162, 204–08.
34. Hammond, 'Behind the Camera', p.700.
35. Arthur Hiller, 'Dialogue on Film', *American Film*, 5, 1 (1979), p.46.
36. The use of witnesses to raise such controversies is used more extensively but to similar effect in Shaw's novel. See Robert Shaw, *The Man in the Glass Booth* (London: Chatto & Windus, 1967), pp.189–97.

4

The Fallibility of Memory and the Return of the Flashback: Music Box (1989) and Perry Mason: The Case of the Desperate Deception (1990)

> Do you really think I give a damn about punishing an old man? I don't have any vengeance in my heart but ... I care about remembering. It's too late to change what happened, but it's never too late to remember what happened.
>
> Jack Burke (Frederic Forrest), *Music Box*.

While the cinematic courtroom of the immediate post-war period had an apparent preference for evidence provided by the trials of real life – sources which could be considered more credible, authentic and effective – in the light of Eichmann's trial it was the survivor who grew in status as film was used to support testimony rather than vice versa. *QB VII* completed the on-screen rehabilitation of the Jewish witness started by Eichmann's trial, but extended the meaning by specifically linking American-Jewish identity with Israel. This new-found authority of the witness, however, was soon questioned by *The Man in the Glass Booth*, a film which paradoxically placed its trust in survivor testimony over scientific evidence while simultaneously highlighting the effects of trauma and the fragility of memory. In the late 1980s the accuracy of both forms of testimony was to be questioned once again in Costa-Gavras's *Music Box* (USA, 1989) as the passing of time was accompanied by an awareness that memory was fallible. Previous films had used firstly the flashback or the newsreel image to provide unquestioned proof of the Holocaust for the courtroom and cinematic audience; then the survivor's voice had come to the fore as the most authentic and affecting of evidence. But by the 1980s, as *Music Box* shows, both word and image were coming under increased suspicion, prompting a return to the flashback in the second film discussed in this chapter, 1990's *Perry Mason and the Case of the Desperate Deception*.

In the second half of the 1970s the thrillers *Marathon Man* (USA, John Schlesinger, 1976) and *The Boys from Brazil* (USA, Franklyn J. Schaffner, 1978) continued the fictional pursuit of the fugitive Nazi war criminal, while the television movie *The House on Garibaldi Street* (USA, Peter Collinson, 1979) recreated the capture (if not the trial) of Adolf Eichmann. War criminals could show up even in the most unexpected of places, with Martin Bormann appearing in *Willy Wonka and the Chocolate Factory* ((USA, Mel Stuart, 1971) as the face of the man who faked a golden ticket, perhaps the film's notion of evil . But American cinema did not return to a trial involving a suspected war criminal until 1989 when, prompted by the publicity surrounding the trials of Klaus Barbie and, particularly, John Demjanjuk, *Music Box* examined the problems inherent in accusing an elderly individual of crimes that had been committed over forty years before.[1] *Music Box* was one of a spate of films made in the mid-to-late 1980s that, similarly galvanized by contemporary events, rejoined the hunt for the war criminal. In *Any Man's Death* (USA, Tom Clegg, 1990) the trail took the Nazi hunter abroad, whereas in *Descending Angel* (USA, Jeremy Kagan, 1990) the focus was closer to home, as an American Romanian (George C. Scott) was accused of collaborating with the Nazis during the war and of taking part in the slaughter of 800 Jews. Also released were *The House on Carroll Street* (USA, Peter Yates, 1987), a thriller that explored the US Government's involvement in smuggling Nazi war criminals into the USA in the summer of 1951; and *Hotel Terminus: The Life and Times of Klaus Barbie* (USA, Marcel Ophuls, 1988), a documentary from the maker of *The Memory of Justice*, that won the 1988 International Critics Prize at the Cannes Film Festival and the Academy Award for Best Documentary. Similarly, it was more than coincidence that two made-for-television biopics of noted Nazi hunters – *Murderers Among Us: The Simon Wiesenthal Story* (Canada/USA, Brian Gibson, 1989), and *Nazi Hunter: The Beate Klarsfeld Story* (USA/France, Michael Lindsay-Hogg, 1986) – also appeared.

This renewed interest in war crimes was not confined to America. Two other English-language films, one set in West Germany (an

Austrian/American/West German production), the other in Australia, also dealt with the contemporary debates on war crimes and war crimes legislation. Fons Rademakers' *The Rose Garden* (Austria/West Germany/USA, 1989), once again based on an actual court case, recounted the trial of Aaron Reichenbach (another role for Maximillian Schell), a Holocaust survivor accused of attacking Arnold Krenn (Kurt Hubner) at Frankfurt airport. Public defender Gabrielle (Liv Ullmann) seeks justice for Reichenbach after she learns that Krenn was the commandant at Mauthausen, where Reichenbach and his sister were sent during the war. Set on the other side of the world, John Power's *Father* (Australia, 1990) recounted a story more redolent of *Music Box*. Joseph Mueller (Max Von Sydow) is an elderly man who emigrated from Germany to Australia shortly after the end of the Second World War. Apparently a loving father and grandfather, he is accused of being Franz Kessler, a former member of Hitler's SS and a wanted war criminal. Mueller is cleared, but his emotionless reaction to the witnessing of the suicide of the reporter (Julia Blake) who first accused him leaves his daughter Anne (Carol Drinkwater) questioning his innocence.[2]

In the years between *The Man in the Glass Booth* and *Music Box*, American interest in the Holocaust continued to grow, with 'the most important moment in the entry of the Holocaust into general consciousness' coming in April 1978 when nearly 100 million Americans watched the influential NBC miniseries *Holocaust*.[3] This widely known and analysed series, directed by Marvin Chomsky from a story by Gerald Green, 'heightened [the] awareness of both the historical facts and the problems of how to dramatize them on film'.[4] Two weeks after the first airing of *Holocaust*, timed to coincide with the thirtieth anniversary of the founding of the State of Israel, President Jimmy Carter announced the establishment of a commission that would look into the construction of a national United States Holocaust museum. Later that same year, Carter signed the 'Holtzman Amendment', a Congressional amendment to US immigration law that would thenceforth permit the deportation of those American residents who had, 'in association with Nazi Germany or its allies, "ordered, incited, assisted, or otherwise participated in the persecution of any person because of race, religion, national origin, or political opinion" '.[5]

Accusations that former Nazis and Nazi collaborationists were living in America had been made consistently since the end of the war. The campaign for an official search for any such fugitives, however, had only recently gained momentum following a succession of high-profile newspaper articles that culminated in the publication of Howard Blum's *Wanted! The Search for Nazis in America* (1977).[6] In light of the new legislation, a special unit was established within the Immigration and Naturalization Service (INS). In 1979 this became the Office of Special Investigations (OSI), an office in the Department of Justice created 'to bring together in one office all investigative and litigation activities concerning Nazi criminals'.[7] The establishment of a central body was, at last, formal recognition that perpetrators of war crimes had found their way into the United States after the war and had since dwelt there freely as American citizens.[8] These included not only those who, like Franz Kindler in *The Stranger*, had entered illegally amid the post-war confusion, but also those such as the eponymous deranged genius of *Dr Strangelove* (USA, Stanley Kubrick, 1964) who had been granted passage to work secretly for the government in the fight against communism. As OSI agent Jack Burke (Frederic Forrest) says near the conclusion of *Music Box*: 'Our country has always tried to be a haven for those who were persecuted. After the war we let in thousands of its victims, but unfortunately we also let in some of the executioners.'[9]

Since the crimes in the cases brought by the OSI had been committed beyond the United States territorial boundaries, it was necessary for the government to apply for the denaturalization and then deportation of the suspect on the grounds that s/he lied on his/her naturalization application. The suspect would then, in theory at least, be returned to stand trial in either the country where his/her crimes were committed, or to a country willing to prosecute for war crimes. This was an expensive and time-consuming process, likely to take a minimum of eight years to conclude.[10] The first such denaturalization case to come to court did not augur well. In this instance, Chicago resident Frank Walus was accused of having been a Gestapo agent in Poland during the Second World War. Having been tried and found guilty, he was ordered to be denaturalized; however, the Court of Appeals ordered a retrial in the light of fresh evidence, doubts over the accuracy of eyewitness identification, and concerns of judicial prejudice. Rather than face the embarrassment of defeat, the government dropped the case. [11]

The highest profile of the hundreds of cases to be prepared by the OSI remains that brought against John 'Ivan' Demjanjuk. Born in Ukraine in 1920, Demjanjuk came to America with his wife and young family in 1952, being granted citizenship in 1958. Denaturalization proceedings against Demjanjuk had started in 1977, when he was been accused of being 'Ivan the Terrible', a notoriously brutal guard who operated the gas chambers at Treblinka. After four years of legal wrangling his citizenship was revoked on the grounds that 'he had procured his citizenship illegally as well as by wilful concealment and misrepresentation of a material fact; for these reasons, he also lacked the good moral character required by the [Immigration and Nationality Act]'.[12] Demjanjuk was to be extradited to Israel to stand trial, although the lengthy appeals process meant that he did not arrive there until February 1986. Finally, in February 1987, twenty-six years after Eichmann's trial, attention was once again focused on Israeli justice as one man, a former American citizen, stood accused of crimes against humanity and the Jewish people.[13]

After fourteen months in court, Demjanjuk was found guilty and sentenced to hang. However, over five years later, on 29 July 1993, Israel's Supreme Court, as the consequence of evidence recently acquired from the former Soviet Union (evidence which, it has been suggested, had been known to the Americans before the Israeli trial had even begun), expressed 'gnawing doubts' about Demjanjuk's identity as 'Ivan'.[14] This new evidence indicated that 'Ivan the Terrible' had been Ivan Marchenko, not Ivan Demjanjuk. The witnesses were understood to have been mistaken in their identification, while the compelling evidence of an identity card in the name of Ivan Demjanjuk issued at Trawniki, an SS training camp in Poland, was now believed to be inauthentic. With this new information casting doubt on Demjanjuk's guilt, and on the efficacy of human memory to discern and remember accurately after forty years, the Israeli Supreme Court overturned the conviction. In September 1993, sixteen years after the denaturalization case against him was first filed (and after seven years in an Israeli prison), Demjanjuk returned to the United States. As is well known, his case did not end there. It would be another twenty years before he would eventually stand trial in Germany in November 2010 before the proceedings finally came to an end with his death in 2012.

In the midst of this sequence of events, director Constantin Costa-Gavras was completing *Music Box*, a film that depicted the denaturalization trial of a suspected war criminal living in the United States. Although Costa-Gavras would deny that Demjanjuk was the point of departure for his film's plot, suggesting instead that the fictional trial was drawn from more general texts on former Nazis living in America, it clearly parallels the contemporaneous political issues and publicity provided by the Demjanjuk case.[15]

Music Box (1989)

Costa-Gavras, a Greek-born film-maker with a reputation for intense, political films, had won the best director prize at Cannes in 1975 for *Section Specialé* (France/Italy/West Germany, 1978), another film with a Second World War theme and a courtroom setting that was based on a true story.[16] *Music Box* was his fourth American-backed film, and his second in collaboration with the Hungarian-born scriptwriter Joe Eszterhas. Although clearly a film that owes much to the European background and influences of its writer, director and crew, *Music Box* is unmistakeably aimed at the American market and concerned with contemporary American society. Whereas *The Man in the Glass Booth* was divided, literally and metaphorically, between America and Israel, *Music Box* is set predominantly in Chicago and recounts the story of an American citizen being prosecuted under American law.

Music Box tells the story of Ann Talbot (Jessica Lange), a successful criminal lawyer. As the film opens she is shocked to learn that her Hungarian-born father Michael 'Mike' Laszlo (Armin Mueller-Stahl) has been accused of war crimes. It is alleged by the OSI's prosecutor Jack Burke (Frederic Forrest) that prior to immigrating into the USA in 1952 under the Displaced Persons Act – the same year and route taken by Demjanjuk to enter the United States – Michael Laszlo was 'Miska', a member of the notorious (and factual) Hungarian Arrow Cross, a group of 'pathologically antisemitic Hungarian ultra-rightists' who were responsible for, amongst other atrocities, the massacre of thousands of Budapest's Jews before the city was liberated by the Red Army in February 1945.[17] In the ensuing denaturalization case, Ann conducts her father's defence, even though she has no particular knowledge of immigration law. It is a decision that hints at the tension that is to come.[18]

Borrowing from the facts behind Demjanjuk's trial (and made before Demjanjuk's case had been through many of its twists and turns), the case against Laszlo questions both identity and identification. Like Demjajnuk's case it also rests upon the authenticity of two forms of evidence: a photostat of what purports to be Laszlo's Arrow Cross identification card; and the testimony of human witnesses, including Jewish and non-Jewish survivors. In the face of the seemingly overwhelming evidence, Ann wins her father's case, not solely with her skill as a lawyer, but by also obtaining the help of (probably illegitimate) outside agencies. Her triumph, however, is short-lived, for in the course of her own private investigations into her father's wartime activity she uncovers, concealed within the titular music box, photographic evidence of her father's participation in several acts of atrocity. After some brief soul-searching, Ann passes the fresh evidence to the OSI and the case against her father is reopened. As the film ends, Laszlo's fate remains unresolved. Ann is left to piece her life and her family's life back together without the father whom she no longer knows or trusts.

Music Box was well received by critics in both the United States and Europe: Jessica Lange was nominated for a Golden Globe (1990) and an Academy Award (1989) for her performance, while Lukas Haas was nominated as best supporting actor in the Young Artist Awards (1990) for his portrayal of Ann's son Mikey. In contrast to the German silence that greeted *Judgment at Nuremberg*, the film won the Golden Bear award for Best Film at the Berlin Film Festival of 1990. In spite of this critical success, *Music Box* received only a tepid reception at the US box office when it was first released, even though it did go on to gross USD 6.3 million in domestic receipts. Costa-Gavras ascribed his film's relative failure on the paucity of chases and other 'action', and on America's inability to empathize with war crimes and the Holocaust: 'There is no action in the movie: the only action is the strength of relationship between the characters. This is something that's very difficult for Americans to understand ... We have in Europe a much stronger experience about the Second World War, and about criminals and the Holocaust, than there is in America.'[19] Costa-Gavras's words appear to be more an attempt to reclaim the memory of the Holocaust from America than a genuine explanation for the initially low box office receipts. The number of films being released that featured war crimes and war criminals was proof of an active American interest in the subject – even if the 'experience' it symbolized was considered to be less than that found in Europe. Further proof of the degree to which the Holocaust had entered the American consciousness can be seen in the manner in which Costa-Gavras could establish authenticity for his film. Rather than use newsreel footage or foreground the use of courtroom proceedings (although such instances do occur), *Music Box* incorporates references throughout that situate it at a particular place in Holocaust historiography and American history. When Ann first accepts her father's case, for example, her fellow lawyers suggest that she should make way for the man who represented 'that Dem ... Dejoo ... Demjook guy'; she seeks a legal precedent for mistaken identity and cites the Walus case as proof of her father's innocence; and in his opening statement Burke informs the court that 'We are speaking not of the banality of evil', connecting the fictional trial with that of Eichmann through Arendt's infamous phrase.

In other ways, however, Costa-Gavras's film is similar to those films that have already been discussed. In an echo of *Judgment at Nuremberg* and *Verboten!*, for example, Costa-Gavras stressed in interviews the particularity of German guilt, even though his film centred on atrocities committed in Hungary by Hungarians. 'I think it's important to see this movie with a German audience', he told journalist Matt Wolf, 'and particularly a German audience over 60.'[20] This was almost entirely at odds with the views of scriptwriter Eszterhas: 'I was proud of the film on a very personal level. I, who was Hungarian-born, had showed the world what the Hungarians themselves ... not occupying Nazi forces but the Hungarian people themselves ... had done to the Jews at the end of the war.'[21]

In background context, too, the film showed little change from thirty years before. Again with reference to *Judgment at Nuremberg,* in Kramer's 1961 appraisal of 1948, American/Soviet enmity and mutual distrust had been used as the explanation for the lenient sentencing, non-prosecution and non-pursuit of Nazi criminals. Such measures, it was intimated, had been instrumental in, and necessary for, the successful post-war recuperation of a German nation that was to be the west's bulwark against communism. In the early 1980s it emerged that the Cold War was also the justification for coded operations such as 'Project Paperclip' that offered refuge in America to German scientists, collaborators and assorted personnel from other European countries who, US intelligence reports suggested, would be invaluable in the battle against the Soviet Union. The most infamous of these came to light in 1983 when Erhard Dabringhaus, a member of the US Military Intelligence Service from 1942 to 1950, revealed how, after the war, Klaus Barbie, the 'Butcher of Lyon', had been employed and protected by the US Army Counter Intelligence Corps (CIC) for the same reason.[22]

The Cold War had also played a significant part in the case against Demjanjuk. From the outset the trial had been beset by accusations of a communist conspiracy to discredit the accused who was, like many of those who immigrated to the United States from Displaced Persons camps, a vehement anti-communist. Mark O'Connor, Demjanjuk's lawyer, had long claimed that Israel was simply 'prosecuting an innocent man on behalf of the KGB because he had fought against the Russians'.[23] This was a deep-rooted and reciprocated distrust. Writing in February 2000, journalist Gitta Sereny noted that the support and financial backing Demjanjuk had received from the 'huge American and Canadian Ukrainian community [was given] not because they did not believe he had done what he was accused of doing', but because he was 'one of their own who ... was being attacked by their traditional enemies, the communists and the Jews.'[24] Likewise, in *Music Box*, demonstrators outside the courthouse (many of whom are recognizable as members of Laszlo's church and Hungarian-American community) carry placards that read 'STOP SOVIET JUSTICE IN US COURTS' and 'DEPORT SOVIET INFILTRATORS NOT LOYAL CITIZENS'. The most vehement of the anti-communist voices in *Music Box*, however, belongs to Harry Talbot (Donald Moffat), Ann's ex-father-in-law and a respected member of the Chicago WASP community whose connections go 'all the way to the White House'. In the aftermath of the Second World War, Talbot was directly involved in the US Government's recruitment of former Nazis as they prepared to fight the new enemy by whatever means possible. He is as vehement in his rebuttal to those who question his morality as Hans Rolfe had been in *Judgment at Nuremberg* when citing 'My country right or wrong': 'The communists were Satan's army on earth ... We needed [Nazis to spy for us], we used them. If the communists haven't taken over ... it was because we did a damn good job ... None of the men I knew were monsters. They were all salt of the earth types like your old man.' In the character of Henry Talbot there is, therefore, an acknowledgement of the flaws and prejudices of America that had once been denied. He is openly anti-Semitic and, in the words of Costa-Gavras, 'part of that generation ... Anti-Semitism was everywhere. [He] comes from that generation and he hasn't changed his mind.'[25] It is Talbot, for example, who is uncomfortable with the appointment of a Jewish judge to the trial and it is he who tells Ann's son Mikey that the Holocaust was an 'exaggeration' and 'all made up'. Even the advice he offers to Ann as a lawyer is tinged with and tainted by his anti-Semitism: 'You don't have a prayer, you know that. The Holocaust is the world's sacred cow. Holocaust survivors are secular saints. You'd be better off pissing on the tomb of the unknown soldier than trying to cross-examine them.' His comments establish the Holocaust's cognizable presence in contemporary American life and memory, but suggest that, for the white Anglo-Saxon elite at least, it is an unwelcome presence and one that is deemed to detract from the memory of the most sacred of American war dead.

John Demjanjuk, Jr, like Ann Talbot's son Mikey, was 11 years old when his father was first accused of war crimes. Speaking many years later after his father had been sentenced, Demjanjuk, Jr, gave his own evaluation of Ivan the Terrible and his father:

> The sort of person who could kill in that way would be a psychopath who couldn't stop killing. He could not change profoundly to be the kind and gentle person my father is. He couldn't hurt anybody. When I was a boy we never went fishing because he couldn't bear to put a worm on a hook … The man who did those things should hang, whoever he is. But he is not my father.[26]

At the opening of *Music Box*, Ann is similarly unequivocal in defence of her father. She is convinced that the OSI have got 'the wrong Michael J. Laszlo', later telling the court that 'My father is a good man.' Ann's brother Karchy (Michael Rooker) agrees, though he offers a more forthright declaration when he tells Ann, 'There ain't no fucking case: he's Pop.' Laszlo himself is sanguine in the affirmation of his innocence. In the courtroom he declares: 'It's not me. It's not me, Anni. It's not me, I didn't do this … I am not a beast, I am a father. I loved my wife, my family. I couldn't do this to you … This man didn't do this. It's not me! It's not me! It's not me!' Non-family members, however, appear less certain of Mike's innocence. Mack Jones (Albert Hall), Ann's partner at her law firm, asks her: 'What do you know about what happened forty years ago in some part of the world you never even been? What do we know about our parents?' And Dean Talbot (Ned Schmidtke), Ann's former husband, advises her: 'I wouldn't represent him. What if he did it? It's not just another case to win. He's still your dad. Blood's thicker than spilled blood.'

Nearly thirty years before, one of Robert Shaw's inspirations for writing *The Man in the Glass Booth* had been, 'What would it be like if the Jews had got the wrong man?'[27] It was a question of identification that prompted an examination of identity. Now *Music Box* asks what it would be like if the accused did not accept that he could or should be held responsible for crimes committed over forty years before. As Costa-Gavras explained to Matt Wolf, 'When he [Laszlo] says, "This man didn't do that", he means, "this man in front of you". He has a curtain between himself and the past; he speaks about two different persons.'[28] By the end of the film there appears little doubt that Mike and Miska are, in one sense, the same man. Laszlo, however, is determined to fight on because he considers himself to be an innocent victim. Laszlo's defence from the film's outset has been that he is an upstanding American citizen and hence it is ridiculous even to suggest that he could be guilty of war crimes. He is an integrated member of society who dresses in a bear-cap, talks of the virtues of Coca-Cola (albeit for cleaning rust from handlebars) and confronts his enemies with a baseball bat. It may have been emigration from Europe that provided Miska with the tabula rasa with which to begin again, but it was his destination that has defined his new identity. He is an American citizen with an American family (the 'perfect alibi', according to Burke, in a phrase that recalls Frank Kindler's description of his marriage to Mary as 'perfect camouflage' in *The Stranger*) and an American past: 'I work as a miller, I raise my kids. It's my country ... I've been here thirty-seven years ... I'm a citizen ... I'm a good American ... My boy was an American soldier; he fought in Vietnam. I'm proud ... [my daughter's] an American lawyer.' 'If you're a good American', Burke tells Laszlo, 'then this country's in big trouble.' But his American identity is responsible for Laszlo's feeling that he cannot be guilty. As Costa-Gavras explained: 'The man described in court, recalled in such vivid detail, is a sadistic monster; the old man we see is roughly respectable ... Laszlo is the model American he claims to be [because he believes] that it's always possible to discard the past and begin all over again.'[29] Much has been written of the Americanization of the Holocaust and its victims, but in *Music Box* it is the perpetrator who is redeemed.

In the extensive courtroom scenes that form the main body of the film, the case against the accused is made through a combination of photographic evidence and witness testimony. The Walus and Demjanjuk cases had shown that forty years after the perpetration of the crimes in question, establishing guilt of the accused through witnesses was proving increasingly difficult:

> Is it possible for men and women who witnessed such deeds happening in front of them for months on end ever to forget the face of a man who committed them? Or could a half-century of agonizing need for retribution against the figure of 'Ivan' – the personification of the monstrosity that was Treblinka – have drawn them unconsciously into identifying a physically similar but different man, as a symbol of that horror.[30]

As Primo Levi had summarized just before his death, the difficulties faced were increasing every year: 'The greater part of witnesses, for the defence and the prosecution, have by now disappeared, and those who remain, and who (overcoming their remorse or, respectively, their wounds) still agree to testify, have ever more blurred and stylised memories; often, unbeknown to them, influenced by information they gained later from readings or stories of others.'[31] *Music Box* could obviate this problem by turning to cinematic convention and proving Laszlo's guilt through flashback, but in common with its predecessors this is a narrative device that goes unused. Interviewed by the BBC in 1990 to mark the UK release of *Music Box*, Costa-Gavras recalled how the omission of flashbacks was deliberate. The flashback, he argued, 'kills both present and the past'.[32] Instead, as in *QB VII*, six witnesses appear for the prosecution as Jack Burke endeavours to prove that Laszlo and Miska are the same man. The first witness is Mr Nathanson (Felix Shuman), a forensics expert who works for the INS. He is to testify to the authenticity of the photostat of Laszlo's identification card and to confirm that, in his opinion, the photograph and signature on this and Laszlo's 'Green Card' issued in 1952 are of and by the same man. As his name suggests, Nathanson is part-Jewish and Ann uses this in her endeavours to establish that the card is fraudulent.[33] She contends that Nathanson's testimony is governed not by his identity as a forensic scientist but through his primary loyalty to his Jewish roots. It is an accusation that is allowed to stand in spite of Burke's objections. The second witness, Mrs Hollo (Magda Szekely Marburg), speaking through an interpreter, recalls how in 1944 'three men in black uniforms', one of whom was identified as 'Miska', murdered her neighbour and her neighbour's son because they were Jewish. 'Is this the man that shot the mother and the boy?' asks Jack Burke, melodramatically spinning an enlargement of the identification card to face Mrs Hollo. 'Yes', she replies, looking at the picture, 'that's the man.' Ann sarcastically applauds Mrs Hollo's 'amazing memory', but she does not pursue the cross-examination on the question of memory. Instead, she insinuates that Mrs Hollo has been coerced into giving this evidence by her son, an official in the communist government. Again, Burke's objection is overruled.

As a resident of the Budapest Ghetto, the next witness, Mr Boday (Sol Frieder), would have been subject to the most brutal of the Arrow Cross's treatment. In his testimony, Mr Boday recounts how one day in December 1944 he and his family were stopped and searched by four Arrow Cross members, led by their 'big boss Miska': 'You got jewel? Diamond? All you Jews got gold ... Open mouth, pig ... he say plenty gold.' They were then bound together with wire, before being thrown into the Danube and left for dead. Again turning the enlargement of the identity card to face Mr Boday, Jack Burke asks for confirmation that the photograph is of the man responsible. 'Yes, that is Miska ... I seen forty years each night I close eyes. That is

Miska.'[34] Ann, moved to tears by what she has heard, does not challenge Mr Boday's testimony on the grounds of his Jewishness, although as we have seen in the case of Mr Nathanson it is a proven tactic. Instead, she accuses him of being a communist and of being mistaken in his identification of her father by errors in the process used by the OSI.[35] It is the only occasion when her strategy fails, an implicit affirmation of Talbot's advice that to cross-examine a survivor is a waste of time. Likewise, the fourth witness, Mr Vamos (Michael Shillo), a former cleaner at the Lanchid Interrogation Centre in Budapest, had seen Miska kill twenty to thirty times: 'Everybody know Miska ... everybody afraid ... Miska worst because he enjoy. Miska liked kill Jew; liked kill gypsy more than Jew.' Burke asks him, 'Is this the man that you knew as Miska at the Lanchid Interrogation Centre?' Vamos confirms that 'It is him.' Once again, Ann devalues his testimony through a personal attack rather than by intellectual perspicacity, now suggesting that he and Mr Boday had compared their testimony the night before. It is an attack that leaves Mr Boday stunned.

The most damning testimony delivered in court once more comes from a female victim. Ms Khalman (Elzbieta Szyzewska), a psychiatrist who specializes in rape trauma, was only 16 years old in 1944 when she was accused by members of the Arrow Cross of being Jewish. In her testimony she recounts how Miska and his comrades repeatedly raped her before leaving her for dead.[36] She identifies Mike as Miska. As she stands to leave the witness box, Mike denies that he is the man responsible. 'Yes, you are!' she exclaims as she spits on him. This is the moment that seems to establish Laszlo's guilt beyond question and yet, even with such unconditional affirmation, doubts remain. These doubts had been more apparent in the earlier testimony. When, for example, Mr Boday states 'Yes, that is Miska ... I seen forty years each night I close eyes', his statement brings the perpetration and process of remembering into the present. But it is a subjective identification that as an audience we are unable to verify. Similarly, Mr Vamos can only confirm that the photograph is of the man he 'knew as Miska'. The problematic nature of this evidence is emphasized by Costa-Gavras when the court travels to Hungary to hear the evidence of the final witness, the terminally ill Mr Horwath. This final witness may be speaking truthfully when asserting 'I have no doubt *in my mind* it is Laszlo', but for *Music Box* this does not establish Laszlo's guilt. Ann herself makes just such a point when she reads to the court a statement made by Horwath in 1973 in which he repeats the phrase almost word for word, as he swears that 'I have no doubt in my mind that the man who committed these crimes is Michael Bato.'

Forty-five years on, therefore, memory is considered imperfect but so too, it emerges, is the photographic and documentary evidence, for the proof of the identification card is discredited by the testimony of Vladimir Kostav (George Pusep), a KGB agent who tells the court that the card was fraudulent, made to discredit anti-communist émigrés. By 1989, in a world of frail memories and Cold War machinations, neither testimony nor documentary evidence are infallible or sufficient.[37] If they cannot be trusted then how can one prove the guilt or innocence of the accused? It is a challenge that is easier to meet in film than it is in reality. For *Music Box* it necessitates the convergence of oral and visual testimony as witness testimony is combined with photographic evidence, both diegetic and non-diegetic, to guide the film and its audience to their verdict. It is true of all courtroom thrillers that, once accused, the defendant is subject to additional audience scrutiny throughout and is on trial not only when in the courtroom, for the stigma of accusation remains. In this sense the cinematic audience has a privileged position, as we are privy to how the accused behaves outside the courtroom. It is this combination that condemns Mike as Miska. As part of his testimony Mr Vamos re-enacts, for the camera and the court, a 'game' that Miska and the Arrow Cross used to make their victims play involving push-ups and a bayonet. He tells the court: 'Miska like push-up. He do push-up, too. With bayonet, too.' Later Ms Khalman remembers how she, too, was forced to participate in the same 'game'. The Arrow Cross leader, Miska, told her: 'A healthy body makes a healthy spirit.' For the audience it recalls an earlier scene when Laszlo used the same phrase to his grandson Mikey as they went through their daily routine of push-ups – that is, the visual and oral testimonies combine to provide the necessary evidence for the cinematic audience. It is a similar combination of evidence that within the film's story also convinces Ann of her father's guilt. When Ms Khalman tells of the horrific treatment she received from the Arrow Cross, she recalls how 'Someone took my picture. The flash would awaken me.' When Ann examines the photographs she has found in the music box, the camera lingers over several shots which recall earlier testimony, including one in particular of a young girl holding her hand out in front of her eyes to shield herself from the brightness of the camera flash. Clearly identifiable, not only from the photograph on the suspect identity card, but also from the photographs of his wedding that adorn his home, is the young Michael

J. Laszlo. This is the proof that confirms to Ann her father's guilt. When she confronts her father the accusation is delivered in a triplet of short sentences that recalls in structure as well as content Franz's words to David Brent at the conclusion of *Verboten!*: 'It was you, Papa. You killed them all. I saw the photos.'

By the director's own admission, *Music Box* was not about the Holocaust but 'crime and punishment ... relationships between fathers and daughters and sons – though, of course, there's no doubt that the war-criminal problem makes it much stronger'.[38] It is also about betrayal, truth and justice, and the fallibility of the law as well as memory. Although I have argued above that Laszlo's guilt is established through the use of visual and oral testimony, by the end of the film we still cannot say unequivocally what the truth is of the story that we have watched or how it will end. It was an intentional ambiguity on behalf of Costa-Gavras, for whom the trial of Laszlo reflected his feelings about the trial of Klaus Barbie. He was ambivalent towards the outcome of Barbie's trial because, for him, the fact that the trial was being held was more important than any verdict. It was, as Jack Burke told Ann Talbot (quoted above) in *Music* Box, 'about remembering'. We may not know the truth of either man's crimes, Costa-Gavras said in interview, but 'maybe truth doesn't matter. Maybe as in *Antigone* ... there is a public need from time to time to convict a war criminal, or someone who might have been a war criminal, to remind us of this dreadful past.'[39]

One year after *Music Box* was released came the uncomfortable realization that art was mirroring fact as Joe Eszterhas's father was arrested on suspicion of war crimes committed during the war in his native Hungary – he was now under investigation by the OSI. Eszterhas recounts in his autobiography *Hollywood Animal* the struggle to come to terms with his father's past and how, like Ann Talbot, although he had helped to get his father off the charges, he 'felt like a piece of my heart had died. I'd lost my mother at thirteen, when her madness began, and now, at age forty-seven, I felt like I'd lost my father as well.' It altered his view on *Music Box*: 'I had seen the movie dozens of times, but never from this perspective. It was the saddest movie I've ever seen ... I will never watch *Music Box* again.'[40]

Music Box continues, therefore, the trend of questioning the evidence, and particularly photographic evidence. Once considered as the most credible form of proof, it was now being treated with suspicion by the film-maker, just at the same time that the fragility of human memory was also being questioned more regularly as the crimes of the Holocaust began to recede further into the past. Perhaps that is why the next film, one that was made for television and aired shortly after *Music Box*, was the first feature-length film since *None Shall Escape* to use flashback to represent survivor testimony, with the film-maker seeking the security of the medium's own conventions.

Perry Mason and the Case of the Desperate Deception (1990)

The success of the *Perry Mason* franchise on television is one of the reasons sometimes cited as an explanation for the fall in the number of courtroom dramas made for the big screen in the 1960s.[41] Based on the novels of Erle Stanley Gardner, with Raymond Burr as the eponymous defence attorney, it ran initially for nine series and proved so popular that it would return regularly in the subsequent decades. In the mid-1980s it was resurrected in a series of films made for NBC, with Burr reprising his role as Mason, but now moving beyond the streets of Los Angeles as seen in the original series. In *Desperate Deception*, Mason defends a captain in the US Marines who is accused of the murder of an ex-Nazi in present-day France. Set in Paris, the Eiffel Tower, Arc de Triomphe and Notre Dame all feature in an opening sequence of establishing shots. Captain David Berman (Tim Ryan) is searching for ex-SS officer Dieter Krugman who 'did something terrible to his family'. He has engineered a transfer to Paris on the basis of a tip-off from a friend in the OSI and has made contact with Elsa Ramsey, a Majdanek survivor who can identify Krugman. Ramsey, however, is murdered in a hit-and-run accident before she can testify. Shortly afterwards, Berman is taken at gunpoint by Carl Meyerhoff (Paul Freeman), an apparently freelance Nazi hunter who is also looking for Krugman.

Meyerhoff leads Berman to Krugman, who is living in Paris under the alias of Felix Altmann. Berman is confused by Altmann's appearance, taken aback that he is 'a pathetic old man' rather than the 'vicious monster' he expected. While the two men talk, Altmann is shot by an unknown assassin. As the only suspect, Berman is arrested and placed on trial before a court martial. Mason, an old friend of the family, believes Berman to be innocent because of his often-voiced desire to see Krugman placed on public trial in France for crimes against humanity. As part of his investigations, which take up half of the film, Mason meets with Meyerhoff's boss Otto Rosen (Ian Bannen), a former inmate of Treblinka who works unofficially in the shadows because he is wanted by Odessa, the organization of former

Nazis made famous by *The Odessa File* (1974). During their discussion, Rosen passes Mason a photograph of Krugman, a piece of evidence that will be crucial in bringing the murderer to justice.

The court case that follows only begins after this extensive and largely unnecessary lead-in. This military trial itself takes place in an ornately furnished room in the US Embassy, for it is not French justice, in spite of Mason's assertion to the contrary. Like *Music Box*, the case concerns the identity of a war criminal, and like *Music Box* the case is built around photographic evidence, although this time the documentary evidence provided by the east is genuine, a suggestion of the contemporary thawing of the Cold War. A key witness in the trial is Berman's mother (Teresa Wright), flown to Paris to testify to her experiences as a child in Majdanek. This has no bearing on proving that her son did or did not kill Altmann, and yet is crucial to the film's and the trial's conclusion. There is no prologue as her testimony begins:

> We were on the train for three days: my mother and father, my two brothers and me. And probably 70 others in one box car, and no food or water the last day and a half. Finally at dawn of the fourth day the train stopped. At Majdanek, they forced us to jump off the train and I saw my mother and father shoved into a group of people and marched away. There were no goodbyes. I learned later they were taken directly to the gas chambers. Then my brothers and I along with many other children … were marched to some kind of holding area.

During this narrative, for the first time since *None Shall Escape*, memories of this kind are presented as a flashback. As Mrs Berman remembers the audience is given a sanitized and stylized memory – of how her brothers were murdered by Krugmann. Again this is more mindscreen than objective flashback, with the camera confirming her memory, including how she used a shard of glass to cut the back of Krugmann's hand in her unsuccessful attempt to save her brothers. It also confirms that she only escaped thanks to the intervention of another SS officer. Would she be able to recognize the man who killed her brothers? 'I will remember his face until the day I die', she concludes. It is another affirmation of the persistence of memory and trauma which presents further intertextual similarities with *Music Box*.

After finishing recounting this story she looks at the evidence provided by the defence for the court. Photograph A is of the SS officer identified as Krugmann and seen by Mason, Rosen and Berman. But now Mrs Berman testifies that it is the officer who saved her life, not Krugmann. In the group photograph provided by Else Ramsey – photograph B – she identifies the same man: Felix Altmann. But in that photograph she recognizes Krugmann, an identification confirmed by photograph C, a picture of Krugmann provided by the Russians. In a twist, Altmann's widow, who has previously said that her husband and Krugmann were the same man, takes to the stand and confesses that she had lied, coerced into a false statement by Meyerhoff. The camera cuts to Meyerhoff in the witness box. He now testifies that he, in turn, was only obeying orders, acting on the instructions of Rosen. Rosen is then called to the stand and, in a not unexpected conclusion, confesses that he is neither a Jew nor a Nazi hunter: he is Dieter Krugmann, The proof of this comes from the scar on the back of his hand, a scar made by the shard of glass in Majdanek according to Mrs Bergman's evidence, and supported by the papers provided by the Russians. To confirm beyond any doubt, Rosen removes his glasses and Mrs Berman identifies 'the eyes of the Devil – Krugmann'.

Rosen is taken away by the police, but this does not clear Bergman of guilt – none of the above disproves the case and is, in fact, largely irrelevant to the case at hand. In the final scenes the real killer is identified as Mitchell (Terry O'Quinn), a friend of Berman's who is revealed in the final unmasking to be Kurt Johann Krugman, the blood nephew of Dieter Krugman and a member of Odessa. Mitchell's confession leads to a directed verdict of not guilty.

Desperate Deception is, as this rather cursory description suggests, not a profound or even especially good film, but it is significant for the return of the flashback within the context of the courtroom, a move which comes alongside a wider awareness of the fragility of memory seen in *Music Box* and *The Man in the Glass Booth*. The change in the film-maker's attitude towards the evidence is however only one of the changes noticeable in the relationship between film, the courtroom and the Holocaust in the 1980s. *Desperate Deception* and *Music Box* are not films about the Holocaust in the same way as, for example, *QB VII* and *The Man in the Glass Booth*, with both suggesting that American citizens could now be seen as perpetrators as well as victims, bystanders and liberators. This ever-increasing complexity of America's relationship to the Holocaust was also evident in the two films which are to be the subject of the next chapter. Made for the domestic market, these films confirmed that by the 1980s the Holocaust was no longer a European event but an American one, with

American heroes using American law to fight neo-Nazis and Holocaust deniers.

NOTES

1. Tom Bower, *Klaus Barbie: Butcher of Lyons* (London: Corgi Books, 1985); and Yoram Sheftel, *The Demjanjuk Affair: The Rise and Fall of a Show-Trial* (London: Gollancz, 1994).
2. John Epstein, 'Fathers and Daughters', *Cinema Papers*, 81 (1990), pp.28–31, provides a good comparison of the two films. It was a story also explored in Allan Massie, *The Sins of the Father* (London: Sceptre Books, 1992).
3. Peter Novick, *The Holocaust and Collective Memory*, p.209.
4. Annette Insdorf, *Indelible Shadows: Film and the Holocaust*, 3rd ed. (Cambridge: Cambridge University Press, 2002), p.4.
5. Eli B. Rosenbaum, 'The Investigation and Prosecution of Suspected Nazi War Criminals: A Comparative Overview', *Patterns of Prejudice*, 21, 2 (1987), p.18.
6. Howard Blum, *Wanted! The Search for Nazis in America* (Greenwich, CT: Fawcett, 1977). See also Alan S. Rosenbaum, *Prosecuting Nazi War Criminals* (Oxford: Westview Press, 1993), for a brief introduction.
7. Henry Friedlander and Earlean M. McCarrick, 'Nazi Criminals in the United States: The Fedorenko Case', *Simon Wiesenthal Centre Annual*, 2 (1985), p.66. See also Matthew Rinaldi, 'The Disturbing Case of Feodor Fedorenko', *Judaism: A Quarterly Journal*, vol. 28, 3 (Summer 1979), pp.293–303
8. Rosenbaum, 'Investigation and Prosecution of Nazi War Criminals', p.17.
9. Ruth Gruber, *Haven: The Dramatic Story of 1000 World War II Refugees and How They Came to America* (Three Rivers, MI: Three Rivers Press, 2000).
10. This is the assessment of the OSI's then director Allan A. Ryan, cited in *Jewish Telegraphic Agency Bulletin*, 3 June 1980.
11. The case against Walus was brought prior to the establishment of the OSI but the procedure would remain the same. For an overview see Gitta Sereny, *The German Trauma: Experiences and Reflections, 1938–2001* (London: Penguin Books, 2001), pp. 309-57 'The Case of John Demjanjuk'; and Friedlander and McCarrick, 'Nazi Criminals', pp.63–85.
12. Friedlander and McCarrick, 'Nazi Criminals', p.50.
13. Technically the trial started in November 1986 but the hearings only commenced in 1987. For a synopsis of the events leading up to the trial and the trial itself, see Tom Teicholz, *The Trial of Ivan the Terrible: The State of Israel vs John Demjanjuk* (London: MacDonald, 1990).
14. There remains the concern that Demjanjuk's trial in Israel took place to justify the considerable expense the United States government had gone to in committing itself to the denaturalization of suspected war criminals. By the early 1980s the OSI had organized 350 investigations and 50 civil trials but none had led, as yet, to a war crimes trial held abroad. See, for example, Sereny, *German Trauma*, pp.309–57.
15. Gary Crowdus, 'Keeping Alive the Memory of the Holocaust: An Interview with Costa-Gavras', *Cineaste*, 17, 3 (1990), p.5. According to this interview, Costa-Gavras's sources were John Loftus, *The Belarus Secret*, ed. Nathan Miller (London: Penguin Books, 1983); Allen A. Ryan, *Quiet Neighbors: Prosecuting*

Nazi War Criminals in America (San Diego: Harcourt Brace Jovanovich, 1984); and Christopher Simpson, *Blowback: America's Recruitment of Nazis and its Effect on the Cold War* (London: Weidenfeld & Nicolson, 1988).

16. *Section Specialé* recounts the case of four young French men who were placed on trial during the war as terrorists by the Vichy government in order to appease the Nazis. Costa-Gavras has since gone on to direct *Amen* (France/Germany/USA, 2002), a film version of Rolf Hocchuth's *The Deputy* (1963; New York: Grove Press, 1964).
17. Gabriel Milland, 'The BBC Hungarian Service and the Final Solution in Hungary', *Historical Journal of Film, Radio and Television*, 18, 3 (1998), p.354. For reviews of *Music Box* see Gary Crowdus, 'Music Box', *Cineaste*, 17, 3 (1990), pp.45–47 and George Perry, 'Opening Pandora's Music Box', *The Sunday Times*, 6 May 1990.
18. Reality can be similarly strange. Mark O'Connor, Demjanjuk's Chief Counsel from 1982 to June 1987, held a law degree but had never pleaded a major case in court prior to accepting Demjanjuk's case. Such a storyline would surely be considered unrealistic if used in a Hollywood film. See Sereny, *German Trauma*, p.328.
19. Matt Wolf, 'Believe You Me', *Listener*, 123, 3163 (3 May 1990), pp.36–37.
20. Ibid.
21. Joe Eszterhas, *Hollywood Animal: A Memoir* (London: Arrow Books, 2005), p.478.
22. Tom Bower, *A Blind Eye to Murder* : *Britain, America and the Purging of Nazi Germany – A Pledge Betrayed* (London: Warner Books, 1997), pp.108–14; Tom Bower, *The Paperclip Conspiracy: The Battle for the Spoils and Secrets of Nazi Germany* (London: Michael Joseph, 1987). See also those works cited by Costa-Gavras as being the inspiration for his film in n.15. For works that more specifically focus on Barbie, see Erhard Dabringhaus, *Klaus Barbie: The Shocking Story of How the US Used This Nazi War Criminal as an Intelligence Agent: A First Hand Account* (Washington, DC: Acropolis Books, 1984); Tom Bower, *Klaus Barbie: Butcher of Lyons* David Ruzie, 'The Klaus Barbie Case: War Crimes versus Crimes against Humanity', in *Patterns of Prejudice*, 20, 3 (1986), pp.27–33; Alain Finkielkraut, *Remembering in Vain: The Klaus Barbie Trial and Crimes against Humanity*, trans. Roxanne Lapidus with Sima Godfrey, introduced by Alice Y. Kaplan (New York: Columbia University Press, 1992); Ted Morgan, *An Uncertain Hour: The French, the Germans, the Jews, the Barbie Trial, and the City of Lyon, 1940–1945* (London: Bodley Head, 1990); and Brendan Murphy, *The Butcher of Lyon: The Story of Infamous Nazi Klaus Barbie* (New York: Empire Books, 1983).
23. Cited in *The Times*, 17 December 1987.
24. Sereny, *German Trauma*, p.309.
25. Crowdus, 'Keeping Alive the Memory', p.5.
26. Cited in *The Times*, 26 April 1988.
27. John French, *Robert Shaw: The Price of Success* (London: Nick Hern Books, 1993), p.89.
28. Wolf, 'Believe you Me', p.36.
29. Margaret Walters, 'Sins of the Father: The Power of the Past in War Crimes Trials', *Listener*, 124, 3169 (14 June 1990), p.41.

30. Sereny, *German Trauma*, pp.315–16, originally published in *The Sunday Times*, 20 March 1988, pp.22–23.
31. Primo Levi, *The Drowned and the Saved*, trans. Raymond Rosenthal (London: Michael Joseph, 1988), p.8.
32. *The Late Show*, 'Screening the Holocaust', BBC2, tx. 18 December 1990.
33. A similar tactic of discrediting the witness had been used in *Judgment at Nuremberg* when Colonel Lawson implied that Mrs Lindnow's testimony was questionable because she had been a member of the Nazi Party.
34. Although Costa-Gavras claimed not to have been influenced by Demjanjuk's trial, this piece of evidence recalls that of Pinchas Epstein who, at Demjanjuk's trial, spoke of how 'I see Ivan every single night ... I dream about him every night.' Cited in Lawrence Douglas, *The Memory of Judgment: Making Law and History in the Trials of the Holocaust* (New Haven, CT, and London: Yale University Press, 2001), p.204; and Sereny, *German Trauma*, p.316.
35. For an evaluation of the flawed identification process in the case of Demjanjuk, see William A. Wagenaar, *Identifying Ivan: A Case Study in Legal Psychology* (Hemel Hempstead: Harvester Wheatsheaf, 1988).
36. There is the implicit and disturbing suggestion that Ms Khalman's degradation as a child prompted her subsequent choice of career. It suggests that only through the catalyst of male sexual violation has she realized her potential. Similarly, Ann was 'touched' as a teenager during her first kiss and this experience seems to have prompted her decision to practise law. Both of these women represent the use of female moral goodness as a means by which to redeem male violation, not only for themselves, but in respect of all of Miska's crimes.
37. This suspicion of photographic evidence is ironic, given that Eszterhas made his name through the publication of colour photographs of the My Lai massacre in *The Plain Dealer* newspaper: see Kendrick Oliver, *The My Lai Massacre in American History and Memory* (Manchester: Manchester University Press, 2005), p.21.
38. Costa-Gavras, cited in Wolf, 'Believe You Me', pp.36–37.
39. Cited in Iain Johnstone, 'Timely Reminder of the Evil Men Do', *The Sunday Times*, 17 June 1990.
40. Eszterhas, *Hollywood Animal*, pp.496–97.
41. Television from the late 1950s onwards began to share film's interest in the war criminal, with a number of shows on both sides of the Atlantic seeking to bring them to justice. For example, this included not only the *Playhouse* version of *Judgment at Nuremberg*, but episodes of popular series such as *The Defenders*, *The Twilight Zone*, *Columbo*, *Canon*, *The Saint*, *Callan* and *Special Branch*, to name but a few.

5

The Domestication of the Holocaust: Skokie (1981) and Never Forget (1991)

'This time it's different: What we do this time is fight.'
Max Feldman (Danny Kaye), *Skokie* (1981)

Released either side of *Music Box* and *Desperate Deception* were two made-for-television movies that saw the convergence of the courtroom and the Holocaust, but confronted neither war crimes nor the pursuit of the fugitive war criminal. Instead, in these films, again based on real-life events, the Holocaust was once more the backdrop for an examination of modern-day America. The first of these films, *Skokie* (USA, Herbert Wise, 1981), told of the struggle of 1977–78 when a group of Holocaust survivors opposed the proposed march of a group of neo-Nazis through their home town of Skokie, Illinois. The second, *Never Forget* (USA, Joseph Sargent, 1991), depicted one man's opposition to the invidious and craven attacks of Holocaust deniers in the early 1980s. Together they illustrate how the Holocaust began to impact on the present in a way superficially similar to – but in fact markedly different from – the films discussed in the previous chapters.

Skokie (1981)

In 1976, Frank Collin's National Socialist Party of America (NSPA) announced that they were to march in uniform through Marquette Park, Chicago.[1] In order to prevent this unwanted demonstration, the City of Chicago insisted that Collin firstly pay a prohibitive amount in insurance before he and his followers be permitted to march. Protesting this as an abuse of the right to free speech and expression, the NSPA's case was taken up by the liberal American Civil Liberties Union (ACLU). They would provide counsel for the neo-Nazis on the basis that the right to march, regardless of the offensive nature of NSPA's beliefs, was guaranteed by the First Amendment. In the meantime, Collin, in an attempt to generate further publicity for his organization, wrote to the civic leaders of the towns and villages in the Chicago area in search of an alternative venue. This included Skokie, a middle-class area to the north of Chicago and home to the 'highest number of Holocaust survivors of any city in the nation outside New York City'.[2] The Skokie authorities, aware of the high proportion of Jewish survivors who populated the town, attempted to stop the NSPA from marching, passing three ordinances and obtaining a preliminary injunction that barred any such demonstration. In July 1977, the Illinois Appellate Court modified the injunction: the Nazis would be permitted to march but they would not be allowed to display the swastika. Following a further appeal, the Illinois Supreme Court ruled in January 1978 'that neither the march nor the swastika emblem could be prohibited'.[3] The injunction was thus vacated and the ordinances passed by the Skokie civic authorities deemed unconstitutional. However, now that Collin and his followers were free to march through Skokie they never did: the ruling had simultaneously removed the impediments to the Chicago march that had always been their preferred option.

Skokie is a predominantly faithful dramatization of these events. It begins like *None Shall Escape* and many other films about Nazi and neo-Nazis, with the image of a swastika on a flag, but as the camera pulls back we can see that this is not 1940s Europe but contemporary America. The flag adorns Rockwell Hall, the Central Headquarters of the NSPA, the group of neo-Nazis fronted by Frank Collin (Geroge Dzundza). Inside the building, with the film allowing no time for further explanation, assembled members of the NSPA discuss their plans for a march through the 'damned Jew town' of Skokie.

Although *Skokie* opens in the office of Frank Collin, the central character of this recreation is the fictional Max Feldman, a Holocaust survivor played by comedian Danny Kaye in his last screen role.[4] The opening dialogue and mise en scène establish that Feldman has integrated into American life in the years since the war without losing his Jewish faith or heritage. His home, for example, contains both a menorah and a copy of Alistair Cooke's popular 1970s coffee-table book *America*. This personal integration is also evident on a collective level. At an interfaith meeting in the village's synagogue to discuss the proposed march, Skokie's mayor Albert Smith (Ed Flanders) reassures the assembled Jewish community that they need take no action, for 'Your Christian neighbours here in the village of Skokie hold hoodlums like Frank Collin and his ilk in the utmost contempt.' It is a statement that not only presents a united front against the shared enemy of intolerance, but one that again equates on-screen Nazis to gangsters, creating parallels between 1930s Nazi Germany and 1970s America, the work of Brecht and the films of the 1940s.

The playing out of the scene that follows also indicates knowledge of both the historical and filmic past. Feldman interrupts Smith to tell him that, with respect, he has heard such talk before. He removes his jacket and points to the tattoo on his arm, a gesture that is in marked contrast to the shame and stigma attached to the tattoo in earlier films such as *The Search* and *The Pawnbroker*, but very much in common with the renewed pride in one's identity that emerged from the 1960s and was also evident in *QB VII*. Feldman tells Smith: 'I will not go home, I will not pull down the window shades, not this time, not in my own town where I made a business and a home. Where I raised my child. If a Nazi marches here in Skokie you can believe me I will be here. I will be here with baseball bats, with a gun, anything.' In previous chapters we have seen how in the post-war period the survivor could be reluctant to speak, or could be overlooked, but here, provoked by the threat of the NSPA, Feldman speaks willingly to an attentive audience that wants to listen and to act. He does so with an aggression that dismisses the allegations of Jewish timidity that had confronted and overwhelmed Arthur Goldman in *The Man in the Glass Booth*. This defiance is shared by the rest of the community: 'You want us to walk into the gas chambers again? Is that what you want?' asks a man in the audience. 'I am an old man but I would fight.' Moments later, Feldman proclaims the film's central message, one that would be shared with *Never Forget* and one that signifies the empowerment that has come through the Americanization of the Holocaust survivor: 'This time it's different: What we do this time is fight.'

For Feldman, a survivor not a victim, America has offered protection (symbolized here and in *Music Box* with the baseball bat) and opportunity, not only for him and his wife (Kim Hunter), but for their teenage daughter, Janet (Marin Kanter). Feldman has previously asked 'What should a child born in America have to do with that suffering?' but the proposed march has been a catalyst not only for resisting, but also for remembering and sharing. Feldman now tells Janet of his experiences in the camps, briefly mentioning slave labour and the *kapos*, the dehumanizing process and the 'selections'. Similarly, in one of the four brief courtroom re-enactments, Holocaust survivor Sol Goldstein (David Hurst), the leader of Skokie's Jewish community, tells the court: 'When I see the swastika I know that even here in this country I'm not safe with my life; that my children are not safe ... even here.' The neo-Nazi rally has forced a reassessment of identity for the wider American-Jewish community as well. Morton Wiseman (Lee Strasberg), a benefactor of the ACLU, tells the ACLU's lawyer Herb Lewisohn (John Rubenstein) that he is a native of Chicago and a conservative Republican,

> but as used to be occasionally suggested to me at various clubs and social events, I am a Jew. The other day I saw a man on television ... the Holocaust survivor from Skokie [Feldman] and it came to me. In a way I too am a survivor of the Holocaust. Must one defend the right to speak for those if they came to power would deny the right to freedom, indeed of life, to others.

Other significant Jewish characters in the film, however, are advocates of free speech. The young lawyer Lewisohn is a Jew, as too is his colleague at the ACLU, Aryeh Neier (Stephen D. Newman). Moreover, Neier is also a Holocaust survivor. His family died in 'in those gas chambers at Auschwitz, Treblinka, Bergen-Belsen. I escaped. In spite of that, no because, I support First Amendment rights.'[5] It is the latter group who emerge victorious from the courtroom, with Lewisohn affirming in the now anticipated universal fashion that 'The only defence for Jews, for blacks, for anybody, is freedom with the protection of law.'

Skokie is therefore a celebration of American law and the freedoms inherent in the American Constitution, but it is one that also sympathizes with and respects the Holocaust survivor. Even though Feldman is defeated in the legal outcome, it is he who has the last word. Spoken directly to the camera, he laments that 'those bastards have got free speech'; perhaps more significantly, he acknowledges that what matters is that 'this time we stood up to them and we fought them right back and we told our story ... We were witnesses.' He concludes, speaking for both the dead and the living: 'This time I stood on my feet and I showed them. This time they couldn't wipe their feet on me. This time they couldn't spit on me. This time they couldn't kill me.'[6] It was a message that would be repeated ten years later in *Never Forget*, a film that, like *Skokie*, showed the effect the Holocaust had on American law and how another assimilated American, Mel Mermelstein, fought back, this time against Holocaust deniers.

Never Forget (1991)

The phrase 'Never Forget' is a proactive call to memory, one of the 'most central injunctions to have become linked with the aftermath of the Holocaust' and, in conjunction with the similar 'Never Again' (the phrase that had been used by the Jewish community in *Skokie*), often taken as symbolic of the fear that to forget the past leads to repetition.[7] In 1945 a special edition of the British newspaper the *Daily Mail* featured extensive photographs of the camps, including the now infamous photograph of the racks of emaciated prisoners at Buchenwald, and had used the phrase in explaining the purpose behind the use of such horrific images:

> Here will be found dreadful facts, and even more dreadful pictures. We may shudder, but we dare not look away.
>
> Some of these grim scenes have appeared in the newsreels which have been shown in cinemas all over the country. In at least one place the film has been withdrawn after a few performances because it was found that many members of the audience walked out.
>
> Such a response is understandable, but it is nevertheless to be deplored. It displayed a reluctance to face facts which we shall encourage at our peril. Nothing is ever gained, but everything shall be lost, by running away from the truth.
>
> To refuse to look at these abominations may do credit to the heart, but it does no credit to the mind. Nor does it reflect the determination to keep the national pledge that these things shall not be repeated. It is our children who will suffer if we weaken in this resolution.
>
> Let us therefore remember … Let us, therefore, never forget.[8]

Pertinently, the magazine's final question asked of the anonymous and homogeneous faces captured in the photographs, 'Can they forget?' The proceeding chapters and the weight of memoirs and testimonies written since have shown that some could not. Elie Wiesel, for example, one of the faces in the Buchenwald photograph and probably the most famous of all American Holocaust survivors, wrote in his autobiographical work *Night*: 'Never shall I forget that night … Never shall I forget that smoke. Never shall I forget the little faces of the children ... Never shall I forget these things, even if I am condemned to live as long as God Himself. Never.'[9] Similarly, Mel Mermelstein, another of the faces later identified in the Buchenwald photograph, could not forget what happened. But for him, to 'never forget' was a promise he made to his father that, should he survive, he would 'bear witness to the world of the crime that has occurred here, for all of us who cannot speak'.[10] The dramatization of the court case is, therefore, an extension of the promise made by Mermelstein to his father that he would be 'a witness to the world' so that 'people will never forget'. It is about past, present and future; a warning that freedom should not be taken for granted – even in America.

At neither the IMT in Nuremberg nor the Eichmann trial – the two major Holocaust trials for the American public – had there been a denial of the existence of an extermination programme or that Jews were gassed to death at Auschwitz, but that was the accusation raised in a Californian courtroom in October 1981 as Mermelstein sought to redress the claims of Holocaust revisionists and deniers – that 'tiny band of cranks, kooks, and misfits who deny that the Holocaust took place' – with an acknowledgment in law of the Holocaust as fact.[11] The first practitioners of Holocaust denial to be found in the United States did not, in fact, issue an explicit denial that the attempted extermination of European Jewry had taken place. Rather, adopting the arguments already being used by their European counterparts, early American revisionists contended that the killing of so many was logistically impossible. The putative dead, it was suggested, were in fact alive and well and living elsewhere, many in America as illegal aliens. Historian Deborah Lipstadt's synopsis of the history of Holocaust denial has shown how, over the next thirty years, revisionist theories proved capricious in their search for publicity and credence, malleable both to the evolving understanding of the Holocaust and the revisionists' own changing demands. In the wake of the Eichmann trial, for example, the revisionist gaze turned inwards, with the United States being condemned for its apparent complicity in creating the 'myth of the Holocaust', with the coverage afforded to the trial by the media cited as evidence of America's 'gullibility and excitability ... relative to German wartime crimes, real or alleged'.[12] By contrast, revisionism in the early 1970s had grown increasingly explicit. Austin J. App, for example, in his influential pamphlet *The Six Million Swindle: Blackmailing the German People for Hard Marks with Fabricated Corpses* (1973), presented eight 'incontrovertible assertions' which 'demonstrate[d] the fallaciousness of the figure of six million' and were intended to 'prove' that the Holocaust was nothing other than a hoax, 'inspired and nurtured by Communists and Jews' in which the USA, in collusion with Israel, had played a leading role.[13] Although revisionism had therefore maintained a continual presence in post-war America, it was not until 1976 and the publication of Arthur R. Butz's *The Hoax of the Twentieth Century* that Holocaust denial entered into mainstream American consciousness. In this so-called 'revisionist bible', Butz, an associate professor of electrical engineering and computer sciences at Northwestern University, Illinois, produced his own series of fallacious arguments to support the assertion that the Holocaust was a hoax, including the implication that Zyklon B had been used simply for delousing and never for extermination. Like his predecessors, he concealed his lack of empirical evidence behind an obfuscation of scientific and pseudo-academic language.

Two years later, Butz's arguments, along with App's eight axioms, were taken up by the Institute for Historical Review (IHR) for its own malefic purposes. As its name suggests, the IHR purported to be an authentic historical organization. Founded in California in the winter of 1978 by Willis A. Carto (a director of Noontide Press, the California-based private publisher of Butz's *The Hoax of the Twentieth Century*) and British fascist David McCalden, the IHR presented itself as a 'non-political' organization created to 'encourage the re-examination of "accepted" accounts of twentieth century events', specifically the Holocaust.[14] As with Frank Collin's neo-Nazis, much of the IHR's time and resources were devoted to a series of self-promotional publicity gimmicks, including the organization of conferences, talk shows and radio broadcasts, and most notably a series of adverts, distributed across university and college campuses, which called for an open dialogue on the Holocaust. Although the latter proved mildly successful in generating publicity, the majority of this, as with the Skokie incident, centred on First Amendment rights rather than on denial per se. To quote Peter Novick's damning indictment: even though 'this kept the pot boiling … in no case known to me was the Holocaust itself ever debated on campuses; rather it was a question of whether boycott or exposure was the best strategy for dealing with these screwballs. So far as one can tell, it was only fellow screwballs that they ever attracted.'[15] At the time of writing, the IHR's profile and influence have continued to wane as internal disagreements and financial irregularities hasten its – and Holocaust denial's – return to the margins.

It had been at the institute's first conference held in the summer of 1979 that director David McCalden, speaking under the pseudonym of Lewis Brandon, announced a $50,000 'reward' payable to anyone able to 'prove that the Nazis operated gas-chambers to exterminate Jews during World War II'. Any claimant would be required, inter alia, to provide exact dates for the gassings, be able to describe fully the mechanics of the killing procedure, and provide conclusive 'forensic evidence'.[16] Any claim, therefore, would have perforce to indulge the deniers' accusations. This was, as Brandon later freely admitted, simply another gimmick, one intended, in his words, to trap the 'naive zealot' and generate publicity for the IHR.

In December 1980, Mel Mermelstein, an Auschwitz and Buchenwald survivor who was by then living and working in California, formally applied for the reward. Mermelstein had been deported to Auschwitz with the rest of his family by the Hungarian Militia (the Arrow Cross, the anti-Semitic organization that had already featured in *Music Box*) in the spring of 1944 when he was 17 years old. He was the only one of them to survive. From Birkenau he was transported first to Gleiwitz-I Labour Camp (a satellite of Auschwitz) and then to Buchenwald, from where he was liberated in April 1945. After a period spent recuperating and searching for any trace of his missing family, he emigrated from Europe to the United States, arriving in New York on 31 August 1946. Over the next thirty years he assimilated into American life as he fought for the US Army in Korea, started his own business and raised a new family with his American Christian wife. Unlike Arthur Goldman in *The Man in the Glass Booth*, Mermelstein chose to display his experiences as he strove to educate about the Holocaust rather than conceal. He spoke regularly on his experiences and established a museum dedicated to the Holocaust at his workplace in California , where he exhibited memorabilia and his own artwork, pieces of which were often created from camp remnants and other assorted ephemera.

Mermelstein had written to the *Jerusalem Post* in August 1980 denigrating the IHR and its 'reward':

> these university professors, some of them former Nazis of the old Hitlerite regime, have taken upon themselves to use and abuse our colleges and universities throughout the western world, in particular the United States, to spread lies, hatred and bigotry vis-à-vis the subject known as the 'Holocaust' ... They are teaching our new generation that the chimneys of Auschwitz were only

> those of the bakeries. That there were no gas chambers at Auschwitz-Birkenau. That Dachau was a peaceful town within Nazi Germany and that the 'six million' European Jews fled Nazism and have been living peacefully in Israel ever since ... These 'prestigious' gentlemen ... as well as the bigoted organizations they represent, have the gall to offer any survivor of the Holocaust a $50,000, and possibly $100,000 award if he or she can prove that indeed gassings of men, women and little children had actually taken place.[17]

In response, in both an open letter published in the IHR's newsletter and in correspondence undertaken with Mermelstein directly, McCalden, again under the guise of Lewis Brandon, offered to reopen the recently closed $50,000 reward, should Mermelstein wish to apply. Any evidence produced, he explained, would 'be judged along the same standards as evidence in a US criminal court; not the standards of the Nuremberg Trials'. If Mermelstein chose not to accept the challenge, then, Brandon continued, 'we will be obliged to draw our own conclusions, and publicise this fact to the mass media'.[18] This was a familiar tactic, well known to the Los Angeles offices of the Anti-Defamation League (ADL) and the Simon Wiesenthal Center (SWC). When approached by Mermelstein, both offices advised him that the appropriate response was to take no further action. Any reply, they assured him, would simply generate publicity for, and therefore be beneficial to, the IHR. In spite of this advice, Mermelstein decided to pursue the matter and in December 1980 sent a notarized declaration to the IHR in which he formally applied for the reward. In this missive, Mermelstein's lawyer William Cox advised the Institute:

> Mr Mermelstein fully accepts your offer and through the attached Exhibits ... fully complies with your requirements of proof.
>
> Inasmuch as your offer letter establishes that the standard of proof shall be that which prevails in the United States Criminal Courts, Mr Mermelstein assumes that the sufficiency of his evidence will be judged by an impartial fact finder, that all proceedings will be open to public and media observation, and that the matter will be resolved in a timely manner.
>
> It is suggested that the proceeding be televised under a system which allows viewers to vote on the outcome and which ensures all parties a just and fair basis for determining whether the contract now entered into has been satisfied.[19]

In conclusion, Cox called the IHR's bluff, advising them that should no response be received by 20 January 1981 then civil proceedings would be instituted against them for breach of contract. In due course, on 19 February 1981, Mermelstein brought a lawsuit against the Institute for Historical Review et al. for over 17 million dollars. The case, however, never came to a formal trial as both sides instead filed cross-motions for, and agreed to, a summary judgment. At the hearing on 9 October 1981 the Honourable Thomas T. Johnson of the Superior Court of California in Los Angeles found in Mermelstein's favour and declared:

> Under Evidence Code Section 452(h), this court does take judicial notice of the fact that Jews were gassed to death at the Auschwitz Concentration Camp in Poland during the summer of 1944 ... It just simply is a fact that falls within the definition of Evidence Code Section 452(h). It is not reasonably subject to dispute and it is capable of immediate and accurate determination by resort to sources of reasonably indisputable accuracy. It is simply a fact.[20]

It was not until the summer of 1985 that the Superior Court finally ordered the IHR to pay USD 90,000 in settlement, and 'to issue and execute' a letter of apology to Mermelstein 'and all other survivors of Auschwitz for the pain, anguish and suffering he and all other Auschwitz survivor have sustained relating to the $50,000 reward offer for proof that "Jews were gassed in gas chambers at Auschwitz" '.[21]

Six years later, only three months after the protracted legal wrangling between Mermelstein and the IHR was finally concluded, Joseph Sargent's docudrama telemovie *Never Forget*, a well-intentioned factional recreation of the case, brought Holocaust denial directly into American homes. The prime mover behind this adaptation was *Star Trek* stalwart Leonard Nimoy.[22] His interest in Mermelstein's story had been initiated at a chance meeting with a lawyer acquainted with the case. Soon afterwards, Nimoy, in his own words,

> went to visit Mel Mermelstein to discuss it further. I was so moved by what he had to say – and show, in the case of the memorial he had created for camp victims – that I contacted my long-time friend, [producer] Robert Radnitz. I was very interested in not only portraying Mel, but also in helping to bring the project to the screen.[23]

The project had been accepted in the first instance by NBC, but the original script proved to be, according to Nimoy, 'unusable'. A second draft, a 'sensitive, lovely script' by Ronald Rubin which 'In a straightforward, honest way, without sensationalising ... told a very touching story about a man who makes a stand', proved more to Nimoy's and producer Radnitz's liking. However, this second script failed to satisfy NBC and the project was dropped. It would prove to be only a temporary setback, for shortly afterwards the film was taken up by the Turner Network, receiving its premiere on 8 April 1991.[24]

Following the by now familiar pattern for a Holocaust-related drama, the film was well received by the critics and was duly nominated for an award, in this case the 1992 Cable Ace Award. Like other actors in Holocaust dramas before and after him, Nimoy, who had been granted his wish to play Mermelstein, was effusive in his praise for the production: 'For me, Mel's story goes beyond the Nazi/Jewish issue – it addresses the fundamental issues of the human spirit ... If every project brought me the same sense of fulfilment that *Never Forget* did, I would truly be in paradise.'[25] Nimoy's position, however, although sincere and laudable, encapsulates the Americanization of the Holocaust as the horror of mass murder is supplanted by a cathartic and redemptive response that is predicated in the universal. The focus of the story for Nimoy is Mermelstein's victory in the present and the protection offered by the law for the future.

The majority of the film's action takes place in California in the 1980s, long after the perpetration of the original crime. The opening prologue, however, is set, as we are advised by an on-screen title, in 'Hungary 1944'. Our temporal and geographical location is important. An establishing shot follows a group of people – later identified as the Mermelstein family – at play in a seemingly pastoral idyll where the sun breaks through the branches of the trees to glint off the smiling, laughing faces which the camera then shows in close-up. It is a scene that recalls similar moments in previous Holocaust films, most notably the opening to *The Pawnbroker*. Off-screen the sound of an engine invades this tranquillity. The camera cuts to the arrival in tandem of Nazi and Hungarian Arrow Cross troops and trucks. In the trucks a group of Jewish prisoners, identifiable by the Orthodox dress of the adults, watch in quiet resignation as the Mermelsteins are forced to join them. The sun-dappled faces of the doleful children gape between the slats of the truck while the adults stand behind them wearing expressions of bemused acquiescence. In marked contrast to *None*

Shall Escape this deportation takes place in bright sunshine: symbolically, the perpetration is no longer a clandestine event undertaken by the cover of night.

The camera settles in close-up on the face of the young Mel Mermelstein (Carl Steven) who stands with hands raised in surrender. The frame dissolves to be replaced by a black-and-white photograph of people and cattle trucks. The camera pans to the right, away from the photograph, and the words 'SOUTHERN CALIFORNIA 1980' are superimposed onto the screen. Both narrative and audience have jumped forward thirty-six years. The continued presence of the noise of the engines creates a sound bridge between the two scenes as we traverse time and space, in the process establishing a connection between sound and memory similar to that made in *QB VII* and *The Man in the Glass Booth*. The previous scene, at first understood as an objective recreation of 1944, is now explained as analepsis, a flashback from the memories of the adult the boy became, the film's protagonist Mel Mermelstein (Leonard Nimoy). The adult Mermelstein is addressing a group of high school children, and for both the children and the cinematic audience it is thus his memories – and his desire to remember – which bring the Holocaust into the present day, for they are contained within him, just as he is trapped within them. In presenting the sequence chronologically, this subjective flashback is interpreted as objective: it establishes the accuracy of Mermelstein's memory at a time when survivor memory was being questioned. As we have seen, at the Jerusalem trial of John Demjanjuk the evidence of those who survived foundered on the frailty of memory, but *Never Forget* can accept no such frailties because this is a film about Holocaust denial. Perhaps with this in mind, *Never Forget* is the first of the case studies to be prefaced with a statement of authenticity that foregrounds the factual sources of what follows:

> *This film is based on events culminating in the lawsuit entitled Mel Mermelstein v Institute for Historical Review, et al, Los Angeles Superior Court case no. C356542. While certain scenes are adapted from incidents in the lives of the Mermelstein family and other individuals, all legal proceedings are based on actual transcripts and documents.*

In one obvious sense this is simply a facade of authenticity (particularly in acknowledging that scenes are 'adapted' and 'based on'), but

Leonard Nimoy confirmed in an interview with *Reform Judaism* that 'Almost every word' of the pivotal and uncomfortable deposition scene was based verbatim on the transcripts.[26] This deposition lasts approximately ten minutes in a film only ninety minutes long. Although not presented in a courtroom, a deposition is a statement given under oath that has the same standing as evidence given in court. For the duration of this interview the IHR's lawyer Richard Fusilier (Paul Hampton) openly ridicules Mermelstein and questions his memory. Firstly he suggests that Mermelstein's interpretation of past events is flawed. Those families and individuals who were arrested by the Nazis had been so not because they were Jewish, Fusilier claims, but because they were anti-German. Then he questions Mermelstein as to the gassings at Auschwitz. How, asks Fusilier, can Mermelstein prove that what he claims is true?

Mermelstein:	My father and my brother were worked to death, and I can prove to you that my mother and my sisters were gassed at Auschwitz-Birkenau. I saw them going in the gas chamber, but I didn't see them coming out ... These very two eyes have seen men, women, little children lured, drawn into gas chambers ... They were told they were going to be taking showers.
Fusilier:	Did you hear anybody say, 'You are going to be taking a shower'?
Mermelstein:	Yes, yes, I was told.
Fusilier:	Did you take a shower?
Mermelstein:	I am not one who returned from the dead ... You don't want me to tell you that I was in a gas chamber with a group who were gassed. I was not gassed – that's why I'm here today and they are not. Anybody who was inside the gas chamber couldn't be alive today to talk about it, could he?

This unobtainable proof was exactly the kind of evidence demanded by deniers for, as Jean-Francois Lyotard explained when talking of France's 'main propagator of Holocaust denial', Robert Faurisson: 'In order for a place to be identified as a gas chamber, the only witness [he would] accept would be a victim of this gas chamber ... there is no victim that is not dead; otherwise this gas chamber would not be what he or she claims it to be. There is, therefore, no gas chamber.'[27] Fusilier next coerces Mermelstein into validating one of Holocaust denial's more infamous claims:

Fusilier:	Was Zyklon B used for any other purpose besides extermination? ... Have you ever heard of it being used for delousing? ... In Buchenwald, Mr Mermelstein, was there a typhus epidemic going on? ... You had your hair shaved? ... You were dipped in a solution?
Mermelstein:	Yes, before you went in the shower.
Fusilier:	Oh, you did take a shower.
Mermelstein:	Yes, but it was for delousing.

He then suggests that it was physically impossible for Mermelstein to have witnessed that which he claims to have seen:

Fusilier:	You have said that in Auschwitz-Birkenau you saw people including your mother and sisters go into a chamber.
Mermelstein:	Yes, they were gas chambers disguised as shower-rooms, that's correct ... I saw this with my own eyes. They went in ... they went in, and I looked at the other end to see if people were coming out and [*begins to cry*].
Fusilier:	So you watched your mother and sisters enter and you're watching the backdoor and they never come out. Could you see the back door? ... Was there a stairway coming out of the back? ... There was no back door there?
Mermelstein:	No.
Fusilier:	But you just said you watched the back. Was that a wrong expression you used?

For the final one-and-a-half minutes of the deposition the camera remains fixed in close-up on Mermelstein's face as he comes to realize that his testimony may not be sufficient proof for a third party. Sargent's direction and Rubin's script, however, combine to emphasize to us, the watching judge and jury, who must share this decision, that Mermelstein's testimony is not to be doubted. To prove this, *Never Forget* could, as *Operation Eichmann* did thirty years before, recreate the gas chambers. We have seen in *None Shall Escape* how the film-maker uses film as proof, and the prologue to this film has already established Mermelstein as a reliable narrator. Yet Sargent eschews any further use of the flashback. I have spoken previously of how the courtroom genre permits the circumvention of the horror of the camps, but for *Never Forget* the obviation of the replication of these experiences stresses the film's reliance and belief in the eyes and testimony of Mermelstein who 'saw this with [his] own eyes'. It is a remarkable transition from the reliance on the film evidence of Nuremberg. Where once the newsreels spoke for the witness and was deemed more credible, *Never Forget* deliberately does not return to the camps and gas chambers in flashback because it emphasises an unquestioned belief in the truth of Mermelstein's words and what he has seen. In choosing not to replicate the murder of Mermelstein's family, *Never Forget* refuses to engage with the IHR's twisted logic and with the notion that only those who died in the gas chambers can provide irrefutable evidence. Similarly, although we watch Mermelstein collect 'derogatories, depositions, statements of witnesses, causes of action, documented evidence' to be submitted to the court in evidence (indeed, they are visible on a table in front of Judge Johnson in the film's finale), none of this material is to be seen or verified by the cinematic audience. Judge Johnson acknowledges the influence of the collected material on his decision, but it is not produced as evidence for the cinematic judge. Film continues to present itself as incontestable proof, but now there is an unequivocal belief in the spoken testimony of the witness. In *None Shall Escape*, André de Toth had filmed the murder of the Jews of Litzbark to prove to the audience what was happening in Poland in 1944; in *Never Forget*, in contrast, it is the fact that the mass murder is *not* filmed that is proof of the veracity of the testimony.

The trust in Mermelstein's testimony does not mean that *Never Forget* is without any familiar visual referents. In 1988, Ilan Avisar identified several images that had become 'quintessential' in the American representation of the Holocaust:

> [They] include the liberated prisoners of Buchenwald, multitudes of shadows of human beings lying on the three-storey bunks inside long, dark barracks, wearing dazed eyes and striking skeletal bodies; the gate at Auschwitz, with its satanically deceiving title *Arbeit Macht Frei*; and, perhaps the most famous picture of the Holocaust, ironically taken by a Nazi photographer following the final liquidation of the Warsaw Ghetto, featuring a

> small boy raising his hands with horror before the arrogant, overpowering German soldiers.[28]

Each of these appears in the film's opening minutes, the moments when the film's authenticity is to be established.[29] In particular, when the young Mel is captured by the Nazis, he is seen with his hands raised in surrender in a gesture that deliberately replicates that of the young boy photographed in the Warsaw Ghetto. The connection between the two is enhanced when in a subsequent scene the adult Mermelstein uses an enlargement of this famous photograph to illustrate his life story. This picture first came to prominence at the IMT when, as part of the Stroop Report, it was used to illustrate the horror of the fall of the Warsaw Ghetto in 1943, but Mermelstein gestures to the photograph whilst describing his arrival at Auschwitz in 1944. The subreption of the image as 'what awaited us at Auschwitz' misleads both on-screen and off-screen audiences and undermines the trust placed in Mermelstein's memory which the remainder of the film strives to establish.[30] By linking the young Mermelstein to the boy in the photograph – indeed by suggesting that he is the boy in the photograph - an identity is created for Mermelstein as an archetypal and iconic victim. It is an association which recalls the connection made between Mrs Shulman and the footage of Auschwitz in *QB VII*. This association is clearly intentional and yet unnecessary for, as we have seen and as *Never Forget* itself later elucidates, Mermelstein was already a part of one of Avisar's other quintessential (if less appealing to replicate) images: the liberated prisoners of Buchenwald.[31] In making the connection to the Warsaw Ghetto photograph however, the authority of both the film and the image in terms of historical accuracy are lessened.

Mermelstein's story is of one man's struggle to stand up for his rights and to preserve the memory of the Holocaust. As he explains to his son Bernie (Jason Presson), this is 'not what I want to do, it's what I have to do'. It is something he has the opportunity to do only because of his identity as an American, for the suffering of the survivor has become an American suffering and his decision to fight is predicated upon his identity as an American citizen. As the real Mel Mermelstein explained to the *LA Times* in March 1981, in a sentence that could have come from Max Feldman in *Skokie*, 'This time I fight back.'[32] Mermelstein may cling to football as a reminder of his past but he goes bowling with the Greenspans and shares an interest in the Dodgers with an employee. Indeed, when the family decides to celebrate, Mel suggests that they go out for hamburgers. In 1944 the passive Mermelsteins were nearly all annihilated by the Nazis; now the family that survives is the one which assimilates and fights. Mermelstein regularly offers reminders to the watching audience of both his own love for the country and its superiority when compared to Europe. 'This is not Nazi Germany, this is not Munkacs, this is the United States', he tells the SWC; 'This is some country', he says, almost purring, to his wife as they reflect on the past; and 'This can't happen here, not in America', he shouts at Cox as he struggles to find a lawyer who will accept his case. These paeans are not only a eulogy to freedom, but also a warning against complacency, for this is a film about prejudice in modern-day America – a reminder, in the words of Ernst Janning in *Judgment at Nuremberg*, that 'this horror can arise anywhere, in any place'. Ten years earlier, in *Skokie*, Janet Feldman had told her father that she had ridden on the Chicago Loop train and imagined that she was 'bound for Auschwitz'. Now, immediately after Mermelstein delivers a description of the arrival of the cattle trucks at Auschwitz, a truck door slides open. The scene cuts to the reverse shot from the perspective of the truck's interior looking outwards. The sun blinds and disorientates the camera, and as the camera regains its orientation it focuses on a distant chimney from which a plume of smoke can clearly be seen. We are, by implication, in Auschwitz, and yet we also remain in Southern California, 1980. As the two locations merge in our imagination, the threat posed by unchecked Holocaust denial is made explicit.

Both *Never Forget* and *Skokie*, based on the efforts made by US law to protect the memory of the Holocaust from denial, have a justification for the way in which they Americanize the Holocaust. However, it is the choice of such a story which is indicative of the way in which American culture has consciously commemorated and propagated the memory of the Holocaust. These are not films about the Holocaust, but rather the repercussions of the Holocaust on the United States and America's self-image as the land of liberty. With Judge Johnson's ruling, US law provided a legal buttress for survivors against the invidious calumny of Holocaust denial; but the little solace such a judgment provided must be considered against the irony that the case and the film show survivors celebrating the establishment of the Holocaust as fact. When one is forced to celebrate such things then the victory is pyrrhic at best. Instead of dwelling on this spiralling entrapment, *Never Forget* intentionally proffers a universal meaning in its concluding remarks, delivered by voice-over rather than the personal message given by Cady at the conclusion of *QB VII*: 'As a result of Mermelstein versus Institute for Historical Review, the Holocaust became a recognized fact in the United States Court for the first time ... However ... the institute maintains that there were no homicidal gas chambers at Auschwitz... The fight against racism, hate and prejudice continues.' Like Nimoy, we emerge from the film with the memory of a happy ending in which the survivors of the Holocaust celebrate proving the fact that Jews were gassed to death at Auschwitz. Hitting the deniers with the law has forced an acknowledgement that the Holocaust occurred, and affirmed America's self-belief: it has not given justice to the survivors.

To conclude, in *Skokie* and *Never Forget* the survivor comes to the fore as an American, an individual willing to fight and survive. These films do not focus on the perpetration of the Holocaust, but highlight that the guilt and suffering has no end for many survivors and their families. In *Skokie*, Janet Feldman exclaims 'I'm sorry I'm not dead ... like Grandma, because then I could be important to you', and similarly, in *Never Forget*, Bernie Mermelstein asks 'How are we supposed to compete with them; we're alive and they're dead.' Thus, while both films are intent on showing the continued effect that the Holocaust exerted on American citizens, American life and American law, they do not add to our understanding of the perpetration itself. In a sense the film-maker has come almost full circle. In the first chapters of this book I examined how the use of liberation footage stifled explanation, with the focus being on the audience as witness rather than the crimes being depicted. Move forward to the 1980s, to the period of growing Holocaust consciousness, and once again film is being used to reflect upon the audience and how Holocaust memory and education can be used to create a 'better' citizen. It is perhaps fitting, therefore, that the final film of the twentieth century and the final chapter of this book complete the circle by taking the viewer back from Hollywood to Nuremberg.

NOTES

1. This is a highly simplified account. For a more detailed background, see James L. Gibson and Richard D. Bingham, *Civil Liberties and Nazis: The Skokie Free-Speech Controversy* (New York: Praeger, 1985), pp.22–34; Donald Alexander Downs, *Nazis in Skokie: Freedom, Community and the First Amendment* (Notre Dame, IN: University of Notre Dame Press, 1985); Philippa Strum, *When the Nazis Came to Skokie: Freedom for Speech We Hate* (Lawrence, KS: University of Kansas Press, 1999); and local press reports (*Chicago Sun-Times*, *Skokie*

Review, *Life: Skokie Edition*) held at Skokie public library and available online at www.digitalpast.org under the sections 'Attempted Nazi Rally in Skokie: 1976–1977'; ''; '', a retrospective; and 'Attempted Nazi Rally in Skokie: Recordings', a selection of recordings from the village Board of Trustees meetings from 1977–78.

2. Gibson and Bingham, *Civil Liberties and Nazis*, pp.22–23.
3. Ibid., p.32.
4. Martin Gottfried, *Nobody's Fool: The Lives of Danny Kaye* (New York: Simon & Schuster, 1994), p.325. Although Max Feldman and his family are fictional, the majority of the characters are based on the town's inhabitants. In fact, the cast included many survivors (mainly as crowd-scene extras) who, only three years after having been affronted by being forced to remember the past, were now happy to re-enact scenes of protest for the cameras. As one resident told a local paper, 'there will be videotape machines rolling when the film airs next month'. See *Chicago Sun-Times*, 4 May 1978.
5. The assertion that there were gas chambers at Bergen-Belsen is a mistake that continues to be made. See Joanne Reilly, David Cesarani, Tony Kushner and Colin Richmond (eds), *Belsen in History and Memory* (London: Frank Cass, 1997), pp.7–8, 42–43, 188–89.
6. For a similarly brief analysis of the survivor's role in *Skokie*, see Jonathan Pearl and Judith Pearl, *The Chosen Image: Television's Portrayal of Jewish Themes and Characters* (Jefferson, NC: McFarland, 1999), pp.124–25.
7. Michael F. Bernard-Donals and Richard R. Glejzer, *Between Witness and Testimony: The Holocaust and the Limits of Representation* (New York: State University of New York Press, 2001), p.1.
8. *Lest We Forget: The Horrors of Nazi Concentration Camps Revealed for All Time in the Most Terrible Photographs Ever Published* (London: *Daily Mail*, 1945).
9. Elie Wiesel, *Night*, trans. Stella Rodway (1960; Harmondsworth, Penguin Books, 1991), p.32.
10. Leonard Nimoy, *I Am Spock* (London: Centenary, 1995), p.305.
11. Peter Novick, *The Holocaust and Collective Memory: The American Experience* (London: Bloomsbury, 2001), p.270.
12. Deborah E. Lipstadt, *Denying the Holocaust: The Growing Assault on Truth and Memory* (New York: Free Press, 1993), p.74. Unless otherwise stated, the background to denial in the United States and details of the Mermelstein case are taken from this book. See esp. pp.137–56, 'The Institute for Historical Review'.
13. App, a professor of English at the University of Scranton and La Salle College, had been actively peddling anti-Semitism and 'playing the numbers game' since the 1940s. The link between denial and revisionism is generally accepted to have been provided by Harry Elmer Barnes who, in the mid-1960s, although 'not yet willing to deny the Holocaust, did cast doubt on it by declaring it a theory at best'. See Lipstadt, *Denying the Holocaust*, pp.75, 99.
14. Institute newsletter, December 1981–January 1982, cited in Institute of Jewish Affairs, *Research Report*, no. 4, May 1982, p.1.
15. Novick, *Holocaust and Collective Memory*, p.270.
16. Lipstadt, *Denying the Holocaust*, p.140.
17. Mel Mermelstein, *By Bread Alone: The Story of A-4685* (Huntington Beach: Auschwitz Study Foundation, 1979), p.270.

18. Ibid.
19. Ibid., p.273. The offer to have a trial in the public domain via televised justice was not taken up.
20. http://www.nizkor.org/ftp.cgi/people/m/mermelstein.mel/mermelstein.text.
21. Lipstadt, *Denying the Holocaust*, p.156.
22. For an examination of Nimoy's upbringing, see Sonia Levitin, 'A Conversation with Leonard Nimoy: The Vulcan is a Real Jew', *Reform Judaism*, 2 (1998).http://reformjudaismmag.org/past/
23. Nimoy, *I Am Spock*, p.320. Nimoy had already been involved in a Holocaust-related story in the original *Star Trek* series. See Jeffrey Shandler, 'Aliens in the Wasteland: American Encounters with the Holocaust on 1960s Science Fiction Television', in Hilene Flanzbaum (ed.), *The Americanization of the Holocaust* (Baltimore, MD, and London: Johns Hopkins University Press, 1999), pp. pp.39–43.
24. Nimoy, *I Am Spock*, p.307.
25. Ibid., pp.310, 322.
26. Levitin, 'Conversation with Leonard Nimoy'.
27. Cited in Yosefa Loshitzky (ed.), *Spielberg's Holocaust: Critical Perspectives on Schindler's List* (Bloomington, IN: Indiana University Press, 1997), p.129.
28. Ilan Avisar, *Screening the Holocaust: Cinema's Images of the Unimaginable* (Bloomington, IN: Indiana University Press, 1988), p.5.
29. The 'Arbeit Macht Frei' sign forms part of Mermelstein's artwork, while the Buchenwald photograph is a part of the display visible behind Mermelstein as he speaks.
30. Burton Andrus, the Nuremberg jailer, wrote in 1969 that one scene of *Nazi Concentration Camps* 'showing how they [the SS] cleared out the Warsaw ghetto' was particularly memorable. 'I shall never forget the sight of a little boy of about seven coming out of the ruins with his mother; his arms were raised and he looked bewildered. A few moments later the camera panned down to the boy's body on the ground. He had been shot to death.' No such moment exists in this film. See Burton Andrus, *The Infamous of Nuremberg* (London: Leslie Frewin, 1969), pp.134–35.
31. At the conclusion of the court case described below, Mermelstein was photographed for US magazine *Newsweek* in October 1981, holding a copy of the Buchenwald photograph with an accompanying caption describing his 'painful victory'. See Barbie Zelizer, *Remembering to Forget: Holocaust Memory Through the Camera's Eye* (Chicago, IL, and London: University of Chicago Press, 1998), pp.186–87.
32. *LA Times*, 12 March 1981, cited in Mermelstein, *By Bread Alone*, p.282.

6

Re-Viewing the Situation: Nuremberg (2000) and the Crime of the Century at the End of the Century

In an edition of the BBC's arts programme *The Late Show* in 1990, director Marcel Ophuls spoke of how it was impossible to apply 'criteria of good taste' to Holocaust films, including the recently released *Music Box* and *Triumph of the Spirit*: 'Let's just think of what words mean ... Nobody's forcing these people to make these films. Who does? Anybody ... out there in the wilderness crying "We want to see a boxer at Auschwitz!" I haven't heard anybody. There doesn't seem to be a terrible demand for it.'[1] And yet, unquestionably, the early 1990s saw an increase in America's and American cinema's interest in the subject, reaching a peak in 1993, the so-called 'year of the Holocaust'.[2] This was the year in which the United States Holocaust Memorial Museum finally opened to the public after fifteen years of delays; the seminal 1978 miniseries *Holocaust* was rebroadcast on prime-time television; and *Schindler's List* (USA, Steven Spielberg, 1993) went on general release in cinemas across the country and then worldwide. Twenty years after its release, *Schindler's List* remains one of most widely discussed of films on the Holocaust, while Spielberg's status has continued to grow. *Schindler's List* won seven Oscars at the 66th Academy Awards, including Best Picture and Best Director, and, while not necessarily a barometer for critical success, the awards remain a gauge for mainstream American opinion. In the final years of the century the Academy would regularly acknowledge films with a Holocaust theme. In 1996 the Oscar for Best Actor was awarded to Geoffrey Rush for his portrayal of traumatized pianist David Helfgott, the son of a Holocaust survivor (Armin Mueller-Stahl, previously seen as Michael Laszlo in *Music Box*), in Scott Hicks's Anglo-Australian production *Shine*. In 1998, Roberto Benigni's *Life is Beautiful* – marketed somewhat bizarrely as a 'truly exceptional, utterly unique motion picture [which] will lift your spirits and capture your heart' – collected three Academy Awards. The success of cinematic documentaries such as *The Last Days* (USA, James Moll, 1998), *Into the Arms of Strangers: Stories of the Kindertransport* (UK/USA, Mark Jonathan Harris, 2000) and *The Long Way Home* (USA, Mark Jonathan Harris, 1998), each of which won the Academy Award for Best Documentary Feature, attested to the sustained level of interest. The 1990s also saw the continued pursuit in American film of the Nazi fugitive, with war criminals being brought to justice, most usually without redress to a visible courtroom, in such films as *Apt Pupil* (USA, Bryan Singer, 1998), *Mother Night* (USA, Keith Gordon, 1996), *The Man who Captured Eichmann* (USA, William A. Graham, 1996) and the Dan Aykroyd/Jack Lemmon comedy *Getting Away with Murder* (USA, Harvey Miller, 1995), which is as appalling as the title suggests.

The prominence of the Holocaust on the screen in the 1990s was in part the consequence of contemporary events in Europe. It was in 1993, nearly fifty years after the IMT had convened at Nuremberg, that UN Security Council Resolution 827 (S/RES/827 [1993]), in response to the continuing reports of 'ethnic cleansing' and 'widespread and flagrant violations of international humanitarian law occurring within the territory of the former Yugoslavia', approved the establishment of 'an international tribunal for the sole purpose of prosecuting persons responsible for serious violations of international humanitarian law committed in the territory of the former Yugoslavia'.[3] For Joseph Persico, author of *Nuremberg: Infamy on Trial* (1994), there was a direct link between the resurgent demand for the establishment of an international tribunal and the Holocaust, even though the IMT had not focused on the latter. For Persico it was not just the nature of the crimes but how they were being reported and how they were presented on screen that was important, as it linked the act of witnessing then with that of nearly fifty years before, confusing the tribunal's aims with the power of the evidence used:

> After over one hundred wars, insurrections, civil conflicts, and revolutions that have racked the world over the past forty-five years and claimed more than 21 million lives, after hardly a

> breath of outrage over atrocities committed in the name of ideology, liberation, independence and religion, people at last have begun to cry out for justice that can penetrate national borders, for a Nuremberg-style prosecution of war criminals. The cry arose in 1990 after Saddam Hussein seized Kuwait, then bloodily suppressed Iraq's Shiite and Kurd minorities. The cry for justice, for a new Nuremberg, became full-throated with the black-and-white images of Auschwitz and Buchenwald updated in colour in Serbian concentration camps in the former Yugoslavia.[4]

Six years later those black-and-white images would feature as the IMT at Nuremberg was itself transformed into colour, when Persico's book became the basis for *Nuremberg* (Canada/USA, Yves Simoneau, 2000), a two-part $24 million miniseries produced and filmed in Canada for Turner Network Television and given its world premiere over Sunday 16 and Monday 17 July 2000. By 2000, fifty-five years after the liberation of the camps, the Holocaust had become firmly established in the popular imagination as the paradigmatic crime of the century. The IMT had in turn become the trial of the century and now, as the century drew to a close, the camera turned again to both, combining crime and process of justice in a miniseries which witnessed a return to Nuremberg as the trial of the Nazi leaders was at long last adapted for the cinematic courtroom .[5] It would reinterpret the events of 1945–46 to present the IMT as the forum in which the Holocaust was first established as America's moral paradigm in order to define and hence control and contain 'evil'. In this adaptation we come full circle, as the questions of authenticity and representation that beset the IMT presented a challenge to the film-maker once again. It marks the return of the newsreel footage of liberation, now being used retrospectively as proof of the Holocaust. As the brief introduction to the filming and contemporary interpretation of the trial that follows will evidence, the trial always seemed destined for a filmic adaptation. However, while the 2000 miniseries strove to foreground its verisimilitude through this use of film footage, the extensive, verbatim use of transcripts, and painstaking attention to detail in rebuilding the courtroom set, the trial itself is markedly different. In particular, the trial's understanding of the Nazi policy against the Jews is transformed, turning it from a trial which subsumed the policy of extermination within the Nazis' many crimes, to one in which the Holocaust had become the moral centre of the prosecution's case.

From Hollywood to Nuremberg: The Cinematic Idiom

> The crimes enumerated ... are so incredible, so monstrous, that they read like scenes from a horror film.
>
> Werner Maser[6]

> By dint of much American ingenuity the small courtroom was completely transformed ... There was far more of Hollywood about the [new] lay-out than of a British court.
>
> Robert Cooper[7]

The city of Nuremberg has long been associated with the Nazi regime.[8] It was, for example, the venue for the annual *Parteitag* (Party congress) and thereby the location in 1935 for the proclamation of the eponymous laws on citizenship and race that were a significant step on the way to genocide. Moreover, as the venue for these choreographed rallies, Nuremberg also has a place in film history as the setting for Leni Reifenstahl's *The Triumph of the Will*, the celluloid celebration of the Nazi Party filmed there in 1934. Yet today Nuremberg is perhaps more commonly a metonym for international justice and a word that recalls the IMT and the iconic images of the interior of the courtroom, in particular those of Hermann Göring and his fellow defendants seated in the dock.

The IMT at Nuremberg was always intended to be a highly visible trial and the camera was to be there to record the events for posterity, a record of the reaffirmation of the rule of law. A month before the trial's opening day, Lord Birkett, the British Alternate Judge, had cause to note in his diary that there had been 'Cinema and flashlight photographs galore' at a preliminary meeting of the judiciary.[9] In the courtroom itself, moving picture cameras –encircling the renovated room at eye level on tripods and looking down on proceedings from apertures located just below the ceiling – would record all bar one of the public sessions of the eleven-month trial, providing a visual record of this grand enactment of justice to accompany and complement the written transcript that was to be one aspect of its lasting legacy.[10]

One of the most enduring images of the IMT was a direct consequence of the camera's presence. To allow the cameras to record with greater efficiency and quality, the courtroom's curtains were kept permanently drawn, with spotlights providing the necessary additional lighting. These lights caused considerable problems for those present, meaning that many of the defendants would insist on wearing dark glasses to counter the glare and alleviate the physical discomfort. But this explanation barely concealed the psychological reasons for the defendants' unwillingness to be placed before the cameras: 'Most of them reached for their black glasses when the sharp and acid lights were switched on, with a sullenness which meant that they were doing more than merely trying to save their eyes; and those who most often resorted to those black glasses were those who had manifested the greatest repentance.'[11]

This evident reluctance to appear before the camera and the glare of publicity was to be expected, but it was also a new sensation for the accused who, as the senior-ranking remnants of a famously narcissistic regime, had until recently been far from camera-shy. As Liliana Cavani, director of *The Night Porter* (Italy, Liliana Cavani, 1973), noted in an interview in 1975:

> The Nazis really loved the cinema and adored filming everything; they did it very well – they had some very good cameramen. A lot of the SS possessed Leicas ... They just loved filming. Everything, even the worst scenes of torture. Not just the reporters – the professionals – but all of them. It was a hobby ... It seems to me an attempt to become more objective, to 'distance' oneself from what is going on ... In an interview with Speer a couple of years ago, he talked about one of the last reunions at Nuremburg [sic]. The Nazi hierarchy had become rather fat and out of condition and Speer didn't know what to do. So he arranged for the lighting for the rally to be at ground level – from below the participants. This made them look slimmer and fitter.[12]

At Nuremberg, now bereft of the flattering angles demanded by Speer, the Nazi hierarchy was no longer content to be paraded in front of the lens, preferring to hide away from the publicity the trial afforded them.[13] There were moments when the old energy and belligerence returned, but in general, especially as the trial dragged on, those accused who had once exuded charisma and power now looked broken, nervous and tired. Moreover, they appeared mundane, something that came as a shock to many observers, not only because of the horrific nature of the crimes, but precisely because of how expertly their appearance had once been orchestrated:

> In spite of the care with which they had been dressed ... the defendants' appearance in court came as a great anticlimax to the spectators. The image everyone had of them was as the central characters of the Nazi newsreels, the heroes of the Leni Reifenstahl films; they had been given stature by the flattering camera angle, glamour from the skilfully placed lights ... They were all so much smaller than anyone had imagined.[14]

The relationship between the trial and the cinema also extended further, with the film world being an idiom that seemed to offer a way for the participants to connect to the events in the courtroom. In his memoir of the trial, Airey Neave, who attended the proceedings as a clerk to the court and served the indictments on the accused, would, for example, describe Hermann Göring as the 'fat man in endless screenplays who leads the gang of killers from his expensive dinner table ... [although] he was far more shrewd and dangerous than any celluloid character'; Hans Frank wore the expression 'of a shyster lawyer in the Hollywood tradition, all sweetness and light'; and old photographs of Franz von Papen 'showed him looking like a villain in an early film with sleek hair and spats', invoking once more the familiar vision of the accused as hoodlums which married popular notions of domestic villainy with the horror of world war.[15] As already noted, similar comparisons had already been made in films such as *Confessions of a Nazi Spy* (USA, Anatole Litvak, 1939) and *The Hitler Gang* (USA, John Farrow, 1944), and were also to be found in the RKO Pathé News report of the IMT's opening day entitled 'The Hitler Gang goes on Trial', a title which established the footage of the trial and the trial itself as a part of a cinematic continuum.[16] The allusion to film was also used in in connection with the prosecution. Neave, for example, was critical of Jackson's closing speech because he felt it 'was emotive, sometimes violent. It created the atmosphere of a Hollywood trial.'[17] The members of the tribunal were also portrayed as film characters by Allied observers, but because they were the 'good guys' the comparisons were more favourable. During the trial, Judge Parker, the US Alternate, was known as the 'Andy Hardy' judge, after the character in the popular movie series of the time; and Justice Lawrence's stature in the courtroom was such that an American lawyer declared that 'Hollywood would have cast him.' Even the executioner, Texan Master Sergeant John C. Wood, 'was almost typecast by Hollywood'. The ultimate retrospective accolade, however, was reserved for the Nuremberg jailer Burton C. Andrus who in film 'would undoubtedly have to be played by John Wayne with all the stops pulled out'.[18]

Eighteen months after the opening day, a trailer for the US release of the first *Nuremberg*, a Soviet documentary, would remind audiences of the trial's imperative to *see* justice done. Cursive script unmistakably redolent of the popular weekly matinee serials such as *Flash Gordon* demanded that the public attend the showing of this 'timely film of terrible significance in which the fate of mankind is being decided ... See! the secret documents of the Nazi masterplan ... See! the graphic, terrifying evidence ... See! the archcriminals ... brought to justice in the people's court ... A warning to all warmongers ... Get a ringside seat!'[19] Such febrile excitement is ironic, for the trial itself was a famously boring undertaking. Even those involved directly in the day-to-day proceedings found few 'highlights' to keep them interested as the prosecution utilized the seemingly endless supply of documentation with the intention of establishing a momentous record of Nazi barbarity. As Ron Chapman, a clerk at Nuremberg, later recalled, to 'present only the exciting and dramatic incidents ... would be to distort both the actual nature of the trial, which was gradual, slow-paced and often tedious, and the picture of Nuremberg'.[20] However, as we have seen over the preceding chapters, such an elision is what must occur if a trial is to work as a piece of cinematic or televisual entertainment, and this is precisely what does occur in the Alliance Atlantis/Productions La Fête version of the trial adapted for television by David W. Rintels in 2000 as a three-hour, two-part miniseries.

Nuremberg (2000)

> I didn't really understand until I saw those films.
> Justice Robert Jackson (Alec Baldwin), *Nuremberg*.

Whereas *Never Forget* gave prominence to its factual basis through an explicit citation in its opening credits to the film's judicial origins, *Nuremberg*'s titles attest simply that it is 'based on the book by Joseph E. Persico', a distancing rather than embracing of the historical origins. *Nuremberg*'s initial reference to its authenticity is in fact visual, drawn through a montage of newsreel images which are taken from the same sources as *The Nazi Plan*. In this visual echo of the IMT – one which is unrecognized by the majority of the audience – film once again charts the rise of the Nazi party and the gradual move towards world war. This concludes with the demagogic Hitler filmed at the Party Congress of 1934 as made famous in *The Triumph of the Will*. As the camera focuses on the connotative swastika, the footage is interwoven with original film, as firstly in black-and-white and then fading into colour the viewer is transported back into the present of 1945 for a modern re-evaluation of a past event.[21]

In the introduction to his book on which the miniseries is based, Joseph Persico observed that the majority of the material previously written on the IMT had concentrated, with good reason, on the jurisprudential aspects of the trial. What these works failed to do, he contended, was 'to satisfy [one's] curiosity about the human drama that must have been unfolding'. Persico elected, therefore, to accentuate the individual sub-dramas of the IMT in an account of the tribunal which personalized the proceedings and played on 'the high theatre [of] the Nuremberg trial itself'. The resulting book, albeit replete with endnotes, and photographs from the trial, and evidently based on the transcripts, memoirs and historical writings of the preceding fifty years, is a factional account of the trial, deliberately written in the style of a courtroom thriller: 'intended for the lay reader and general student of history more than the academic or legal historian ... The account is narrative supported by historical fact.'[22] The hybridity of the text which this produces is exacerbated in the Simoneau/Rintels screen adaptation in which fact and fiction continue to converge as the trial and the lives of its protagonists are abbreviated and then embellished by dramatic flourishes.

It would be disingenuous to suggest that an undertaking the size and duration of the Nuremberg trial could be replicated without considerable ellipsis. For *Nuremberg*'s director Yves Simoneau, it was to be this compression of the proceedings which would be the 'real challenge' of the dramatization: 'We're shrinking [the trial]. We're combining characters. We're combining events. But it's amazing to see how close we are to what happened. We kept the spirit, that's for sure. I mean, the courtroom is an exact replica of what they had. You look at the defendants. I mean they really look like the original guys.'[23] For *Judgment at Nuremberg* a similar commitment to the accurate replication of the Nuremberg courtroom had given the film the accretion of authenticity that was clearly desired by Simoneau. But that was a setting in which to create a fact-based, fictional story populated by composite characters. In contrast, in Simoneau's film the attempted realism highlights more differences than it conceals. Although the courtroom is an 'exact replica', beyond the physical similarities this is a much-altered court whose 'reconstitution' is not – and could not be – as precise as Simoneau avers. On a superficial level, for example, the IMT courtroom normally contained six fixed microphones only: one placed with each principal judge, one for the witness stand and one on the speaker's podium. There were portable microphones used in the court, notably for the defendants' opening and closing statements, but these were cumbersome devices. Crucial to the *Nuremberg* courtroom, however, is the cinematic convention of perambulatory freedom afforded to Justice Jackson (Alec Baldwin). Whereas in Simoneau's film the speaker moves and all else remains static, archive footage reveals a reality in which the speaker would remain stationary while the business of the court went on all around. Similarly, while in the replica courtroom background noise is kept to a minimum, the IMT was, as all trials are, full of coughing, laughter, murmurs, multiple voices and long silences. The IMT was a process whose constituent parts created a whole of far greater import; but in the televisual courtroom, especially one cast with 'stars' (regardless of their magnitude), the individual and not the trial is often the focus.

There are similar differences evident in how the trial was filmed. At the IMT, the cameras, like the microphones, were fixed and the lenses would need to be swapped between shots rather than through the zoom/crane/track of modern cinematography; shots could not be as quickly framed; and the supply of film would run out at inconvenient moments. This was not a trial performed for the camera but rather one at which the camera – like the principal players – was subservient to the process of law. The camera was neither omnipresent nor omnipotent; it recorded events but did not control the proceedings. At *Nuremberg*, in contrast, the camera is as a cicerone, as the action stops and starts at its behest and a voyeuristic justice is enacted, including for the first time the witnessing by the camera of the sentencing and execution. The authenticity provided by the replica set and lookalike cast is, therefore, fallacious, but to an audience it is a tenacious facade because the images of both courtroom and accused are so recognizable.

A more insidious duplicity is created in the illusional veracity of the courtroom dialogue, 'the overwhelming majority' of which, as Alec Baldwin stressed in interview 'is excerpted from the actual trial transcripts'.[24] The opening moments of *Nuremberg*'s version of the trial, for example, amalgamate the proceedings of 20 and 21 November 1945 into one eight-minute section. The IMT had begun with the reading of the indictment, a laborious and time-consuming but necessary process. For the year 2000 this is omitted and the trial begins instead with the pleas of the defendants. Hermann Göring (Brian Cox) is the first of the accused to speak. He attempts to impose his personality on the court by reading a prepared statement. When prevented from so doing, he states, 'I declare myself in the sense of the indictment nicht shuldig – not guilty', in a mixture of German and English. The majority of the other defendants answer simply, 'Nicht shuldig.'[25] At the IMT and in this film version, Rudolph Hess (Roc LaFortune) answers 'Nein. Nein', a response which Lawrence instructed should be recorded as 'not guilty'. Lawrence's instruction was greeted with laughter in the courtroom in 1945 but this laughter has now been removed as the projected earnestness of the courtroom takes precedence over humour.

Aside from these brief moments of German, this modern IMT is conducted in English as an attempt is made to reduce the complexities of the trial. In watching the footage of the IMT, in comparison, one is struck by the obvious presence of the translators, and the effect the process of translation would have on the trial. Often, for example, a question would be asked in one language and replied to in another. On other occasions the use of headphones would mean that one could hear a female voice speaking the translation of a male participant, or due to technical faults the participants would hear the wrong language or two languages simultaneously. The use of simultaneous translation could also lead to discrepancies with the authorized record. For example, the official transcript for 12 March 1946 which details the cross-examination of Paul Korner, former State Secretary in the Prussian Ministry, records Justice Jackson asking Korner to expand on the 'unauthorized concentration camps' that had previously been mentioned. In the footage of the trial, however, it can be seen and heard that Jackson, obviously having received a different translation through his headset, actually asked Korner for more information on the 'wild concentration camps'.[26] It is a minor aberration that highlights the pitfalls of such a system and the potential inaccuracies of the written record.

The pleas are followed with an abbreviated version of Justice Jackson's opening address. This acclaimed piece of oratory, reduced in duration from hours to minutes, is quoted verbatim, abridged, amended and paraphrased, quoted in chronological and achronological order.[27] In an interview, Alec Baldwin, executive producer as well as leading player, felt it necessary again to stress the film's authenticity while justifying the changes: 'The overwhelming majority of what is said in the film is excerpted from the actual trial transcripts, but in the case of Jackson's opening argument, the actual document was somewhere between 40 and 60 pages in length, which would have been a mini-series in itself. So we had to abbreviate.'[28] In condensing Jackson's speech it is that which is omitted that proves revealing, for every decision made in the present about what to include or not to include projects a contemporary distortion onto the past. For example, at Nuremberg Jackson declared: 'We know that the Nazi Party was not put in power by a majority of the German vote. We know it came to power by an evil alliance between the most extreme of the Nazi revolutionists, the most unrestrained of the German reactionaries, and the most aggressive of the German militarists'; whereas in *Nuremberg*, the celluloid Jackson argues that 'Hitler did not achieve power by a majority of the vote but seized it by an evil alliance of revolutionists, reactionaries, and militarists.' These changes have a small but important effect on the film's – and hence the trial's – meaning which is controlled not by the paucity of time available but by the film's – and not necessarily the trial's – aims. Whereas culpability once lay with the Nazi Party in general, it is now solely Hitler's responsibility, for it was he who actively 'achieved' power, rather than being passively 'put in' by a minority of the electorate. The references to the extremes of 'German' society have been removed and the 'evil alliance' is formed not by German society but by the accused, as the camera cuts to show, in turn, Dönitz ('revolutionists'), Von Papen ('reactionaries') and Jodl ('militarists') as Jackson's speech envelops the men in the dock.

A similar simplification of guilt occurs in the rewriting of witness testimony. Mme Vaillant-Couturier, a French newspaper photographer, took the stand at the IMT on 28 January 1946. She was to testify to the conditions in the camps, recounting her experiences at both Ravensbruck and Auschwitz: 'Her testimony tumbled out so quickly that the interpreters could not keep up with her. Biddle could only note: "It is hard to give the impression of the long monotony of horror." '[29] This bears scant similarity to a description of her testimony as presented in *Nuremberg*. As played by Charlotte Gainsbourg her delivery is in English, slow and measured. This revised testimony is again a combination of verbatim, paraphrase and abridged quotations from the transcripts; again it presents a simplified, if no less gruesome, version of events: 'One night we were awakened by horrible cries. The next day we learnt that the Nazis had run out of gas and the children had been thrown into the furnaces alive.' In comparison, the more detailed recollection in the official transcript would require a greater knowledge of its audience as to the way in which the camps were operated: 'One night we were awakened by terrifying cries. And we discovered, on the following day, from the men working in the *Sonderkommando* – the "Gas Kommando" – that on the preceding day, the gas supply having run out, they had thrown the children into the furnaces alive.'[30]

As early as the second day of this factional trial, David Maxwell-Fyfe (Christopher Plummer) had recounted to the court the destruction of the Jews of Dubno as recorded in the affidavit of 'one Hermann Friedrich Gräbe', who by January 1946 was an employee of the United States Government in Frankfurt but during the war had been a 'construction manager who in a civilian capacity was employed by the German army in the occupied Ukraine from 1941 to 1944'.[31] Read into the record on 2 January 1946, the first day after the Christmas recess, Gräbe's affidavit was, in fact, the final document to be presented in connection with the actions of the Einsatzgruppen in the Eastern Occupied Territories, rather than one of the trial's opening gambits. It is the same testimony as that briefly quoted by Arthur Goldmann in *The Man in the Glass Booth* to describe the humiliation of the Jews of Europe. The use of a signed affidavit – a statement of authenticity on behalf of the film-maker – does not prohibit emendation of its contents, as once again the chronology and factual details are changed to reflect the film-maker's aims. There are several minor inaccuracies and abridgements, but whereas Gräbe made reference in the original to the Ukrainian militia's involvement in the mass murder (they were responsible for guarding the prisoners and for driving the trucks to and from the pit under the supervision of an SS man), all reference to them has been removed in the film's version as the responsibility again is that of the SS alone.

It is ironic that a production which tampers with the evidence in this fashion so as to isolate Nazi guilt also makes clear that the IMT was not created solely as a forum for establishing Nazi guilt. As Sam Rosenman (Max von Sydow), formerly Roosevelt's special legal advisor, tells Jackson at the film's outset, the IMT is also the opportunity to 'establish a basis for conduct among nations'. Symbolically thereafter the American legal team's discussion of the trial's remit is conducted aboard a plane bound for Europe, a journey east, into a new dawn as the new world returns to the old to re-establish the rule of law. As a radioman broadcasting from the trial on Christmas Eve later announces: 'as we're filled with thoughts of peace on Earth, it is here that the future of peace may well be determined.' If it is, then it is a peace that is to be determined by the romanticized version and vision of Justice Jackson.

The Pennsylvania-born Jackson was 53 when appointed Chief Counsel on 2 May 1945; Alec Baldwin was only 41 when filming on the series commenced. In the film, Jackson is wanted by President Truman as a 'tough but impartial' prosecutor. He is from the outset the champion of civilization, opposed to anything but a fair trial for the Nazi leaders. Baldwin's Jackson is the charismatic driving force behind the trial's creation and dominant figure of the prosecution. As Samuel Rosenman tells him, 'The trial is yours to create Bob ... [you] even get to pick the defendants.' Jackson is also the lawgiver, responsible for drafting the indictment, 'the secular equivalent of the Ten Commandments'. The Decalogue's importance to Jackson is reinforced when he and his secretary Elsie Douglas (Jill Hennessy) enter the damaged Nuremberg courtroom for the first time. Together they observe a carved medallion over the door:

Douglas: Bob. The Ten Commandments.
Jackson: The Ten Commandments on the same building where the Nuremberg Laws were decreed that deprived all German Jews of their rights. This is it. This is the place to hold the trial.

Baldwin's Jackson is also the conscience of the trial. He is to ensure that this 'is not the triumph of superior might but the triumph of superior morality'. Yet his morality and integrity is compromised by the film's creation of a romance between him and his secretary. Elsie Douglas, an 'attractive, blond ... slightly plump widow of early middle age who managed to combine a good nature with brisk efficiency', bore as little resemblance to the 29-year-old Jill Hennessey as Baldwin did to Jackson.[32] In none of the texts on the IMT is there a suggestion that any impropriety occurred between Jackson and Douglas, but the two become on-screen lovers in order to provide the stagnant courtroom with a distracting romantic subplot. Their relationship becomes tied to the success of the IMT in securing a conviction against the accused and particularly Göring. It is Douglas who provides the confirmation of faith Jackson needs when she refuses to take a telegram of his resignation, telling him: 'Bob, you are this trial. Everything it is, everything it represents is from inside you: your thoughts, your values.'

The defeat of Göring precipitated by Douglas's faith in Jackson is pivotal to establishing Allied morality over the immorality of the Nazis. For Persico, at the time of the trial a boy of 16, the IMT seemed to say that good must triumph over evil, yet Brian Cox's portrayal of Göring is the highpoint of the production precisely because Cox refuses to accept the black-and-white boundaries of good and evil which the film is suggesting. As he says of Göring in a statement that recalls the question of identity posed of Michael Laszlo in *Music Box*:

> He was a loving father – he wasn't a monster. I hope I don't play him as a monster. I'll play him as someone who is tough and someone who has a very hard point of view ... He's vain – he's very clever, intelligent and incredibly bright. And there are humane elements to him, you know. I mean, you don't see it as much in the trial but you certainly see it when he's in prison.[33]

Elsewhere, the moral ambiguity and nuances of the accused are lost in favour of caricatures that allow for a largely romanticized and simplistic evaluation of the trial and the nature of evil. As the accused assemble at Bad Mondorf, they are classified collectively as both 'war criminals' and 'Nazi bastards' by prison commander Burton C. Andrus (Michael Ironside). But during the trial the heterogeneity of the principal members within this group identity is also apparent: the anti-Semitic, foul-mouthed Streicher (Sam Stone) is loathed by all; Schacht (James Bradford) professes his innocence; Speer (Herbert Knaup) is intelligent and apparently contrite; Keitel (Frank Fontaine), Dönitz (Raymond Kloutier) and Jodl (Bill Corday) are honourable soldiers; Sauckel (Ken Kramer), cowardly and frightened; Ley (Julien Poulin), drunk and desperate; Frank (Frank Moore) corrupt but penitent; the deranged Hess can only whisper his name; Ribbentrop (Benoit Girard) is dismissed as stupid; Kaltenbrunner (Christopher Heyerdahl) vicious; and Funk (Erwin Potitt) obsequious.

I have noted in the beginning to Part One that at Nuremberg the details of what would become known as the Holocaust were lost amid all of the horrors of the Nazis. It would be wrong to suggest that the crimes against the Jews were neither considered at all nor deemed to be of any importance to the prosecution. As part of his opening address, for example, Justice Jackson stated unequivocally the severity of these crimes:

> The most savage and numerous crimes planned and committed by the Nazis were those against the Jews ... It is my purpose to

> show a plan and design, to which all Nazis were fanatically committed, to annihilate all Jewish people. These crimes were organized and promoted by the Party leadership, executed and protected by the Nazi officials, as we shall convince you by written orders of the Secret State Police itself.[34]

But the crimes against humanity, which included the case for 'Crimes against the Jews', were prone to being misunderstood as they were downplayed in favour of evidence which supported the primary charge of waging aggressive war. In this stripped-down *Nuremberg* courtroom, however, the Holocaust is far more prominent, although it is noticeable that in this rewriting of the IMT, a recreation in which one absent witness is made flesh and the Holocaust given increased prominence, there is still no room for a Jewish witness, not even one of the handful who actually appeared for the Russian prosecution.[35] That aside, in virtually every courtroom scene the persecution of the Jews is referred to either explicitly or implicitly as it gains pre-eminence. The Holocaust, for example, has a pivotal role in the defeat of the hitherto undaunted Göring. At the IMT Jackson's considerable oratorical skill was not matched by his skill in cross-examination, a shortcoming that was exposed in his confrontations with Göring. Now Jackson is once again exposed as underprepared, but he is given a weekend in which to formulate a more effective approach. It is Maxwell-Fyfe who advises Jackson that the way to beat Göring is to treat him as the 'vile, conniving, bloody, fascist bastard that he is'. On the Monday Jackson keeps the court waiting before sweeping in without offering anything in the way of explanation or apology. He turns immediately to the subject of Jewish life in Germany as gradually he silences Göring:

> Jackson: You were Hitler's second-in-command, you were in charge of the economic four year plan so you know all about the gold wedding rings and the gold teeth and the gold eye glasses that the victims left behind, and you have heard that it took five extra minutes to kill the women because they had to cut their hair off to be used in making mattresses and nothing was told to you about this material that came from these people that had been murdered?
>
> Göring: No, no. How can you imagine such a thing? I was laying down the broad outlines of the German economy.

Jackson:	Witness is excused.
Göring:	I am not finished.
Lawrence:	The witness is excused.
Göring:	I am not finished.
Lawrence:	The witness is excused.[36]

In spite of these various omissions and simplifications, *Nuremberg* represents a well-intentioned attempt to represent what was an important and significant event. For John Q. Barrett,

> the movie accurately depicts how Jackson proved his case and, for history, the reality of the Holocaust. Jackson demonstrated the defendants' guilt using Nazi documents and other objective evidence rather than the testimony of deal-making witnesses. In the movie, as in the real trial, Jackson plays film taken at liberated death camps in the spring of 1945. This evidence – showers; crematoria; piles of bodies; emaciated survivors – shocked and shaped world opinion at the time. The movie performs a real, if horrifying, public service by using the actual footage relied on by Jackson.[37]

Barrett's assessment – understandably concerned with the film's portrayal of the legal arguments presented at Nuremberg – replicates the misunderstanding of the trial's use of liberation footage as evidence of something already understood as the Holocaust. As in *The Stranger* and *Judgment at Nuremberg* the footage used in the dramatization is taken from *Nazi Concentration Camps*, but now this footage is shown as this seminal film and not simply a montage utilizing its images. Any emendation to the original therefore constitutes a reworking of the court proceedings as openly as a rewriting of testimony.

On the day that the film is introduced into testimony, an unshaven, agitated Tom Dodd disturbs Jackson in his office:

Dodd:	The film came in late last night and I was up until dawn watching it. Now, very few people have seen this film. Bob, you have got to enter this into evidence this morning.
Jackson:	What's the film?
Dodd:	You're not going to believe this.

Dodd's prescient admonition is to both viewer and Jackson, but of course his statement is really hindsight, a knowing acknowledgement of the contemporary public reaction to reports of Nazi atrocities. As we have seen in Part One, the prosecution and the defence counsel had already viewed the film and many of the images it contained were already known through newsreels. Lawrence Douglas and Jefffrey Shandler inter alios have spoken of how the viewing of the liberation footage from today's perspective does not enable a modern audience to connect with the shock and horror felt in first seeing these films, and in what appears to be a direct attempt to counter the atrophying of surprise and repulsion – and assuming a level of audience awareness since the film's content is undisclosed at this point – the film is introduced as a surprise piece of evidence. In the process it becomes a concession to the courtroom's and the film's melodrama.[38] As the camera focuses on Dodd's face, it cuts to the interior of the now crowded courtroom to find Dodd sitting at the prosecution tables. His gaze is fixed away from the front of the courtroom, away from the camera and the screen on which the film is to be shown. He has a clear and unambiguous reluctance to confront the horrors of the liberation footage again. It is Telford Taylor (Christopher Shyer) who introduces the footage to the court: 'May it please the Tribunal, the United States now offers a film into evidence. It was compiled from motion pictures taken by allied military photographers as their armies liberated into areas where concentration camps were located.'[39]

This marks the return to the use of film within a film, and while the purpose and their meaning has changed, in some ways the way in which they are used has not. At times the images are once more relegated to an out-of-focus background, with the camera more interested on the courtroom's reaction, adhering to the precedent established in *The Stranger*, *Verboten!* and *Judgment at Nuremberg*. The camera captures how the Nazis in the dock turn away from the screen, often also turning their faces away from the watching audience, as if they are hiding twice, once from the crime and once from the witness. The timing of these reaction shots, which form a significant proportion of the next four minutes, is telling: the first one comes, after a picture of Zyklon B canisters and pile of bodies. A view along the line of the back row of the dock allows a comparison of reactions. Von Neurath cries; Speer looks guilty and penitent; Kaltenbrunner, the stereotypical Nazi in appearance and manner, is shown in close-up, his expression changing from casual disregard to the realization that this evidence is damning.[40] Some of the diegetic audience sob and feel compelled to leave and Douglas blinks nervously; Jackson, although facing the screen head-on, puts his hand to his mouth. Dodd, who has seen the film before, now shields his eyes from even the flicker of the screen.

Nuremberg also complicates the relationship between the diegetic and non-diegetic audiences. It begins by showing *Nazi Concentration Camps* as a film projected within a film, emphasising the courtroom setting by including shots from the rear of the courtroom and then the view from the judges' bench. But on occasion the footage fills the whole screen without the use of any border, assimilating the non-diegetic audience into the courtroom as vicarious witnesses. This confuses the viewer's relationship with the images and the trial, asking us simultaneously to feel empathy with the courtroom audience as viewers while stressing the imperative to observe not only the footage but also the reactions, of which the most graphic are the shots of the audience members leaving the courtroom.

What of the content of the film itself? Originally an hour in length, *Nazi Concentration Camps* has been reduced to only three minutes and fifty-five seconds in duration, although proportionally this increases the percentage of the trial it occupies. There is no extraneous material added as in *Judgment at Nuremberg* but neither is there a narrative nor diegetic soundtrack attached to the footage. I noted in Part One how the lack of engagement with the content of the film was evident in Commander Donovan's introductory remarks at the IMT that these 'motion pictures *speak for themselves* in evidencing life and death in Nazi concentration camps'.[41] By 2000, after sixty years of representation and film history, they again speak for themselves, but now as evidence of a crime already recognised, and known as the Holocaust.

The film begins with a map of Europe on which are displayed the name and position of these concentration camps. There is an audible gasp from the audience as the extent of the camp system becomes clear. In this abridged version the named camps are, in order, Dachau, Mauthausen, Nordhausen and Belsen, although, true to the original, the footage used includes material shot at Buchenwald, Hadamar, Ohrduf, Breendonck, Penig and Arnstadt. Amid this confusion of camps and images the footage is also edited and presented in new ways. For example, the caption for 'Dachau Concentration Camp' is followed, as in the original film, with an establishing shot of the camp. In a divergence from the original, we cut immediately to a close-up shot of a canister labelled Zyklon B, the gas now synonymous with Nazi mass murder. This is one of several examples of the inclusion of previously unseen close-ups which significantly emphasis sections of the original frame.[42] The manipulation of the images, another example of cinema's continual re-editing of history, also tampers with the sequence of images. For example, the editing of images taken at Belsen reverses the order in which they appeared in *Nazi Concentration Camps* to give the illusion that a corpse being swung and a body being placed in a cart are one and the same.[43] Most noticeably, this revised version ends not with the bulldozer and mass graves of Belsen but with images of liberated women smiling for the camera, originally taken at the camp at Penig (a sub-camp of Buchenwald) and now attributed to the liberation of Belsen. In choosing to conclude with these images of rescued women (who were, according to the original commentary, 'able to smile for the first time in years'), the once shocking film has been edited to conclude with a message of redemption and hope rather than horror and despair. In place of the gruesome pictures of cadavers tipped into mass graves, the film, playing to stereotypical gender roles, ends with the smiling faces of the liberated women.

The women are not the only ones to be liberated; once the film has finished, the courtroom's curtains are drawn open in a metaphorical casting-out of the demons, allowing the sunlight to extricate the courtroom from the horror of what has just been witnessed. It is at this point that Jackson exhibits his only moment of doubt as to the value of the civilization he represents:

Jackson:	I didn't really understand until I saw those films.
Douglas:	I still don't. I don't think I ever will. How could civilized human beings do that to other civilized human beings?
Jackson:	Maybe civilization's overrated.

It is a realization which recalls that seen in *Verboten!* forty years before, but it is also a moment which misrepresents not only the trial but the contemporary relevance of the Holocaust more generally. Moreover, while the images may have shown Douglas the horrors of Nazi Germany, this does not equate to an understanding of the persecution of the Jews of Europe. Indeed, in spite of the film's underlying message, this moment highlights that what one fights for is not the same as what one fights against.

By the end of the century, therefore, the courtroom had returned to the use of newsreel footage as evidence. But now it was used as evidence of the Holocaust, a crime which had become a moral paradigm instantly recognisable by the audience. In *Nuremberg* the use of the Holocaust in this way, coupled with the caricatures presented of the Nazi leaders, facilitates an understanding of the 'evil' that drives men to commit such crimes, as if to provide an assessment that would prohibit repetition. It is the prison psychologist, the assimilated American Jew Gustav Gilbert (Matt Craven), who is to be the conduit through which this resolution is achieved and then articulated to the watching audience. It is Rudolf Höss (Colm Feore), the former commandant of Auschwitz who provides the testimony that enables Gilbert to reach his conclusion. In an out of court interview, Höss describes to Gilbert his 'perfectly normal family life even during the period of extermination', explaining how he had always been taught that the 'Jews were the enemy of Germany ... I was an SS man, trained to obey without thinking. Does a ratcatcher think it is wrong to kill rats?' Gilbert is thus able to conclude that the Holocaust – the crime that now circumscribes 'evil' – was the consequence of a series of necessary factors. Firstly, it was made possible by the German proclivity for obedience. Secondly it was possible thanks to the Nazi system of propaganda in which the Jews were classified as subhumans. Finally, and most importantly, was the psychological make-up of the perpetrators. Each was predisposed to such acts and each displayed a 'lack of empathy ... a genuine incapacity to feel with their fellow man.' 'Evil, I think,', concludes Gilbert, 'is the absence of empathy.' This final statement concludes a remarkable transition. Fifty-five years before, the Jewish witness was virtually absent from the IMT and the Jewish suffering marginalized as the trial's focus remained on the perpetrator. In contrast, *Nuremberg* is a film that foregrounds the Nazi persecution of the Jews of Europe. The crime intended to destroy all memory of European Jewry has become the trigger for a trial in which, through our empathy with Gustav Gilbert, the Jewish psychologist who provides our perspective on the inner workings of the trial, each member of the watching audience becomes a Jewish witness to the past for the future.

NOTES

1. *The Late Show*, 'Screening the Holocaust', BBC2, tx. 18 December 1990.
2. For a history and evaluation of the United States Holocaust Memorial Museum, see Edward Linenthal, *Preserving Memory: The Struggle to Create America's Holocaust Museum* (New York: Viking, 1995); and Michael Berenbaum, *The World Must Know: The History of the Holocaust as Told in the United States Holocaust Memorial Museum* (Boston, MA: Little, Brown, 1993).

3. For the complete text of UN resolution 827, see http://www.nato.int/ifor/un/u930525a.htm.
4. Joseph E. Persico, *Nuremberg: Infamy on Trial* (New York: Penguin, 1994), p.ix. See also Peter Novick, *The Holocaust and Collective Memory: The American Experience* (London: Bloomsbury, 2001), pp.251–55.
5. It was not, however, the first time that any of the Nuremberg trials had been recreated in colour. In *The 25th Hour* Anthony Quinn plays Johann Moritz, a non-Jewish Romanian peasant who is arrested for being Jewish before then being mistaken for a German war criminal and placed on trial at Nuremberg. There he is prosecuted by Alexander Knox, who had played Wilhelm Grimm in *None Shall Escape* thirty-three years earlier, as accused becomes accuser. For a scathing review of the film, by Bosley Crowther, see *The New York Times*, 17 February 1972, http://www.amused.nl/film/film/1967/25th/index.html.
6. Werner Maser, *Nuremberg: A Nation on Trial*, trans. Richard Barry (London: Allen Lane, 1979), pp.78–79.
7. R.W. Cooper, *The Nuremberg Trial* (Harmondsworth: Penguin Books, 1947), p.147.
8. For more on the relationship between Nuremberg's past and present, see Neil Gregor, *Haunted City: Nuremberg and the Nazi Past* (New Haven, CT: Yale University Press, 2009).
9. Diary entry, 18 October 1946, quoted in H. Montgomery Hyde, *Norman Birkett: The Life of Lord Birkett of Ulverston* (1964; London: Reprint Society, 1965), p.497.
10. Telford Taylor, *The Anatomy of the Nuremberg Trials: A Personal Memoir* (London: Bloomsbury, 1993), pp.227–29; Ann Tusa and John Tusa, *The Nuremberg Trial* (London: BBC Books, 1995), pp.229–30. The one session that went unrecorded by the cameras was the last. For reasons of propriety it was felt inappropriate to record the sentencing, which would condemn many of the accused to death by hanging. See Albert Speer, *Inside the Third Reich*, trans. Richard Winston and Clara Winston, introduced by Eugene Davidson (London: Sphere Books, 1971), p.694.
11. Rebecca West, *A Train of Powder* (London: Macmillan, 1955), pp.43–44. See also Boris Polevoi, *The Final Reckoning: Nuremberg Diaries*, trans. Janet Butler and Denis Bradbury (Moscow: Progress, 1978), p.101.
12. Film director Liliana Cavani in Alexander Stuart, 'Consciousness and Conscience An Interview with Liliana Cavani', *Films and Filming*, 21, 5, issue no. 245 (February 1975), p.13. The Nazis' love of the camera also forms the basis of Don DeLillo's thriller *Running Dog* (London: Sphere Books, 1981) in which similar sentiments are expressed.
13. While there was an obvious reticence about being seen in the formal proceedings, some of the accused could revert to the performers of old when it suited. This is not always apparent in the footage of the trial, much of which captures the lethargy of the proceedings, but is far more obvious in between the sessions, when the cameras capture just how relaxed the accused could be in front of the lens. One such candid moment, for example, shows Ernst Kaltenbrunner look directly into the camera as he stands to leave an already deserted dock during a recess period. There is no sound to capture the conversation, but the camera captures him smile as he says something to his guard. The guard then turns, at Kaltenbrunner's behest, to look and smile at the camera as not only do they share

a joke, but they do so at the camera's expense. *NWT 048*, Imperial War Museum, London. http://www.iwm.org.uk/collections/item/object/1060013166

14. Polevoi, *Final Reckoning,* pp.70–72. See also John Weitz, *Joachim von Ribbentrop: Hitler's Diplomat* (London: Weidenfeld & Nicolson, 1992), p.297; Tusa and Tusa, *Nuremberg Trial*, p.148; William Shirer, *End of a Berlin Diary* (London: Hamish Hamilton, 1947), p.293; Peter Padfield, *Hess: Flight for the Führer* (London: Weidenfeld & Nicolson, 1991), pp.309–10; Burton C. Andrus, *The Infamous of Nuremberg* (London: Leslie Frewin, 1969), p.53; and Taylor, *Anatomy of the Nuremberg Trials*, p.523.
15. Airey Neave, *Nuremberg: A Personal Record of the Trial of the Major War Criminals in 1945–46* (London: Grafton Books, 1989), pp.28, 81, 130.
16. *The Hitler Gang* was the first film to assemble 'the leaders of the Third Reich in one movie' and which used documentary footage and lookalike actors for verisimilitude. The screenplay was written by Frances Goodrich and Albert Hackett, the husband-and-wife team who would later provide the screenplay for *The Diary of Anne Frank* (1959). See Clayton R. Koppes and Gregory D. Black, *Hollywood Goes to War: How Politics, Profits and Propaganda Shaped World War II Movies* (Berkeley, CA: University of California Press, 1987), pp.299–301; and Bernard F. Dick, *The Star-Spangled Screen: The American World War II Film* (Lexington, KT: University Press of Kentucky, 1985), pp.196–199.
17. Neave, *Nuremberg*, p.367. Neave's comment leaves little doubt as to his opinion of Hollywood as well as of Jackson's speech.
18. See ibid., p.181; Leonard Mosley, *The Reich Marshal: A Biography of Hermann Göring* (London: Weidenfeld & Nicolson, 1974), p.326; James McMillan, *Five Men at Nuremberg* (London: Harrap, 1985), p.75; Tusa and Tusa, *Nuremberg Trial*, p.209; Weitz, *Joachim von Ribbentrop*, p.303. There are a total of sixteen films in the Andy Hardy series, beginning with *A Family Affair* in 1937 and ending with *Andy Hardy Comes Home* in 1958. In these films, Mickey Rooney's 'all-American' teenager was a constant worry for his father Judge Hardy, played by Lionel Barrymore for the first film and subsequently by Lewis Stone.
19. Svilov's film was released in the United States on 24 May 1947. The 1930s serials featuring Flash Gordon saw the hero, played by Buster Crabbe, fight a long-running battle to save the universe from the despotic, totalitarian role model Ming the Merciless. See Roy Kinnard, *Science Fiction Serials: A Critical Filmography of the 31 Hard SF Cliffhangers, with an Appendix of the 37 Serials with Slight SF Content* (Jefferson, NC, and London: McFarland, 1998).
20. Gaskin, *Eyewitnesses at Nuremberg* (London: Arms and Armour, 1990), pp.143–46. Nearly all other observers who have written in detail on the trial have spoken of the boredom of the proceedings. Most famously, Rebecca West described the Nuremberg courtroom as a 'citadel of boredom' and the 'symbol of Nuremberg [as] a yawn'. See West, *Train of Powder*, pp.9, 11.
21. The technique of moving from black and white into colour is one used regularly by film-makers to suggest authenticity. It had already been used, for example, in the miniseries based on Albert Speer's memoirs *Inside the Third Reich* (USA, Marvin J. Chomsky, 1982). The process was inverted in *Schindler's List* as the film moved from colour to black and white to suggest a different kind of authenticity. *Nuremberg*'s second part opens in a similar fashion, but Hitler's

presence has been replaced by Churchill's. Against images of the devastation of Nuremberg and Germany, and liberation footage of the camps as seen in *Nazi Concentration Camps*, Churchill speaks of the Cold War and the need to rehabilitate Germany. This balance is lost in the DVD release, which has only one set of titles.

22. Persico, *Nuremberg*, pp.xii-xiii.
23. http:/turnerlearning.com/tntlearning/nuremberg/index.html.
24. Alec Baldwin, quoted in Ivor Davis, 'Nuremberg War Trial: New Drama is Must-See Watching', http:/www.jewishfamily.com.culture/films/Nuremberg.txt. The courtroom scenes in *Nuremberg* are based on the proceedings as follows: 20–21 November 1945, Pleas and Jackson's opening address; 27 July 1946, Gräbe's affidavit (originally mentioned 2 January 1946, but the section recited in the film was not read out at that time); 12 December 1945, document 294-PS; 20 August 1946 Pachelogg's testimony (although part of this evidence was presented on 20 December 1945); 28 January 1946, Mme Vaillant-Couturier; 29 November 1945, the screening of *Nazi Concentration Camps*; 13 March 1946, Göring testimony, followed by 18 March 1946 and 19 March 1946, his cross-examination; 20 March 1946, Jackson and Göring; 21 March 1946, Jackson and Göring continued; 1 April 1946, von Ribbentrop in the stand; 26 April 1946, Streicher; 6–7 May 1946, Funk; 12 April 1946, Kaltenbrunner; 15 April 1946, Höss; 28 May 1946, Sauckel; 20 June 1946, Speer; 3 April 1946, Keitel; 24 May 1946, Schirach; 18 April 1946, Frank; 26 July 1946, Jackson's closing speech; 31 August 1946, the defendants' final statements; 30 September 1946, reading of the Judgment; and 1 October 1946, sentencing.
25. 21 November 1945, *IMT*, vol. 2, pp. 97–98. The exceptions are Hess and Kaltenbrunner. The latter was, in fact, absent from the court's opening day owing to ill-health and did not enter a plea until 10 December 1945, his first day in court.
26. *NWT 24*, Reel 3; *IMT*, vol. 9, p. 157. http://www.iwm.org.uk/collections/item/object/1060013152
27. The abridged version of Jackson's speech used in the film is drawn from *IMT*, vol. 2, pp.98, 102–03, 99, 130, 99, 155.
28. http:/alt.tnt.tv/movies/originals/Nuremberg/intro.html.
29. Tusa and Tusa, *Nuremberg Trial*, pp.193–94.
30. *IMT*, vol. 6, p.216.
31. Affidavit of Hermann Gräbe, dated 10 November 1945 (USA494, 2992-PS). The incident at Dubno, although recorded in this affidavit, was not read in court until 27 July 1946 as part of Sir Hartley Shawcross's summing up (*IMT*, vol. 19, pp. 501–07) and was subsequently quoted by US Alternate Parker in the judgment (*IMT*, vol. 22, p.479, 494). Shawcross incorrectly attributed events to October 1943 and not 1942. Jackson later conceded that the testimony would have made a greater impact if Gräbe had appeared in court in person. See Rober E. Conot, *Justice at Nuremberg* (London: Weidenfeld & Nicholson, 1983), p.231.
32. Persico, *Nuremberg*, p.7.
33. Cited at http:/alt.tnt.tv/movies/originals/Nuremberg/intro.html.
34. *IMT*, vol. 2, pp.118–19.
35. Anton Pachelogg (Robert Joy) appears in *Nuremberg* as a witness for the prosecution, whereas at Nuremberg he was absent and only his words appeared

in the form of an affidavit. His testimony is one of the few in the film that is not concerned with crimes against the Jews.

36. Göring's cross-examination by Jackson, was followed by the considerably more successful cross-examination by David Maxwell-Fyfe, who proceeded to unsettle Göring with questions about the murder of the escaped prisoners of Stalag Luft. See 19–20 March 1946, *IMT*, vol. 9, pp.492-574
37. http://writ.corporate.findlaw.com/commentary/20000714_barrett.html.
38. The shock of the images' introduction is lessened when, as when premiered in the UK, the break for adverts that immediately precedes this part of the trial is accompanied with a warning that 'what follows contains graphic and disturbing images of the Holocaust'.
39. See Chapter 2 for how this differs from the actual introduction of the film.
40. In fact, when *Nazi Concentration Camps* was shown at Nuremberg in November 1945, Kaltenbrunner was still absent through illness. He arrived in court only in December of that year.
41. See Part One, n.34.
42. These are, in the order in which they appear in *Nuremberg*: a shot of a showerhead, followed by a close-up (appearing in the original film after 46m 44s in the footage shot at Dachau); a close-up of a Zyklon B can (47.10 Dachau); a close-up of an oven interior (39.27 Buchenwald); a naked man lying down (48.15 Dachau); a solitary clothed man (26.17 Nordhausen); woman with headscarf in close-up (5.25 Pegnig); a close-up of a group of young men who face the camera (37.20 Buchenwald).
43. Frames 52 and 53 of the new film originally appear fifteen seconds apart and in the reverse order after fifty-five minutes of *Nazi Concentration Camps.*

Conclusion

The case studies in this book take us from Nuremberg to Hollywood in presenting a cultural history of those American fictive films of the twentieth century in which the courtroom and the Holocaust converge. It is a study bookended by *None Shall Escape* and *Nuremberg*, two films which feature international tribunals at which the defendants stood accused of war crimes and crimes against humanity, but not specifically crimes against the Jews. Unusually for a wartime film, and in spite of the lack of a specific indictment, *None Shall Escape* explicitly and graphically identified the Jews of Europe as the victims of Nazi persecution and was free to imagine the crimes. This changed in light of liberation and the use of film as witness at the IMT. The power of precedent was seen first in the quasi-courtroom of *The Stranger* in which atrocity footage was used to provoke a reaction without really educating. Then *Sealed Verdict*, looking to establish its authenticity and credibility as a process of justice, used documentary footage of the IMT to ensure its authority, simultaneously recalling the IMT's construction of evidence through the use of film within film. As the 1950s ended and the 1960s began, the two courtrooms of *Verboten!* and *Judgment at Nuremberg*, recreating the IMT and the subsequent proceedings of the Nuremberg Military Tribunals, examined collective and individual guilt, apportioning a responsibility that extended beyond Nazism and Germany to include the Allies.

These first films all focused on the perpetrator and the accused, endeavouring to establish guilt and exact punishment. In the decades that followed, however, it was to be the victims of Nazism – and particularly the Jewish victims who were absent from those first films – who came to the fore as the cinematic courtroom moved to consider how the Holocaust was being remembered, rather than how it had been perpetrated. Following on from Eichmann's trial, from the early 1970s onwards the cinematic courtroom became the forum for dialogue concerning survivor guilt and trauma, and questions of identity and identification. In the 1980s and early 1990s the continued impact and importance of the Holocaust on contemporary America grew ever more evident as the rise of neo-Nazism and Holocaust denial became the focus of the televisual courtrooms, with once passive European Jewish victims becoming belligerent American survivors. This sequence of films charts, therefore, not only the changing face of justice but the American cinema's gradual embracing of the Holocaust victim. In this reading of these films, the cinematic descendant of Rabbi Levin in *None Shall Escape* is the psychologist Gustav Gilbert in *Nuremberg*, with the culturally and spiritually different Polish Jew transforming into the assimilated US Army officer, one who is able to emphasize with confidence his dual identity as both an American and a Jew without the use of a hyphen and without fear of persecution.

At the same time, these depictions also resonate with domestic concerns beyond the Holocaust, concerns as varied as post-war insecurity and insularity, teenage delinquency and racial inequality, the Cold War, the American–Israeli relationship, the war in Vietnam, and more recently ethnic cleansing in Bosnia, the Gulf War and the 'War on Terror'. There has been, therefore, a clear move towards an Americanization of the Holocaust in the text and context of these films. To make such an observation is not to condemn this as an abuse of the Holocaust or its memory (although that could be argued), but to show that there is an equivalence between the representations of the Holocaust in courtroom dramas with the Americanization evident throughout other aspects of American culture.

At the beginning of this book I asked whether the filmic courtroom could present evidence of the Holocaust in such a way as to satisfy the demands of the cinematic jury. That is, to return to Kathy Eden's translation of Aristotle, how could the film-maker 'make the Audience feel that they, like the jury, can see for themselves the events exactly as they occurred.'[1] The majority of these films are, as we have seen, films in which the audience is expected to participate actively in the process of judgment, be that by an invitation extended directly to the camera as in *None Shall Escape*, or more usually an implicit requirement on behalf of the viewer, as seen in *Music Box*. The different representational strategies they have employed are significant for understanding the relationship between the law, the Holocaust and cinema. In *None Shall Escape*, the evidence of the murder of the Jews of Europe by the Nazis is provided in flashback as non-Jewish Poles and German survivors take to the stand to bear witness to crimes that are not yet beyond the limits or considered taboo.

After 1945 there is an obvious movement towards the projection of the iconic footage of liberation as precedent and the most authentic and credible of visual evidence. But this reliance on documentary newsreel comes at a cost to dialogue and understanding, with the power of the image providing the film-maker with a form of representation which does not detail the complexity of what is being seen. By the Eichmann trial, it is survivor testimony which presents the more compelling picture of the horror of the Holocaust, with the human witness adding an emotional and dramatic dimension into the sterile environment of the courtroom. Similarly, in the first films that followed Eichmann's trial, the survivor spoke of her/his experiences to a world increasingly willing to listen, with the film-maker looking beyond archive footage to tell stories which people wanted to hear. In *The Man in the Glass Booth* the post-war courtroom represents the Holocaust without redress to the newsreel footage, as survivor testimony gains precedence over the images which had for so long supplanted memory. But Hiller's film also showed the persistence of history in its use of sources, and underlined that by the 1970s the complexities of memory and trauma had become a factor in the courtroom. Whereas Colonel Lawson in 1961's *Judgment at Nuremberg* could object that 'the counsel has no right to suggest that the witness's memory is inaccurate', this was a very real problem for Arthur Goldman and the witnesses in *Music Box*. To conclude, the camera returned to the IMT and a trial which had its own singular identity as *Nuremberg*. If the IMT had failed 'to recognize the unique nature of the fate of European Jewry', then *Nuremberg*, the three-hour dramatization of the trial, attempted to rectify what had come to be seen as a mistake, misrepresenting the trial in order to foreground the importance the Holocaust had obtained for American popular memory by the end of the century.[2]

The courtrooms at the heart of the films discussed are based, almost without exception, on real-life cases. They establish their credibility and veracity by buttressing themselves with legal references and historical authenticity through film and documentation, form and content. They do so in order to foreground their factual origins, to accrete authenticity and satisfy the demands of history. But if this is primarily because the subject is the Holocaust then this authenticity is misleading, because the cinematic courtroom achieves only a realistic depiction of the process of justice, not the crime: it is a process which is not – indeed cannot – be beyond the limits. That is, these films tend to focus on the legacy and memory of the Holocaust, not its perpetration. As a whole, therefore, the film and the courtroom, jointly and separately, act as a protective barrier as well as a medium for articulation. Although the regular appearance of the Holocaust in the real-life courtroom has provided a factual locus that assists in the accretion of authenticity and realism that is often desired by the film-maker, the depiction of the Holocaust via the courtroom based on fact produces only a representation of a representation. Barbie Zelizer has argued that the representation of the Holocaust should directly mirror the event and not its retelling, but this is denied by the courtroom genre, even when utilizing flashback.[3] It becomes a forum for narrating and interpreting the past without engagement with the atrocity. It is a representation which is reassuringly civilized and ordered, one which considers an aftermath which permits the Holocaust to be contained through the closure of a decisive verdict. The courtroom drama is therefore a genre which, rather than give the viewer access to the Holocaust, generates a double distancing and a double screen of memory, moving the crime further into the realm of the untouchable.

At the very start of this book I quoted Lawrence Langer's observation of *Judgment at Nuremberg* that 'In the aftermath of such "indecent" dying, the courtroom as mise-en-scène for a comprehension of its enormity seems pitifully inadequate.'[4] I would argue that the preceding chapters have shown that these films seek comprehension or validation of the process of justice rather than the crime. In that sense the cinematic courtroom, like the process of law, acts as both barrier and conduit. Although it is certainly a setting with its limitations in respect of Holocaust representation, it is those limitations which ensure its continued appeal to both audience and film-maker.

NOTES

1. Kathy Eden, *Poetic and Legal Fiction in the Aristotelian Tradition* (Princeton, NJ: Princeton University Press, 1986), p.73.
2. Donald Bloxham, *Genocide on Trial: War Crimes Trials and the Formation of Holocaust History and Memory* (Oxford: Oxford University Press, 2001), p.2.
3. Barbie Zelizer, 'Every Once in a While: *Schindler's List* and the Shaping of History', in Yosefa Loshitzky (ed.), *Spielberg's Holocaust: Critical Perspectives on Schindler's List* (Bloomington, IN: Indiana University Press, 1997), pp.22–23.
4. Lawrence Langer, *Admitting the Holocaust: Collected Essays* (Oxford: Oxford University Press, 1996), p.177.

Epilogue

The public appetite for Holocaust films has remained robust in the first decade of the new millennium. [1] Moreover, the Oscar success of *The Pianist* (France/Poland/Germany/UK, Roman Polanski, 2002), perhaps the most widely praised Holocaust film of the first ten years of the twenty-first century, is testament to a continued desire on behalf of the film-maker and audience for films which suggest verisimilitude and authenticity. Yet, as suggested in the introduction to this book, some of the most successful Holocaust films of recent years have demonstrated an increased willingness on behalf of the film-maker to challenge the traditional perspective of the Holocaust as being a subject that does not lend itself to the imagination. Films such as *Everything is Illuminated* (USA, Liev Schreiber, 2005), *Inglourious Basterds* (USA, Quentin Tarantino, 2009) and *This Must be the Place* (Italy/France/Ireland, Paulo Sorrentino, 2011), for example, have moved towards depictions that appear less reverential to the past, less obsessed by historical accuracy and more willing to embrace fantasy and the imagination, even if still grounded in history in some way. This shift has not gone unnoticed, with the recent works by Jenni Adams and Matthew Boswell, for example, offering respectively magical realism and Holocaust impiety as emergent and increasingly recognizable and important trends in Holocaust representation. Where has this movement towards the imagined left the Holocaust courtroom, an area of mise-en-scène which, as we have seen, has relied even more heavily on factual sources for dialogue, story and setting, and has consciously adhered to legal and cinematic precedent? This brief epilogue considers that question with reference to the courtroom scenes of two transatlantic collaborations from 2008 – Stephen Daldry's adaptation of Bernard Schlink's acclaimed novel *The Reader*, and Andy De Emmony's *God on Trial*. Both films have once again placed the chaos of the Holocaust within the order of the courtroom, but they have done so in ways which reflect not only recent developments in

Holocaust awareness, but also the widening cultural and political context of the new century.

God on Trial (2008)

God On Trial, based in part on the experiences and work of Elie Weisel, is an account of 'the story that prisoners in Auschwitz, their faith tested by their suffering and the barbarity of the Nazis, put God on trial'.[2] It is a film that places theodicy, religion and faith at the heart of its narrative, a focus which reflects a shift in public awareness and attitudes that, as executive producer Mark Redhead explained, was a result of both the 'War on Terror' and natural tragedies such as the Boxing Day Indian Ocean earthquake and tsunami of 2004: 'With the attacks of September 11 and the Iraq war, religion is now centre-stage in a way that has not occurred before in my lifetime; extraordinary atrocities are being committed in the name of God, while natural calamities and man-made disasters claim thousands of lives every year.'[3]

For the screenwriter Frank Cottrell Boyce, too, in spite of the film's context and argument, *God on Trial* went beyond questions about being Jewish or the horrors of the Holocaust; it was a universal story 'about God' and for that reason he 'tried hard to keep the script as theological as possible'.[4] This was a view shared by at least some of the cast, with Stephen Dillane describing the film's setting as being of secondary importance to the central question of faith, with 'the actual business of being in Auschwitz' not feeling like 'a priority'.[5] Furthermore, Antony Sher, an actor with a history of roles in Holocaust-related productions, also felt that the film was about more than Judaism.[6] Once again he made the connection between the film and the events of September 2001 which created a new context for all these issues:

> It's about faith and that's something we can all relate to. On 9/11 when those planes struck the Twin Towers there must have been people of all religions inside the buildings, including some with the same religion as the men flying those planes. The people who survived that attack and the relatives of those who didn't must have had to ask questions like the ones we ask in the film about where God was in this terrible event.[7]

While the film addresses these ontological and theological issues, one cannot, in fact, avoid the centrality of the Holocaust and Judaism, with

Boyce's script focusing specifically on the Jewish experience of the daily routine in Auschwitz. This is, therefore, far more interested in the victim's camp experience than any of the previous films discussed. Indeed, in preparation for the film, Boyce, a Roman Catholic, read 'the Torah, the Talmud, everything' in order to familiarize himself with the Jewish response to God's absence. He also consulted rabbis Dan Cohn-Sherbok and Jonathan Romaine on the 'long Jewish tradition of wrangling with God' that went 'right back to Abraham bargaining with him over the destruction of Sodom, and forward to Elie Weisel's famous declaration that God was hanged on the gallows in Auschwitz' in his memoir *Night*.[8]

Although *God on Trial* has clear links back to that scene in *Night*, its more immediate source is Wiesel's *The Trial of God* (1979), his play set in Ukraine during Purim in 1649, in which God is accused of remaining silent in the face of evil and placed on trial.[9] It was a play which in turn had its basis in the story that a group of prisoners had conducted such trial at Auschwitz, even if Boyce dismissed this as 'almost certainly apocryphal ... one of those stories that persists because it strikes a chord'.[10] Cohn-Sherbok was similarly uncertain as to the story's origins: 'I always thought of it as a received story, and I certainly couldn't say definitively that it happened in the camps. But it could have, and it is such a moving story that I think it should have happened.'[11] Historian Robert Jan Van Pelt has been less equivocal regarding the story's provenance, arguing that there was 'no material evidence whatsoever' for a story that 'has become part of the lore of Auschwitz'.[12] In contrast, Elie Wiesel has been equally as clear in his affirmation of the story as factual: 'Why should they know what happened? I was the only one there. It happened at night; there were just three people. At the end of the trial, they used the word *chayav*, rather than "guilty". It means "He owes us something". Then we went to pray.' Perhaps because of this uncertain provenance, *God on Trial*, unlike many of the previous films discussed, does not begin by establishing its factual authenticity through any foregrounding of its origins. Instead, the authority of the film's story is generated by a combination of word and image, now wilfully manipulating in order to persuade the audience that this drama is a documentary.

Although most of the film, including its trial scenes, takes place at Auschwitz in the 1940s, *God on Trial* begins in the present day. The opening shot, replicating the angles, quality and handheld camera styles of a documentary, follows a coach as it brings a group of tourists to an unidentified concentration camp in the present day. The tourists are a mixture of young and old, men and women, driven to come, one assumes, by a desire to visit a site of memory about which they have heard and read so much but know so little. As the door of the coach opens, a cut transforms the present into the past, with the pneumatic door of the coach becoming a sliding door on a cattle truck, opening to reveal a Nazi guard and his dog. A reverse shot shows the frightened and confused faces of the new arrivals. The camera does not linger, and we return to the present, and to the safe and reassuring images of the visitors, including an older man, Hugo (David de Keyser), and a younger woman, Emily (Louise Mardenborough).

This opening montage directly confronts, therefore, the notion of 'dark tourism', visiting sites of atrocity as places of leisure and pleasure, sites of memory and memorialization. It also confronts the audience's desire and ability to be witnesses, seeing this as problematic rather than an ideal. Moreover, it highlights the ways in which images generate their own authority: in *Operation Eichmann* the images of Buchenwald lent the fictive narrative a degree of documentary authority through authenticity of setting. Here, however, the relationship is more complicated, with any authenticity being illusory, for these scenes were filmed not at a camp but on location at an ex-military base near Glasgow, in Scotland. The visual clues allow the fictive and the factual to merge in the imagination as the sights and sites of memory converge. For this to work the opening montage relies on the audience being at least partially informed, knowing enough to recognize the words and images which have become part of the cultural lexicon. This is confirmed by the words of the tour guide (Agnieszka Liggett) as she distributes tickets to the visitors. As the guide explains: 'This is the typical blockhouse. There would be up to about 1,000 people in here. When a new transport came in they made room for it by ... you can imagine. They would make a *selekja*. Everyone from the blockhouse is given a card by the block elder – the *blockaltester* – and then they go to the selection area.' A parallel scene set in the past then equates the issuance of tickets to the distribution of medical cards to each prisoner prior to the start of the selection process, mimicking the manner in which visitors to modern museums are encouraged to identify with the victims by the issuance of an identity card.

Unlike many of the films discussed in the previous chapters, the trial sequence forms the major part of *God on Trial*. This is not a formal trial, but proceedings held within an Auschwitz blockhouse. In a further example of formal entanglement, these scenes were intentionally shot to resemble a play more than a film. To that end, "director Andy de Emmony undertook to approach the piece in an unusual way, cross-shooting in extra-long ten-minute takes with three cameras on high-speed film with simple, very naturalistic light sources without any of the relighting normal in film drama – a major challenge for the brilliant young Polish Director of Photography Wojciech Szepel – nailing up to fifteen minutes of material per day instead of the usual five, and shooting a ninety-minute film in a remarkable eleven days."[13]

The prisoners who form the court in these flashbacks are those who were introduced through the selection process, plus the twelve new inmates who have recently arrived.[14] They include the pious Kuhn (Jack Shepherd) and the younger Moche (Dominic Cooper), a cynic who has the initial idea to hold the trial. The main figures in the scenes that follow, however, are the three judges: Baumgarten (Stellen Skaarsgard), the Head of the Court, 'a sophisticated, modern and successful professor of Criminal Law in Berlin who taught bright, admiring students and obviously mixed in fairly high circles';[15] Schmidt (Stephen Dillane), the Father of the court, a Jewish political prisoner, 'who is incredibly optimistic, with a strong faith in God'; and Mordechai (Rupert Graves), Kuhn's son, who is named as Dayan.[16]

The evidence set before this impromptu court is anecdotal, provided by the experiences of the prisoners and attempts to provide a balanced debate. Kuhn, for example, speaking in defence of God, argues that 'Bad things have happened before. Read the Torah, read your history. We are Jews: we suffer.' For him, it is not God who is in breach of contract but the Jews: 'God is just, so we must have done something wrong. We should be examining our consciences.' It is a position supported by Schmidt, who argues for these and other acts of God as 'not a punishment but a purification', something to be endured and embraced rather than condemned: 'Our suffering is a privilege if it is a part of God's plan. We are fortunate to be purifying the people through our pain … Hitler will end, the war will end. The people and the Torah will live.' Schmidt's position in this respect is made more complicated by the fact that he has only come to think of himself as a Jew since being defined as one by the Nazis. Moreover, again in line with Nazi ideology, it is an identity he sees in terms of race in spite of his embracing of religious teaching:

> It was just a year ago the Gestapo came for me and that was the first thing I knew of my race. I thought I was a normal German.

> I was a German. I was a Jew-hating German. I knew nothing of your ways. I learned here, I had never heard a word of the Torah before I came here. I grew up learning that the Jews were dirty, deceitful and disorganized and when I came here I saw everything was true ... In order for them to get ordinary Germans to kill us they must show them that we are what ordinary Germans are taught to believe we are: filthy, fearful and Godless.

The philosophical and theological arguments are played back and forth between the prisoners until the three judges agree on a verdict. It is at this point that Akiba (Antony Sher) speaks for the first time. One of the twelve new inmates, Akiba is a rabbi, a healer, one of the 36, the *lamed-vovnik*, 'the secret saints who are carrying us on their shoulders'. Now his words resonate 'with quite surprising anger':[17]

> Who led us out of Egypt? ... What was it like for the people of Egypt when Adonai turned against them? It was like this. Today there was a selection. When David defeated the Moabites, what did he do? He made them lie on the ground in lines and he chose one to live and two to die ... They faced extinction at the hand of Adonai ... they were afraid as we are afraid ... They learned that Adonai, the Lord our God, is not good. He was not ever good, He was only on our side. God is not good ... He is not good, He has simply been strong and on our side. The guards on the train had belts that read 'God is on our side.' Maybe He is. We see His majesty but it is turned against us. He is still God but not our God. He has become our enemy. That's what has happened to the covenant. He has made a new covenant with someone else.

The trial and the flashback sequence ends not with the announcement of the guilty vedict – although that is the verdict – but the death of those already selected at the outset. 'Now that we have found God guilty,' Moche asks, 'what do we do?' Akiba's simple answer is 'We pray.' It is an ending that owes something again to Elie Wiesel, who in *Night* and his other writing has spoken of a questioning but not a loss of faith.[18]

The final scene therefore becomes a re-enactment of the saying of Kaddish in *None Shall Escape*. As the men pray, the camera follows those selected for death as they run across the camp, moving with them as they enter the gas chamber, before stepping back to look from the outside, recalling in turn *Operation Eichmann*. This scene is then intercut with the gas chamber in the present day, the camera angle looking down from above, suggesting both some form of omniscience and that the camera is God and therefore also on trial. The past and the present then converge as the camera tracks from left to right through the faces in the chamber, those of the tourists mingling with the dead who continue to recite scripture. 'And was their prayer answered?' asks Emily. 'They're still here', the guide replies.

God on Trial is therefore unlike any of the films that preceded it, even if it has much in common with them. The others placed on trial either a perpetrator or in some way the Holocaust's memory. Here, however, it is a trial of God, conducted during the perpetration of the atrocities. Whereas the other films which have not been concerned with the perpetrator, in particular *Skokie* and *Never Forget*, have celebrated the law as offering an individual protection from hate crimes, the proceedings in *God on Trial*, taking place during the perpetration, make no difference to the fate of the prisoners. It is an unusual trial in this respect: it does not seek to reassure or to offer the courtroom as a route to a form of redress or security, but rather to illustrate the value of faith, offering prayer as a form of protection and spiritual resistance which is more valuable than the law.

The Reader (2008)

A far more traditional Holocaust courtroom could be seen in Stephen Daldry's *The Reader*. Set in post-war Germany this film returned to the subject of forbidden love and the melodrama seen in *Sealed Verdict* and *Verboten!*, with the romance now taking place between two Germans and provoking questions of generational guilt, internal conflict and reconciliation. Bernard Schlink's novel *Die Vorleser* had been published in Germany to great popular acclaim in 1995. Translated as *The Reader* it became an international success, with Schlink using the metaphor of illiteracy and the central love affair between Hanna Schmitz, a former concentration camp guard, and the much younger Michael Berg, the articulate second-generation perpetrator, to question and explore German responsibility and guilt. Daldry's 2008 film version, adapted by David Hare, was similarly acclaimed, receiving five Oscar nominations, with Kate Winslet winning the award for Best Actress for her portrayal of Schmitz.

The adaptation retells the story of Schmitz and Berg's relationship, from their first meeting in 1958, across her trial in 1966 for crimes committed as a guard during the war, on to their correspondence while she is in prison, and then finally in the days leading up to her suicide. Like *God on Trial* it, too, uses flashbacks to revisit the past, moving backwards from 1995 to recreate the story of their affair in the present, suggesting again that the film-maker of the new century seems willing and able to imagine, although again this does not extend to the crimes being confronted. The first flashback is motivated by the adult Michael (Ralph Fiennes), a successful lawyer, watching a train pass outside his window, the movement and sound of the train transporting him to the memory of his first meeting with Hanna thirty-seven years before. I say flashback, but in fact the past is always present in this film, as many scenes are linked by sound bridges, as if to emphasize that Michael's guilt and memory, past and present, are always intertwined.

The beginning of *The Reader* recounts the early days of the romance between Hanna and Michael, when he would read aloud to her from various works of classic literature. This comes to an abrupt end when she suddenly and inexplicably disappears from his life entirely. The void she leaves is replaced by a legal rather than sexual education and the film moves forward eight years to 1966. Michael is now studying at Heidelberg Law School and is a member of Professor Rohl's (Bruno Ganz) special seminar group, 'a small group and a select one' whose purpose and membership is unclear, but whose subjects for discussion include Karl Jespers and German guilt. There is no further explanation as the scene cuts to show Michael and his group boarding a train which takes them to attend an on-going trial. The exact nature of the case is unknown, but outside the court the students observe a number of demonstrations 'both for and against' whatever is going on inside, proceedings that are described as 'a circus' by one of Michael's fellow students.

Inside the courtroom an out-of-shot voice calls one of the unseen defendants to give evidence. The camera then follows Michael as he takes his seat in the gallery, watching him and not the proceedings as the defendant's name is given as 'Hanna Schmitz'. It seems unlikely that a law student would not have been sufficiently interested in this high-profile trial to be aware of the names and charges facing the accused, but Michael appears shocked to hear Hanna's name and then to see her in person. What this enables, however, is the creation of a scene in which the camera's interest is focused on the audience and not the accused.

Whereas in the previous films we have seen that a trial's opening moments can establish the charges faced by the accused, here there is neither a plea nor any background to the case aside from our knowledge of Hanna and Michael. The case outlines Hanna's biography: born in October 1922, she joined the SS in 1943, taking that role in preference to a promotion at her job with the local Siemens factory, a decision which, it is suggested, came not from ideology but from the shame of being exposed as illiterate. She worked at Auschwitz before moving to 'a smaller camp near Krakow' and in the winter of 1944 she assisted the prisoners on a death march.

The key piece of evidence in the case against Hanna is the testimony of Ilana Mather (Lena Olin), a child survivor who has recently published her account as a memoir, an on-screen acknowledgement of the commercialization of the Holocaust which has been discussed in earlier chapters. Extracts from that memoir are read to Hanna, her only task being to confirm the accuracy of the text as it describes a selection. Unlike the other defendants, Hanna does not attempt to deny her role and even provides more details which confirm her complicity: 'There were six guards, so we decided we'd choose ten people each. That's how we did it every month. We'd all choose ten.' She justifies these actions both to herself and the court as driven by expediency – 'We couldn't keep everyone' – and the need to make room for the new arrivals. In contrast to Hanna's compliance and passivity, an acknowledgement of guilt without actually displaying contrition, Ilana is far stronger. No longer is there the need for a courtroom proxy as Ilana presents her evidence, a vocal and physical Jewish presence which identifies all of the defendants as participants in the selection process, but focuses on the behaviour of Hanna:

> Each of the guards would choose a certain number of women. Hanna Schmitz chose differently ... She had favourites. Girls, mostly young. We all remarked on it. She gave them food and places to sleep. In the evening she asked them to join her and we all thought ... well you can imagine what we thought. And then we found out. She was making these women read aloud to her ... They were reading to her. At first we thought this guard, this guard is more sensitive, she's more human, she's kinder. Often she chose the week, the sick, she picked them out. She seemed to be protecting them almost. But then she despatched them. Is that kinder?'

The story is then taken up by Ilana's mother: 'In the winter of 1944 our camp was closed down. We were told we had to move on, but the plan kept changing every day. Women were dying all around us in the snow. Half of us died on the march. My daughter says in the book, less a death march, more a death gallop.' And she continues by describing 'the night in the church', the event which is pivotal to Hanna's fate: 'That night we thought we were lucky because we had a roof over our heads ... We'd arrived in a village. As always the guards took the best quarters, they took the priest's house. But they let us sleep in a church.' During a bombing raid, the church was hit: 'At first we could only hear the fire: it was in the steeple. Then we could see burning beams and they began to crash to the floor. Everyone rushed ... rushed to the doors but the doors had been locked from the outside ... Everyone was killed.' 'But you survived', says the judge, removing his glasses.

The key component in the case against Hanna is the SS report of that incident, 'written, approved and signed' by all of the defendants immediately after the event. Hanna is accused of writing the document, but we know that this cannot be true, that the illiterate Hanna cannot have done this. But she accepts responsibility, rather than face ridicule for being unable to read and write. When asked for a sample of her handwriting, Hanna is for the first time uncertain in her actions. As Michael watches her anxiety grow, a series of flashbacks show how he remembers that she always refused to read. It is only now that he realizes that she has always been illiterate. She may be guilty of the crimes being described, but she did not write this document, and the audience knows that while the verdict may be just, it is not correct.

The Reader is a film that reflects on how memory and testimony overlap and for that reason there is no objective flashback or subjective mindscreen. Instead, intercut with the courtroom are scenes from Rohl's special seminar, during which the students discuss what they have learnt of the present rather than the past, arguing initially over the trial's purpose rather than the guilt or innocence of the accused. In almost complete contrast to the narrative of *God on Trial*, the process of law and the verdict are important. As Professor Rohl explains in one of the sessions:

> Societies think they operate by something called morality, but they don't. They operate by something called law. You're not guilty of anything merely by working at Auschwitz. 8000 people worked at Auschwitz. Precisely 19 have been convicted and only six for murder. To prove murder you have to prove intent. That's the

law. The question is never 'Was it wrong?' but 'Was it legal?' and not by our laws. No, by the laws of the time.

It is this discussion which is the film's core. Unlike in the first courtroom films, films obsessed with establishing the horror of the crimes and the guilt of the accused, *The Reader* considers the need for understanding. It is this desire for an explanation, in part triggered by his relationship with Hanna, that sees Michael visit a camp. As with *QB VII* and *God on Trial*, the site of atrocity is now a *lieu de mémoire*, for it has become both a memorial and museum. Michael sighs to himself as he wanders around in the half-light, a return to the shadows which most of the previous films had sought to avoid. The camp is no longer a monochrome world but one shot with a blue-and-grey palette, the colour of the camp uniforms, with only the green of Michael's duffel bag offering a rare splash of colour. He sees the bunks and the collection of found shoes on display, ending his journey in front of the ovens where he stands, head bowed. It is an image which takes us back fifty years, back to the face of Franz when confronted by the crimes of his parents' generation in *Verboten!*.

The first films of the new century have looked, therefore, to challenge the boundaries set by the old, but in some ways they are rehearsing familiar debates. *God on Trial*, for example, assumes a level of knowledge and familiarity on behalf of its audience, using visual signifiers of the camp – the barbed wire, the blockhouse, the cattle truck, the uniforms – to draw the audience into a world which is simultaneously familiar and reassuringly distant. Its narrative argues that the present can be explained by the past, but that the past cannot simply be understood by the present, suggesting that the superficial knowledge of visiting the camps conceals ignorance of what lies behind the images. There are echoes here of seventy years ago: the concentration camp liberation footage may no longer be an ever-present component of the Holocaust courtroom, but the power of the visual continues to arrest dialogue, although now the film-maker looks for solutions. For this reason, *God on Trial* gradually draws the audience in to the past, using extended flashbacks to show the confusion and complexity of camp life, including selections, the *Sonderkommando*, theft and camp morality. Likewise *The Reader*, in some ways a traditional courtroom drama in the style of *Sealed Verdict* sixty years earlier, complicates past and present, using a combination of sound and image to demonstrate that they can coexist in memory.

NOTES

1. The most high profile critique of the prevalence of the Holocaust in popular culture and memory at the turn of the century remains Norman G. Finkelstein, *The Holocaust Industry: Reflections on the Exploitation of Jewish Suffering* (London: Verso, 2001).
2. BBC *God on Trial* Press Pack (London: BBC Press Office, 2008), 'http://www.bbc.co.uk/pressoffice/pressreleases/stories/2008/08_august/27/trial.shtml.'
3. Ibid.; Frank Cottrell Boyce, 'Losing my Religion', *Guardian*, 19 August 2008.
4. http://www.bbc.co.uk/pressoffice/pressreleases/stories/2008/08_august/27/trial5.shtml.
5. http://www.bbc.co.uk/pressoffice/pressreleases/stories/2008/08_august/27/trial7.shtml.
6. His previous roles included the lead in *Genghis Cohn* (1993), one of the earliest films to take an imaginative approach to the Holocaust, and *Primo* (2008), an acclaimed version of *If This is a Man* in which he played Primo Levi.
7. http://www.bbc.co.uk/pressoffice/pressreleases/stories/2008/08_august/27/trial6.shtml.
8. Boyce, 'Losing my Religion'.
9. David Tollerton, 'Holocaust Representation and Judicial Proceedings Against God on the Stage and Screen', *Modernism/Modernity*, 20, 1 (2013), pp.95-113
10. Boyce, 'Losing my Religion'.
11. Jenni Frazer, 'Wiesel: Yes, We Really Did Put God on Trial', *Jewish Chronicle*, 19 September 2008.
12. Ibid.
13. http://www.bbc.co.uk/pressoffice/pressreleases/stories/2008/08_august/27/trial4.shtml.
14. Halfway through the trial the prisoners are interrupted by the guards, who have come to take the twelve newcomers to be inducted into the camp. This is perhaps the most disturbing scene in the film, as the camera watches the men being stripped, allocated uniforms, and having their hair and beards trimmed. There are no words, just sounds of gasping and then the noise of the tattoo pen before a cut to the blockhouse where all the men have been returned, now uniform and unrecognizable from those who entered the camp.
15. http://www.bbc.co.uk/pressoffice/pressreleases/stories/2008/08_august/27/trial8.shtml.
16. http://www.bbc.co.uk/pressoffice/pressreleases/stories/2008/08_august/27/trial7.shtml.
17. Anthony Sher, cited at http://www.bbc.co.uk/pressoffice/pressreleases/stories/2008/08_august/27/trial6.shtml.
18. Frazer, 'Wiesel'.

Bibliography and Filmography

Bibliography

Adams, Jenni, *Magic Realism in Holocaust Literature: Troping the Traumatic Real* (Basingstoke: Palgrave Macmillan, 2011).

Adams, Jenni and Vice, Sue (eds), *Representing the Perpetrator in Holocaust Film and Literature* (London: Vallentine Mitchell, 2012).

Andrus, Burton C., *The Infamous of Nuremberg* (London: Leslie Frewin, 1969).

Arendt, Hannah, *Eichmann in Jerusalem: A Report on the Banality of Evil*, rev. and enlarged ed. (1963; London: Penguin Books, 1994).

Aronsfeld, C.C., 'The Institute for Historical Review: "Revisionists" Who Whitewash Nazism', *Institute of Jewish Affairs Research Reports*, 4 (May 1982), pp.1–8.

Avisar, Ilan, *Screening the Holocaust: Cinema's Images of the Unimaginable* (Bloomington, IN: Indiana University Press, 1988).

Avisar, Ilan, 'Holocaust Movies and the Politics of Collective Memory', in Alvin H. Rosenfeld (ed.), *Thinking about the Holocaust after Half a Century* (Bloomington, IN: Indiana University Press, 1997), pp.38–58

Bach, Stephen, *Marlene Dietrich: Life and Legend* (London: Harper Collins, 1982).

Balio, Tino, *United Artists: The Company That Changed the Film Industry* (Madison, WI: University of Wisconsin Press, 1987).

Baron, Lawrence, *Projecting the Holocaust into the Present: The Changing Focus of Contemporary Holocaust Cinema* (Lanham, MD: Rowman & Littlefield, 2005).

Bartov, Omer, *Murder in our Midst: The Holocaust, Industrial Killing and Representation* (Oxford: Oxford University Press, 1997).

Bartov, Omer, *The 'Jew' in Cinema: From 'The Golem' to 'Don't Touch My Holocaust'* (Bloomington, IN: Indiana University Press, 2005).

Bartov, Omer, 'Spielberg's Oskar: Hollywood Tries Evil', in Yosefa Loshitzky (ed.), *Spielberg's Holocaust: Critical Perspectives on Schindler's List* (Bloomington, IN: Indiana University Press, 1997), pp.41–60

Bayor, Ronald H., *Neighbours in Conflict: The Irish, Germans, Jews and Italians of New York City, 1929–1941* (Baltimore, MD: Johns Hopkins University Press, 1978).

Beck, Nicholas, *Budd Schulberg: A Bio-Bibliography* (Lanham, MD: Scarecrow Press, 2001).

Beigbeder, Yves, *Judging War Criminals: The Politics of International Justice* (Basingstoke: Palgrave Macmillan, 1999).

Belhmer, Rudy (ed.), *Inside Warner Brothers (1935–1951)* (New York: Viking Press, 1985).

Belknap, Michal R., *The Vietnam War on Trial: The My Lai Massacre and the Court Martial of Lieutenant Calley* (Lawrence, KS: University Press of Kansas, 2002).

Bennett, W. Lance and Feldman, Martha S., *Reconstructing Reality in the Courtroom: Justice and Judgment in American Culture* (New Brunswick, NJ: Rutgers University Press, 1981).

Berenbaum, Michael, *The World Must Know: The History of the Holocaust as told in the United States Holocaust Memorial Museum* (Boston, MA: Little, Brown, 1993).

Bergman, Paul and Asimov, Michael, *Reel Justice: The Courtroom Goes to the Movies* (Kansas City, MO: Andrews McMeel, 1996).

Bernard-Donals, Michael F. and Glejzer, Richard R., *Between Witness and Testimony: The Holocaust and the Limits of Representation* (New York: State University of New York Press, 2001).

Biddiscombe, Perry, *The Last Nazis: SS Werewolf Guerrilla Resistance in Europe, 1944–1947* (Stroud: Tempus, 2000).

Bigsby, Christopher, *Remembering and Imagining the Holocaust: The Chain of Memory* (Cambridge: Cambridge University Press, 2006).

Birdwell, Michael E., *Celluloid Soldiers: The Warner Bros Campaign Against Nazism* (New York and London: New York University Press, 1999).

Black, David A., *Law in Film: Resonance and Representation* (Urbana and Chicago, IL: University of Illinois Press, 1999).

Bloxham, Donald, *Genocide on Trial: War Crimes Trials and the Formation of Holocaust History and Memory* (Oxford: Oxford University Press, 2001).

Blum, Howard, *Wanted! The Search for Nazis in America* (Greenwich, CT: Fawcett, 1977).

Boswell, Matthew, *Holocaust Impiety in Literature, Popular Music and Film* (Basingstoke: Palgrave Macmillan, 2011).

Bosworth, Patricia, *Montgomery Clift: A Biography* (London: Bantam Books, 1979).

Bower, Tom, *Klaus Barbie: Butcher of Lyons*, rev. ed. (London: Corgi Books, 1985).

Bower, Tom, *Blind Eye to Murder: Britain, America and the Purging of Nazi Germany – A Pledge Betrayed* (London: Warner Books, 1997).

Boyce, Frank Cottrell, 'Losing my Religion', *Guardian*, 19 August 2008.

Brinkley, Robert and Youra, Steven, 'Tracing *Shoah*', *PMLA*, 111, 1 (January 1996), pp.108–27.

Brogan, Hugh, *The Penguin History of the United States of America* (Harmondsworth: Penguin Books, 1985).

Bruzzi, Stella, 'Court Etiquette', *Sight and Sound*, 3, 2 (February 1993), p.4.

Buford, Kate, *Burt Lancaster: An American Life* (London: Arum Press, 2001).

Bull, R. and Rumsey, N., *The Social Psychology of Facial Appearances* (New York: Springer, 1992).

Burk, Michael, *The Tribunal* (Sevenoaks: Coronet Books, 1978).

Burleigh, Michael, *The Third Reich: A New History* (Basingstoke: Palgrave Macmillan, 2000)

Cain, Kathleen Shine, *Leon Uris: A Critical Companion* (Westport, CT: Greenwood Press, 1998).

Callan, Michael Feeney, *Anthony Hopkins: In Darkness and in Light* (London: Sidgwick & Jackson, 1993).

Cameron, Kenneth M., *America on Film: Hollywood and American History* (New York: Continuum, 1997).

Camper, Fred, 'Harsh Master: Films by André de Toth', *Chicago Reader*, 10 (1997). http://www.chicagoreader.com/chicago/harsh-master/Content?oid=894500

Carlen, Pat, *Magistrates' Justice* (London: Martin Robertson, 1976).

Carmean, Karen, *Robert Shaw: More Than a Life* (Lanham, MD: Madison Books, 1994).

Carr, Robert K., *The House Committee on Un-American Activities* (Ithaca, NY: Cornell University Press, 1985).

Carr, Steven Alan, *Hollywood and Anti-Semitism: A Cultural History up to World War II* (Cambridge: Cambridge University Press, 2001).

Carruthers, Susan L., *The Media at War: Communication and Conflict in the Twentieth Century* (Basingstoke: Palgrave Macmillan, 2000).

Cassiday, Julie A., *The Enemy on Trial: Early Soviet Courts on Stage and Screen* (De Kalb, IL: Northern Illinois University Press, 2000).

Cecil, Robert, *The Myth of the Master Race: Alfred Rosenberg and Nazi Ideology* (London: B.T. Batsford, 1972).

Cesarani, David, *Justice Delayed* (London: Mandarin Paperbacks, 1992).

Cesarani, David and Sundquist, Eric J., *After the Holocaust: Challenging the Myth of Silence* (London: Routledge, 2012).

Chaisson, Lloyd (ed.), *The Press on Trial: Crimes and Trials as Media Events* (Westport, CT: Greenwood Press, 1997).

Chambers, John Whiteclay II and Culbert, David (eds), *World War II, Film, and History* (Oxford: Oxford University Press, 1996).

Chaplin, Charles, *My Autobiography* (1964; Harmondsworth: Penguin Books, 1966).

Chapman, James, *The British at War: Cinema, State and Propaganda, 1939–1945* (London: I.B. Tauris, 1998).

Chartock, Roselle and Spencer, Jack (eds), *The Holocaust Years: Society on Trial* (New York: Bantam Books, 1978).

Chiel, Deborah, *Music Box* (New York: Jove Books, 1989).

Clark, Roger S., 'Crimes against Humanity at Nuremberg', in George Ginsburgs and V.N. Kudriavtsev (eds), *The Nuremberg Trial and International Law* (Dordrecht, Boston, MA, and London: Martins Nijhoff, 1990), pp.177–99.

Clover, Carol J., 'God Bless Juries!', in Browne (ed.), *Refiguring American Film Genres*, pp.255–77.

Cohen, Sarah B. (ed.), *From Hester Street to Hollywood: The Jewish-American Stage and Screen* (Bloomington, IN: Indiana University Press, 1983).

Cohn, Marjorie and Dow, David, *Cameras in the Courtroom: Television and the Pursuit of Justice* (Jefferson, NC: McFarland, 1998).

Cole, Lester, *Hollywood Red: The Autobiography of Lester Cole* (Palo Alto, CA: Ramparts Press, 1981).

Cole, Tim, *Images of the Holocaust: The Myth of the 'Shoah' Buisness* (London: Duckworth, 1999).

Colombat, André Pierre, *The Holocaust in French Film* (Metuchen, NJ, and London: Scarecrow Press, 1993).

Columbia Pictures, *Accessories Catalogue and Campaign Book* (1944) for *None Shall Escape*.

Conot, Robert E., *Justice at Nuremberg* (London: Weidenfeld & Nicholson, 1983).

Cooper, R.W., *The Nuremberg Trial* (Harmondsworth: Penguin Books, 1947).

Crowdus, Gary, 'Keeping Alive the Memory of the Holocaust: An Interview with Costa-Gavras', *Cineaste*, 17, 3 (1990), pp.4–7.

Crowdus, Gary, 'Music Box', *Cineaste*, 17, 3 (1990), pp.45–47.

Crowdus, Gary (ed.), *The Political Companion to American Film* (Chicago, IL, and London: Fitzroy Dearborn, 1994).

Dabringhaus, Erhard, *Klaus Barbie: The Shocking Story of How the US Used This Nazi War Criminal as an Intelligence Agent: A First Hand Account* (Washington, DC: Acropolis Books, 1984).

Davies, Philip and Neve, Brian (eds), *Cinema, Politics and Society in America* (Manchester: Manchester University Press, 1981).

Davis, Ivor, 'Nuremberg War Trial: New Drama is Must-See Watching', http:/www.jewishfamily.com.culture/films/Nuremberg.txt.

Davis, Kenneth F., *FDR, Into the Storm, 1937–1940: A History* (New York: Random House, 1993).

Dawidowicz, Lucy S., *The War against the Jews, 1933–45*, 10th anniversary ed. (Harmondsworth: Penguin Books, 1990).

DeLillo, Don, *Running Dog* (London: Sphere Books, 1981).

Denvir, John (ed.), *Legal Reelism* (Urbana and Chicago, IL: University of Illinois Press, 1996).

De Toth, André, *Fragments: Portraits From the Inside* foreword by Martin Scorsese and preface by Bertrand Tavernier (London: Faber & Faber, 1994).

Dick, Bernard F., *The Star-Spangled Screen: The American World War II Film* (Lexington, KT: University Press of Kentucky, 1985).

Dimock, Wai Chee, *Residues of Justice: Literature, Law, Philosophy* (Berkeley, CA: University of California Press, 1997).

Dinnerstein, Leonard, *America and the Survivors of the Holocaust* (New York: Columbia University Press, 1982).

Dinnerstein, Leonard, *Antisemitism in America* (Oxford: Oxford University Press, 1994).

Doherty, Thomas, *Projections of War: Hollywood, American Culture and World War II* (New York: Columbia University Press, 1993).

Donat, Alexander, *The Holocaust Kingdom: A Memoir* (London: Secker & Warburg, 1965).

Doneson, Judith E., 'The American History of Anne Frank's Diary', *Holocaust and Genocide Studies*, 2, 1 (1987), pp.149–60.

Doneson, Judith, *The Holocaust in American Film* (Philadelphia, PA: Jewish Publication Society, 1987).

Doneson, Judith, 'From Hitler to *Heimat*: The Return of History as Film', *Holocaust and Genocide Studies*, 6, 2 (1991), pp.207–13.

Doneson, Judith, '*Holocaust* Revisited: A Catalyst for Memory or Trivialization?', *Annals of the American Academy of Political and Social Science*, 548 (1996), pp.70–77.

Donner, Frank, *The Un-Americans (1935–1951)* (New York: Ballantine Books, 1961).

Douglas, Kirk, *The Ragman's Son: An Autobiography* (London: Pocket Books, 1999).

Douglas, Lawrence, 'Film as Witness: Screening *Nazi Concentration Camps* Before the Nuremberg Tribunal', *Yale Law Journal*, 105 (1995), pp.449–81.

Douglas, Lawrence, *The Memory of Judgment: Making Law and History in the Trials of the Holocaust* (New Haven, CT, and London: Yale University Press, 2001).

Downs, Donald Alexander, *Nazis in Skokie: Freedom, Community and the First Amendment* (Notre Dame, IN: University of Notre Dame Press, 1985).

D.P.J., 'Judgment at Nuremberg', *Monthly Film Bulletin*, 337, 29 (February 1962), p.19.

Eaglestone, Robert, *The Holocaust and the Postmodern* (Oxford: Oxford University Press, 2004).

Eden, Kathy, *Poetic and Legal Fiction in the Aristotelian Tradition* (Princeton, NJ: Princeton University Press, 1986).

Epstein, John, 'Fathers and Daughters', *Cinema Papers*, 81 (1990), pp.28–31.

Erens, Patricia, *The Jew in American Cinema* (Bloomington, IN: Indiana University Press, 1984).

Etheridge, Brian C., 'In Search of Germans: Contested Germany in the Production of *The Search*', *Journal of Popular Film & Television*, 34, 1 (Spring 2006), pp.34–45. Eszterhas, Joe, *Hollywood Animal* (London: Hutchinson, 2004).

Ezrahi, Sidra DeKoven, *By Words Alone: The Holocaust in Literature* (Chicago, IL: University of Chicago Press, 1980).

Feingold, Henry L., *The Politics of Rescue: The Roosevelt Administration and the Holocaust, 1938–1945* (New Brunswick, NJ: Rutgers University Press, 1970).

Felman, Shoshana, 'In an Era of Testimony: Claude Lanzmann's *Shoah*', *Yale French Studies*, 79 (Spring 1991), pp.39–81. Felman, Shoshana, 'The Return of the Voice: Claude Lanzmann's *Shoah*', in Shoshana Felman and Dori Laub (eds), *Testimony: Crises of*

Witnessing in Literature, Psychoanalysis, and History (New York: Routledge, 1992), pp.204–83.

Finkelstein, Norman G., *The Holocaust Industry: Reflections on the Exploitation of Jewish Suffering* (London: Verso, 2001).

Finkielkraut, Alain, *Remembering in Vain: The Klaus Barbie Trial and Crimes Against Humanity*, trans. Roxanne Lapidus with Sima Godfrey, introduced by Alice Y. Kaplan (New York: Columbia University Press, 1992).

Fishgall, Gary, *Against Type: The Biography of Bert Lancaster* (New York: Scribner, 1995).

Flanzbaum, Hilene (ed.), *The Americanization of the Holocaust* (Baltimore, MD, and London: Johns Hopkins University Press, 1999).

Frank, Jerome, *Courts on Trial: Myth and Reality in American Justice* (Princeton, NJ: Princeton University Press, 1949).

Frazer, Jenni, 'Wiesel: Yes, We Really did put God on Trial', *Jewish Chronicle*, 19 September 2008.

French, John, *Robert Shaw: The Price of Success* (London: Nick Hern Books, 1993).

Friedlander, Saul (ed.), *Probing the Limits of Representation: Nazism and the 'Final Solution'* (Cambridge, MA: Harvard University Press, 1992).

Friedlander, Henry and McCarrick, Earlean M., 'Nazi Criminals in the United States: The Fedorenko Case', *Simon Wiesenthal Centre Annual*, 2, 1985, pp.63–85.

Friedlander, Henry and McCarrick, Earlean M., 'Nazi Criminals in the United States: Denaturalization after Fedorenko', *Simon Wiesenthal Centre Annual*, 3 (1986), pp.47–85.

Friedman, Lawrence M., 'Law, Lawyers and Popular Culture', *Yale Law Journal*, 98, 8 (June 1989), pp.1579–606.

Friedman, Lester, *Hollywood's Image of the Jew* (New York: Ungar, 1982). Friedman, Lester D., *The Jewish Image in American Film* (London: Citadel Press, 1987).

Frodon, Jean-Michel, *Cinema and the Shoah: An Art Confronts the Tragedy of the Twentieth Century* (New York: SUNY Press, 2010).

Fuller, Sam, *A Third Face: My Tale of Writing, Fighting and Filmmaking* (New York: Alfred A. Knopf, 2002).

Fyne, Robert, *The Hollywood Propaganda of World War II* (Metuchen, NJ, and London: Scarecrow Press, 1994).

Gabler, Neal, *An Empire of Their Own: How the Jews Invented Hollywood* (London: W.H. Allen, 1989).

Gaskin, Hilary, *Eyewitnesses at Nuremberg* (London: Arms and Armour, 1990).

Gerber, David A., *Anti-Semitism in America* (Urbana, IL: University of Illinois Press, 1986).

Gibson, James L. and Bingham, Richard D., *Civil Liberties and Nazis: The Skokie Free-Speech Controversy* (New York: Praeger, 1985).

Gilbert, G.M., *Nuremberg Diary* (London: Eyre & Spottiswoode, 1948).

Gillett, John, 'Judgment at Nuremberg', *Sight and Sound*, 31, 1 (Winter 1961–62), p.41.

Glancy, H. Mark, *When Hollywood Loved Britain* (Manchester and New York: Manchester University Press, 1999).

God on Trial Press Pack (London: BBC Press Office, 2008),

Goldensohn, Leon N., *The Nuremberg Interviews: Conversations with the Defendants and Witnesses* (New York: Alfred A. Knopf, 2004).http://www.bbc.co.uk/pressoffice/pressreleases/stories/2008/08_august/27/trial.shtml.

Gottfried, Martin, *Nobody's Fool: The Lives of Danny Kaye* (New York: Simon & Schuster, 1994).

Greenfield, Steve and Osborn, Guy, 'Lawyers in Film: Where Myth Meets Reality', *New Law Journal*, 143, 6629 (17 December 1993), pp.1791–92. Greenfield, Steve and Osborn, Guy, 'The Living Law: Popular Film as Legal Text', *Law Teacher: Journal of the Association of Law Teachers*, 29, 1 (1995), pp.33–42.

Greenfield, Steve and Osborn, Guy, 'Where Cultures Collide: The Characterization of Law and Lawyers in Film', *International Journal of the Sociology of Law*, 23 (1995), pp.107–30.

Greenfield, Steve and Osborn, Guy, 'Film, Law and the Delivery of Justice: The Case of Judge Dredd and the Disappearing Courtroom', *Journal of Criminal Justice and Popular Culture*, 6 (2), 1999, pp.35–45.

Greenfield, Stephen , Osborn, Guy and Robson, Peter (eds.), *Film and the Law: The Cinema of Justice*, second edition (Hart, 2010)

Gruber, Ruth, *Haven: The Dramatic Story of 1000 World War Refugees and How They Came to America* (Three Rivers, MI: Three Rivers Press, 2000).

Guttenplan, D.D., *The Holocaust on Trial* (London: Granta Books, 2001).

Hammond, David, 'Behind the Camera on *The Man in the Glass Booth*', *American Cinematographer*, 56, 6 (June 1975), pp.664–65, 700–02, 732.

Hardy, Phil (ed.), *The BFI Companion to Crime* (Berkeley, CA: University of California Press, 1997).

Harriman, Robert (ed.), *Popular Trials: Rhetoric, Mass Media, and the Law* (Tuscaloosa, AL: University of Alabama Press, 1990).

Harris, Thomas J., *Courtroom's Finest Hour in American Cinema* (Metuchen, NJ, and London: Scarecrow Press, 1987).

Hartman, Geoffrey (ed.), *Holocaust Remembrance: The Shapes of Memory* (Oxford: Blackwell, 1994).

Hartman, Geoffrey, *The Longest Shadow: In the Aftermath of the Holocaust* (1996; Basingstoke: Palgrave Macmillan, 2002).

Heimler, Eugene, *Concentration Camp* (1961; London: Corgi Books, 1979).

Higham, Charles, *Warner Brothers* (New York: Scribner, 1975).

Hilberg, Raul, *The Destruction of the European Jews* (1961; New York: Harper Colophon Books, 1979).

Hill, Mavis M. and Williams, L. Norman, *Auschwitz in England: A Record of a Libel Action* (New York: Ballantine Books, 1966)

Hiller, Arthur, 'Dialogue on Film', *American Film*, 5, 1 (1979), pp.41–52.

Hirsch, Joshua, *Afterimage: Film, Trauma and the Holocaust* (Philadelphia, PA: Temple University Press, 2004).

Hirschhorn, Clive, *The Warner Bros Story* (New York: Crown, 1979).

Hocchuth, Rolf, *The Deputy* (1963; New York: Grove Press, 1964).

Horwits, Al (ed.), *Stanley Kramer's Judgment at Nuremberg Souvenir Program* (London: Classics Illustrated, 1961).

Hyde, H. Montgomery, *Norman Birkett: The Life of Lord Birkett of Ulverston* (1964; London: Reprint Society, 1965).

Insdorf, Annette, *Indelible Shadows: Film and the Holocaust*, 3rd ed. (Cambridge: Cambridge University Press, 2002).

Jick, Leon A., 'The Holocaust: Its Use and Abuse Within the American Public', *Yad Vashem Studies*, 14 (1981), pp.303–18.

Johnstone, Iain, 'Timely Reminder of the Evil Men Do', *The Sunday Times*, 17 June 1990.

Jones, J. Walter, *The Nazi Conception of Law* (Oxford: Clarendon Press, 1939).

Kael, Pauline, 'The Intentions of Stanley Kramer: *Ship of Fools*', in Kael, *Kiss Kiss Bang Bang* (1970), pp.203–14.

Kaplan, Brett Ashley, *Unwanted Beauty: Aesthetic Pleasure in Holocaust Representation* (2007). Karpf, Anne, *The War After: Living with the Holocaust* (London: Minerva Books, 1997).

Kelley, Douglas M., *22 Cells in Nuremberg: A Psychiatrist Examines the Nazi Criminals* (New York: Greenberg, 1947).

Kershaw, Ian, *Hitler 1889–1936: Hubris* (London: Allen Lane, 1998).

Kershaw, Ian, *Hitler 1936–1945: Nemesis* (London: Allen Lane, 2000).

Kershaw, Ian, *Hitler, The Germans, and the Final Solution* (New Haven, CT: Yale, 2008).

Kinnard, Roy, *Science Fiction Serials: A Critical Filmography of the 31 Hard SF Cliffhangers, with an Appendix of the 37 Serials with Slight SF Content* (Jefferson, NC, and London: McFarland, 1998).

Kochavi, Arieh J., *Prelude to Nuremberg: Allied War Crimes Policy and the Question of Punishment* (Chapel Hill, NC: University of North Carolina Press, 1998).

Koppes, Clayton R. and Black, Gregory D., *Hollywood Goes to War: How Politics, Profits and Propaganda Shaped World War II Movies* (Berkeley, CA: University of California Press, 1987).

Kramer, Stanley, with Thomas M. Coffey, *A Mad, Mad, Mad, Mad World: A Life in Hollywood* (London: Aurum Press, 1998).

Kushner, Tony, *The Holocaust and the Liberal Imagination: A Social and Cultural History* (Oxford: Blackwell, 1994).

Kushner, Tony, 'Who Do You Think You Are Kidding, Mr Sawoniuk? British Memory of the Holocaust and Kosovo, Spring 1999', in Peter Gray and Kendrick Oliver (eds), *The Memory of Catastrophe*, Manchester: Manchester University Press, 2001), pp.201-15

Lawrence L. Langer, *The Holocaust and the Literary Imagination* (New Haven, CT, and London: Yale University Press, 1975).

Langer, Lawrence, *Admitting the Holocaust: Collected Essays* (Oxford: Oxford University Press, 1996).

Lappin, Elena, 'The Man with Two Heads', *Granta,* 66 (Summer 1999), pp.7–65.

Leonard, Maurice, *Montgomery Clift* (London: Sceptre, 1997).

Levi, Neil and Rothberg, Michael (eds), *The Holocaust: Theoretical Readings* (Edinburgh: Edinburgh University Press, 2003). Levi, Primo, *If This Is A Man/The Truce*, trans. Stuart Woolf (1958; 1963; London: Sphere Books 1987).

Levi, Primo, *The Drowned and the Saved*, trans. Raymond Rosenthal (London: Michael Joseph, 1988).

Levine, Michael G., *The Belated Witness: Literature, Testimony, and the Question of Holocaust Survival* (2006).

Levinson, Julian, 'The Maimed Body and the Tortured Soul: Holocaust Survivors in American Film', *Yale Journal of Criticism*, 17, 1 (Spring 2004), pp.141–60.

Linenthal, Edward, *Preserving Memory: The Struggle to Create America's Holocaust Museum* (New York: Viking, 1995).

Lipstadt, Deborah, *Beyond Belief: The American Press and the Coming of the Holocaust, 1933–1945* (New York: Free Press, 1986).

Lipstadt, Deborah E., *Denying the Holocaust: The Growing Assault on Truth and Memory* (New York: Free Press, 1993).

Loftus, John, *The Belarus Secret*, ed. Nathan Miller (London: Penguin Books, 1983).

Loshitzky, Yosefa (ed.), *Spielberg's Holocaust: Critical Perspectives on Schindler's List* (Bloomington, IN: Indiana University Press, 1997).

Louvish, Simon, 'Witness', *Sight and Sound*, 4, 3 (March 1994), pp. 12–15.

Machura, Stefan and Robson, Peter (eds), *Law and Film* (Oxford: Blackwell, 2001). Manchel, Frank, 'A Reel Witness: Steven Spielberg's Representation of the Holocaust in *Schindler's List*', *Journal of Modern History*, 67, 1 (March 1995), pp.83–100. Manchel, Frank, 'Mischegoss: *Schindler's List*, Holocaust Representation and Film History', *Historical Journal of Film, Radio and Television*, 18, 3 (1998), pp.431–36.

Mann, Abby, *Judgment at Nuremberg* (New York: Signet Books, 1961).

Mann, Abby, *Judgment at Nuremberg: The Script of the Film* (London: Cassell, 1961).

Marrus, Michael R., 'The Holocaust at Nuremberg', *Yad Vashem Studies*, 26 (1998), pp.5–41.

Marrus, Michael R., *The Holocaust in History* (London: Penguin Books, 1993).

Maser, Werner, *Nuremberg: A Nation on Trial*, trans. Richard Barry (London: Allen Lane, 1979).

Massie, Allan, *The Sins of the Father* (London: Sceptre Books, 1992).

McGilligan, Pat (ed.), *Backstory 2: Interviews with Screenwriters of the 1940s and 1950s* (Berkeley, CA, and London: University of California Press, 1997).

McGilligan, Patrick and Buhle, Paul, *Tender Comrades: A Backstory of the Hollywood Blacklist* (New York: St Martins Press, 1997).

McKale, Donald M., *The Nazi Party Courts: Hitler's Management of Conflict in His Movement, 1921–1945* (Lawrence, KS: University Press of Kansas, 1974).

McMillan, James, *Five Men at Nuremberg* (London: Harrap, 1985).

Medoff, Rafael, *The Deafening Silence: American Jewish Leaders and the Holocaust* (New York: Shapolsky, 1987).

Medoff, Rafael, 'New Perspectives on How America and American Jewry Responded to the Holocaust', *American Jewish History*, 84, 3 (1996), pp.253–66.

Medoff, Raphael, 'We Will Never Die: Shattering the Silence of the Holocaust', in *Holocaust Encyclopedia* (Washington, DC: United States Holocaust Memorial Museum), http://www.ushmm.org/wlc/en/article.php?ModuleId=10007036.

Mettraux, Guénaël (ed.), *Perspectives on the Nuremberg Trial* (Oxford: Oxford University Press, 2008).

Milland, Gabriel, 'The BBC Hungarian Service and the Final Solution in Hungary', *Historical Journal of Film, Radio and Television*, 18, 3 (1998), pp.353–73.

Miller, Arthur, *Focus* (1945; Harmondsworth: Penguin Books, 1986).

Miller, Judith, *One by One: Facing the Holocaust* (New York and London: Simon & Schuster, 1990).

Mintz, Alan, *Popular Culture and the Shaping of Holocaust Memory in America* (Seattle, WA: University of Washington Press, 2001).

Morgan, Ted, *An Uncertain Hour: The French, the Germans, the Jews, the Barbie Trial, and the City of Lyon, 1940–1945* (London: Bodley Head, 1990).

Morse, Arthur, *While Six Million Died: A Chronicle of American Apathy* (New York: Random House, 1967).

Mosley, Leonard, *The Reich Marshal: A Biography of Hermann Goering* (London: Weidenfeld & Nicolson, 1974).

Mote, David (ed.), *Contemporary Popular Writers* (New York and London: St James Press, 1997).

Muller, Ingo, *Hitler's Justice: The Courts of the Third Reich*, trans. Deborah Lucas Schneider (London: I.B. Tauris, 1991).

Munn, Michael, *Burt Lancaster: The Terrible-Tempered Charmer* (London: Robson Books, 1995).

Murphy, Brendan, *The Butcher of Lyon: The Story of Infamous Nazi Klaus Barbie* (New York: Empire Books, 1983).

Naremore, James, *The Magic World of Orson Welles* (Dallas, TX: Southern Methodist Press, 1989).

Neave, Airey, *Nuremberg: A Personal Record of the Trial of the Major War Criminals in 1945–46* (London: Grafton Books, 1989).

Neve, Brian, *Film and Politics in America: A Social Tradition* (London and New York: Routledge, 1992).

Nimoy, Leonard, *I Am Spock* (London: Centenary, 1995).

Novick, Peter, *The Holocaust and Collective Memory: The American Experience* (London: Bloomsbury, 2001).

Nyiszli, Miklos, *Auschwitz: A Doctor's Eyewitness Account* (1960; London: Grafton Books, 1978).

Oliver, Kendrick, *The My Lai Massacre in American History and Memory* (Manchester: Manchester University Press, 2005).

Orgeron, Marsha, '"The Most Profound Shock": Traces of the Holocaust in Sam Fuller's *Verboten!* (1959) and *The Big Red One* (1980)', *Historical Journal of Film, Radio and Television*, 27, 4 (October 2007), pp.471–96.

Padfield, Peter, *Hess: Flight for the Führer* (London: Weidenfeld & Nicolson, 1991).

Parish, James Robert and Marill, Alvin H., *The Cinema of Edward G. Robinson* (Cranbury, NJ: A.S. Barnes, 1972).

Pearl, Jonathan and Pearl, Judith, *The Chosen Image: Television's Portrayal of Jewish Themes and Characters* (Jefferson, NC: McFarland, 1999).

Pearlman, Moshe, *The Capture and Trial of Adolf Eichmann* (London: Weidenfeld & Nicolson, 1963).

Penfold, Chris, 'Elizaveta Svilova: Female Authorship in Soviet Cinema' (unpublished PhD thesis, University of Southampton, 2012).

Perry, George, 'Opening Pandora's Music Box', *The Sunday Times*, 6 May 1990. Persico, Joseph E., *Nuremberg: Infamy on Trial* (London: Allison & Busby, 1995).

Polevoi, Boris, *The Final Reckoning: Nuremberg Diaries*, trans. Janet Butler and Denis Bradbury (Moscow: Progress, 1978).

Powers, Steven, Rothman, David J., and Rothman, Stanley, *Hollywood's America: Social and Political Themes in Motion Pictures* (Boulder, CO: Westview Press, 1996).

Priemel, Kim C. and Stiller, Alexa (eds), *Reassessing the Nuremberg Military Tribunals: Transitional Justice, Trial Narratives, and Historiography* (Berghahn Books, 2012).

Reilly, Joanna, Cesarani, David, Kushner, Tony, and Richmond, Colin (eds), *Belsen in History and Memory* (London: Frank Cass, 1997).

Rinaldi, Matthew, 'The Disturbing Case of Feodor Fedorenko', *Judaism: A Quarterly Journal*, vol. 28, 3 (Summer 1979), pp.293–303.

Robinson, Edward G., *All My Yesterdays: An Autobiography* (New York: Hawthorn Books, 1973).

Robinson, Jr, Edward G., *My Father, My Son* (New York: Frederick Fell, 1958).

Roeder, Jr, George H., *The Censored War: American Visual Experience During World War Two* (New Haven, CT, and London: Yale University Press, 1993).

Rosenbaum, Alan S., *Prosecuting Nazi War Criminals* (Oxford: Westview Press, 1993).

Rosenbaum, Eli B., 'The Investigation and Prosecution of Suspected Nazi War Criminals: A Comparative Overview', *Patterns of Prejudice*, 21, 2 (1987), pp.17–24.

Rosenman, Samuel I. (ed.), *The Public Papers and Addresses of Franklin D. Roosevelt: Compiled with Special Material and Explanatory Notes by Samuel I. Rosenman. II: Humanity on the Defensive 1942* (1950; New York: Russell & Russell, 1969).

Rosenstone, Robert A., 'History in Images/History in Words: Reflections on the Possibility of Really Putting History into Film', *American Historical Review*, 93, 5 (December 1988), pp.1173–185.

Rosenstone, Robert A. (ed.), *Revisioning History: Film and the Construction of a New Past* (Princeton, NJ: Princeton University Press, 1995).

Rosenstone, Robert A., *Visions of the Past: The Challenge of Film to our Idea of History* (Cambridge, MA: Harvard University Press, 1995).

Ruzie, David, 'The Klaus Barbie Case: War Crimes Versus Crimes Against Humanity' in *Patterns of Prejudice*, 20, 3 (1986), pp. 27–33.

Ryan, Allan A., *Quiet Neighbors: Prosecuting Nazi War Criminals in America* (San Diego, CA: Harcourt Brace Jovanovich, 1984).

Schlink, Bernard, *The Reader*, trans. Carol Brown Janeway (London: Phoenix, 1997).

Sereny, Gitta, *The German Trauma: Experiences and Reflections, 1938–2001* (London: Penguin Books, 2001).

Server, Lee, *Sam Fuller: Film is a Battleground: A Critical Study, with Interviews, a Filmography and a Bibliography* (Jefferson, NC: McFarland, 1994).

Shandler, Jeffrey, *While America Watches: Televising the Holocaust* (New York and Oxford: Oxford University Press, 1999).

Shaw, Robert, *The Man in the Glass Booth* (London: Chatto & Windus, 1967).

Shaw, Robert, *The Man in the Glass Booth: A Play* (1967), in J.C. Trewin (ed.), *Plays of the Year, Volume 34, 1967–1968* (London: Elek, 1968), pp.115–87.

Sheftel, Yoram, *The Demjanjuk Affair: The Rise and Fall of a Show-Trial* (London: Gollancz, 1994).

Shipman, David, *Judy Garland* (London: Fourth Estate, 1992).

Shirer, William L., *The Rise and Fall of the Third Reich: A History of Nazi Germany* (1960; London: Pan Books, 1964).

Short, K.R.M. (ed.), *Film and Radio Propaganda in World War II* (London and Canberra: Croom Helm, 1983).

Short, K.R.M. and Dolezal, Stephan (eds), *Hitler's Fall: The Newsreel Witness* (London: Croom Helm, 1988).

Shulman, Holly Cowan, 'The Voice of America, US Propaganda and the Holocaust: "I Would Have Remembered" ', *Historical Journal of Film, Radio and Television*, 17, 1 (March 1997), pp.91–103.

Sicher, Efraim, 'The Future of the Past', *History and Memory: Studies in Representation of the Past*, 12, 2 (Fall–Winter 2000), pp. 56–91.

Simpson, Christopher, *Blowback: America's Recruitment of Nazis and its Effect on the Cold War* (London: Weidenfeld & Nicolson, 1988).

Slide, Anthony (ed.), *De Toth on de Toth: Putting the Drama in Front of the Camera* (London: Faber & Faber, 1996).

Slide, Anthony, *Actors on Red Alert: Career Interviews with Five Actors and Actresses Affected by the Blacklist* (Lanham, MD, and London: Scarecrow Press, 1999).

Smith, Bradley F., *The Road to Nuremberg* (London: André Deutsch, 1981).

Speer, Albert, *Inside the Third Reich*, trans. Richard Winston and Clara Winston, introduced by Eugene Davidson (1970; London: Sphere Books, 1971).

State of Israel Ministry of Justice, *The Trial of Adolf Eichmann: Record of Proceedings in the District Court of Jerusalem* , 8 volumes (Jerusalem: Ministry of Justice, 1992).

Steiner, George, *In Bluebeard's Castle: Some Notes Towards the Redefinition of Culture* (London: Faber & Faber, 1971).

Steiner, George, *Language and Silence: Essays 1958–1966* (1967; London: Penguin Books 1979).

Strumm, Philippa, *When the Nazis Came to Skokie: Freedom for Speech We Hate* (Lawrence, KS: University of Kansas Press, 1999).

Stuart, Alexander, 'Consciousness and Conscience: An Interview with Liliana Cavani', *Films and Filming*, 21, 5, issue no. 245 (February 1975), pp.10–14.

Taylor, Telford, *Nuremberg and Vietnam: An American Tragedy* (New York: Bantam Books, 1971).

Taylor, Telford, *The Anatomy of the Nuremberg Trials: A Personal Memoir* (London: Bloomsbury, 1993).

Teicholz, Tom, *The Trial of Ivan the Terrible: The State of Israel vs John Denjanjuk* (London: MacDonald, 1990).
Thomas, Bob, *King Cohn: The Life and Times of Hollywood Mogul Harry Cohn*, with new preface and revised final chapter (1967; Beverly Hills, CA: New Millennium Press, 2000).
Thomson, David, *Rosebud: The Story of Orson Welles* (London: Abacus Books, 1997).
Tollerton, David, 'Holocaust Representation and Judicial Proceedings Against God on the Stage and Screen', *Modernism/Modernity*, 20, 1 (2013).
Toplin, Robert Brent, 'The Filmmaker as Historian', *American Historical Review*, 93, 5 (December 1988), pp.1210–27.
Toplin, Robert Brent, *History by Hollywood: The Use and Abuse of the American Past* (Urbana, IL: University of Illinois Press, 1996).
Trial of the Major War Criminals before the International Military Tribunal, 42 vols, Nuremberg, 1947.
Turim, Maureen, *Flashbacks in Film: Memory and History* (New York and London: Routledge, 1989).
Tusa, Ann and Tusa, John, *The Nuremberg Trial* (London: BBC Books, 1995).
Uris, Leon, *Exodus* (London: Corgi, 1961).
Uris, Leon, *QB VII* (London: Corgi, 1971).
Urwand, Ben, *The Collaboration: Hollywood's Pact with Hitler* (Cambridge, MA: Harvard University Press, 2013).
Van Pelt, Robert Jan and Dwork, Debórah, *Auschwitz 1270 to the Present* (New Haven, CT, and London: Yale University Press, 1996).
Vice, Sue, *Holocaust Fiction* (London and New York: Routledge, 2000).
Vrba, Rudolf, *I Cannot Forgive* (London: Sidgwick & Jackson, 1963).
Wagenaar, William A., *Identifying Ivan: A Case Study in Legal Psychology* (Hemel Hempstead: Harvester Wheatsheaf, 1988).
Walters, Margaret, 'Sins of the Father: The Power of the Past in War Crimes Trials', *Listener*, 124, 3169 (14 June 1990), p.41.
Ward, Ian, *Law and Literature: Possibilities and Perspectives* (Cambridge: Cambridge University Press, 1995). Add to intro
Weitz, John, *Joachim von Ribbentrop: Hitler's Diplomat* (London: Weidenfeld & Nicolson, 1992).
West, Rebecca, *A Train of Powder* (London: Macmillan, 1955).
Wiesel, Elie, *Night*, trans. Stella Rodway (Harmondsworth: Penguin Books, 1991).
Wiesenthal, Simon, *Justice Not Vengeance*, trans. Edward Osers (London: Mandarin Books, 1990).

Wolf, Matt, 'Believe You Me', *Listener*, 123, 3163 (3 May 1990), pp.36–37.

Wyman, David S., *Paper Walls: America and the Refugee Crisis, 1938–1941* (Amherst, MA: University of Massachusetts Press, 1968).

Zelizer, Barbie, *Remembering to Forget: Holocaust Memory Through the Camera's Eye* (Chicago, IL, and London: University of Chicago Press, 1998).

Archive Sources

BBC [British Broadcasting Corporation] Written Archives Centre, Caversham Park, Reading, UK.

British Film Institute, London.

Imperial War Museum, London.

University of Southampton Archives, UK.

Filmography

After the Truth (Germany, Roland Suso Richter, 1999).

Amen (France/Germany/USA, Costa-Gavras, 2002).

Angel of Death (USA, Frank Drew White, 1987). check

Anne Frank (USA, Robert Dornheim, 2001).

Any Man's Death (USA, Tom Clegg, 1989). check

Apt Pupil (USA, Bryan Singer, 1998).

The Boys from Brazil (USA, Franklin J. Schaffner, 1978).

The Big Red One (USA, Sam Fuller, 1980).

Cast a Giant Shadow (USA, Melville Shavelson, 1966).

Confessions of a Nazi Spy (USA, Anatolé Litvak, 1939).

Crossfire (USA, Edward Dmytryk, 1947).

Descending Angel (USA, Jeremy Kagan, 1990).

The Diary of Anne Frank (USA, George Stevens, 1959).

The Divided Heart (GB, Charles Crichton, 1954).

Dr Strangelove (USA, Stanley Kubrick, 1964).

Everything is Illuminated (USA, Liev Schreiber, 2006).

The Execution (USA, Paul Wendkos, 1985). Add to chapt 5 re wc

Exodus (USA, Otto Preminger, 1960).

Father (Australia, John Power, 1990).

Frieda (GB, Basil Deardon, 1947).

Genghis Cohn (GB, Elijah Moshinsky, 1993).

Gentleman's Agreement (USA, Elia Kazan, 1947).

Getting Away with Murder (USA, Harvey Miller, 1995).

God on Trial (UK/USA, Andy de Emmony, 2008).
The Great Dictator (USA, Charles Chaplin, 1940).
The Hitler Gang (USA, John Farrow, 1944).
Holocaust (USA, Marvin Chomsky, 1978).
The House on Carroll Street (USA, Peter Yates, 1987).
The House on Garibaldi Street (USA, Peter Collinson, 1979).
The House on Telegraph Hill (USA, Robert Wise, 1951).
Inglourious Basterds (USA, Quentin Tarantino, 2009).
Inside the Third Reich (USA, Marvin J. Chomsky, 1983).
Judgment at Nuremberg (USA, Stanley Kramer, 1961).
Judith (USA, Daniel Mann, 1966).
Kojak: The Belarus File (USA, Robert Markowitz, 1985). Add mbox
Life is Beautiful (Italy, Roberto Benigni, 1997).
The Man in the Glass Booth (USA, Arthur Hiller, 1975).
The Man who Captured Eichmann (USA, William A. Graham, 1996).
Marathon Man (USA, John Schlesinger, 1976).
Mother Night (USA, Keith Gordon, 1996).
Murderers Among Us: The Simon Wiesenthal Story (USA: Brian Gibson, 1989).
Music Box (USA, Costa-Gavras, 1989).
Nazi Hunter: The Beate Klarsfeld Story (USA: Michael Lindsay-Hogg, 1986).
Never Forget (USA, Joseph Sargent 1991).
None Shall Escape (USA, André de Toth, 1944).
Nuremberg (Canada/USA, Yves Simoneau, 2000).
The Odessa File (GB/West Germany, Ronald Neame, 1974).
Once Upon a Honeymoon (USA, Leo McCarey, 1942).
Operation Eichmann (USA, R.G. Springsteen, 1961).
The Pawnbroker (USA, Sidney Lumet, 1964).
The Pianist (UK/France/Germany, Roman Polanski, 2002).
The Purple Heart (USA, Lewis Milestone, 1944).
QB VII (USA, Tom Gries, 1974).
The Reader (USA/Germany, Stephen Daldry, 2008).
The Rose Garden (Germany, Fons Rademakers, 1990).
Schindler's List (USA, Steven Spielberg, 1993).
Sealed Verdict (USA, Lewis Allen, 1948).
The Search (USA, Fred Zinnemann, 1948).
Shine (Australia, Scott Hicks, 1996).
Ship of Fools (USA, Stanley Kramer, 1965).
Skokie (USA, Herbert Wise, 1981).
The Stranger (USA, Orson Welles, 1946).

This Must Be the Place (Italy/France, Paulo Sorrentino, 2010).
The 25th Hour (France/Italy/Yugoslavia, Henri Verneuil, 1967).
Verboten! (USA, Sam Fuller, 1959).
Willy Wonka and the Chocolate Factory (USA, Mel Stuart, 1971).
The Young Lions (USA, Edward Dmytryk, 1958).

Documentary

'The Hitler Gang Goes on Trial' (RKO Pathé News, November 1945).
The Holocaust on Trial (Channel 4, tx. 29 April 2000).
Hotel Terminus: The Life and Times of Klaus Barbie (USA, Marcel Ophuls, 1987).
Imaginary Witness: Hollywood and the Holocaust (USA, Daniel Anker, 2004).
Into the Arms of Strangers: Stories of the Kindertransport (USA, Mark Jonathan Harris, 2000).
The Last Days (USA, James Moll, 1998).
The Late Show, 'Screening the Holocaust' (BBC2, tx. 18 December 1990).
The Long Way Home (USA, Mark Jonathan Harris, 1997).
The Memory of Justice (UK/USA/France/West Germany, Marcel Ophuls, 1976).
Nazi Concentration Camps (USA, 1945).
The Nazi Plan (USA, 1945).
Nuremberg (USSR, C. Svilov, 1946).
Shoah (France, Claude Lanzmann, 1985).
The Specialist (France/Israel, Eyal Sivan, 2000).
Triumph of the Will (Germany, Leni Reifensthal, 1935).

Index

Please note that page numbers relating to Notes will have the letter 'n' following the page number. Titles with dates following relate to films, while titles with names following relate to publications. Titles beginning with 'A' or 'The' will be sorted under the first significant word.